HANDBOOK OF DRUGS AND CHEMICALS
USED IN THE TREATMENT
OF FISH DISEASES

HANDBOOK OF DRUGS AND CHEMICALS USED IN THE TREATMENT OF FISH DISEASES

A Manual of Fish Pharmacology and Materia Medica

By

NELSON HERWIG

Curator of Fishes
Houston Zoological Gardens
Houston, Texas

With Forewords by

Louis Garibaldi

Curatorial Departments Director
New England Aquarium
Boston, Massachusetts

and

R.E. Wolke, D.V.M.

Comparative Pathologist
University of Rhode Island
Kingston, Rhode Island

CHARLES C THOMAS · PUBLISHER
Springfield · Illinois · U.S.A.

Published and Distributed Throughout the World by
CHARLES C THOMAS • PUBLISHER
BANNERSTONE HOUSE
301-327 East Lawrence Avenue, Springfield, Illinois, U.S.A.

© *1979, by* NELSON HERWIG
ISBN 0-398-03852-X
Library of Congress Catalog Card Number: 78-11764

Printed in the United States of America
N-11

Library of Congress Cataloging in Publication Data

Herwig, Nelson
    Handbook of drugs and chemicals used in the treatment of fish
diseases.

    Bibliography: p. 238
    1. Aquarium fishes—Diseases. 2. Fishes—Diseases. 3. Veterinary
Pharmacology. I. Title.
SF458.5.H47   639'34   78-11764
ISBN 0-398-03852-X

To the living memory of my father
Walter Nelson Herwig (1911–1969)

FOREWORD

SINCE MAN FIRST BEGAN to keep fish in ponds and tanks, he has had to contend with a broad spectrum of disease problems. By "trial and error" methodology, a body of knowledge developed from those trials that were successful. This, in turn, has led to the development of what can be termed, for lack of a better name, fish pharmacology. Over the years, many successful, and some not so successful, disease treatments have been described in a wide variety of publications. However, many of these articles are not readily available, are obscure, or have never found their way into translation from foreign publications. Therefore, professional fish culturists and amateur aquarists (hobbyists) alike have depended on a handful of "medicine cabinet" remedies. Although these remedies are widely used with qualified success, fish fanciers and workers in this field have expressed a need for a comprehensive guide to alternate solutions and remedies.

There are many reference works regarded as indispensable by professionals in various fields. Writers frequently refer to the ever-useful thesaurus, chemists use *The Merck Index,* doctors have their *P.D.R. (Physicians' Desk Reference),* and new parents read Dr. Spock. However, there never has been such a comprehensive reference work for the fish hobbyist or aquaculturist.

From years of research and review of all the available literature, Nelson Herwig has produced a reference that satisfies this need. This amazingly thorough review of the published literature includes almost every remedy imaginable, including, for the sake of thoroughness, some of questionable merit (noted as such). What was begun as a personal compilation of the available literature has been expanded into a comprehensive reference volume to the chemicals and drugs that have been used in the treatment of

vii

fish diseases. Thus, another tool has been added to our resources, one which will be used frequently and will be well appreciated. It is hoped that this work will act as a springboard, inspiring others to contribute to this body of knowledge.

LOUIS E. GARIBALDI

FOREWORD

FOR THOUSANDS OF YEARS man has cultured fish. The species of fish raised have varied from climate to climate and geographic area to geographic area, but the final result has been the same in each instance, an endeavor that has brought food and aesthetic pleasure to mankind. The publication of this book brings to mind the responsibilities of various professions for the health of fish associated with such culture.

Contemporary fish culture has reached new heights of productivity. More and more in the modern world, fish are commercially produced for human consumption and placed in aquaria for their aesthetic beauty. In both instances the animals are raised in confined areas with high population densities. Husbandry of this type may lead to severe disease problems and costly epizootics.

Disease has always been a problem, and the literature surrounding the area is plentiful. The foundation of our knowledge concerning these diseases was laid by investigators from many different scientific fields: fishery biology, bacteriology, virology, parasitology, and ichthyology. The foundation is a firm one, and much is owed to the early and contemporary work of these scientists.

One notes, however, a startling absence of medically trained individuals among the ranks of those concerned with fish health. In fact, the contribution from members of the medical field has been minimal. The major responsibility for the health and welfare of all animals, both companion and food producing, should lie with the veterinary profession. There seems to be little question that medically trained individuals could make a major contribution towards the prevention, diagnosis, and treatment of fish diseases. The veterinarian, with his knowledge of anatomical pathology, clinical pathology, and medical techniques, is in a unique position to assist the culturist. He has been trained to appreciate epizootiological problems and the relationships of large numbers of animals to their environment. The responsibility to make a contribution, however, lies with the veterinary profession. Members of the veterinary profession must recognize this responsibility and join hands with those of other professions who have and will continue to address themselves to fish health problems.

A major problem to culturists and other scientists concerned with fish diseases is access to the literature. Much has been written, but it is literally scattered far and wide and is often out of date or inaccessible. In addition, one of the least carefully investigated areas of fish health is therapeutics. *Handbook of Drugs and Chemicals Used in the Treatment of Fish Diseases* addresses itself to both problems. It brings under one cover much of the knowledge concerning drugs used to treat diseases of fish, and it does so in a logical and easily accessible manner. It is a careful work, encompassing years of painstaking research and attention to detail. Now culturists, hobbyists, and scientists alike can come to one source to gather information on piscine therapeutics. The work will serve as a reference for years to come and is in this respect a contribution of some consequence to the field of fish health.

While this book is essentially a compilation of drugs used to treat fish, it should stand as a challenge to veterinary pharmacologists and all scientists concerned with fish diseases to advance our knowledge in the field and to recognize the contributions that may be made by all, medical and nonmedical scientists alike.

R. E. WOLKE, D.V.M.

PREFACE

THE ART AND SCIENCE of fish medicine is in the dark ages, but it does exist. From the rank amateur hobbyist who comes into the pet store and exclaims, "My fish have all died, how come?," or says, "I think my fish are sick, I need some fish medicine," to the academic expert who is the accepted authority and whose best answer is, "Try it, who knows, it might work," or "Authority No. 256 recommends it in his paper," very few really know how, why, or even if most drugs and medications work on fish. Confusing opinions are rampant. It is into this seething cauldron of confusion that I pour this effort. I know not whether it will fan the flames of controversy or quench the fires of ignorance. But I do know this: I am no authority. I have not written this book because I knew the answers, but because I didn't, and in all too many instances still do not. When I found an answer to my questions or even the remote likelihood of an answer, I wrote it down. Soon, people began coming to me for answers to their fish problems. My "answers" are the product of other authorities' answers with a smattering of my own practical experience of the past twenty-two years of fish keeping thrown in for good measure.

It must be noted that there may be some drugs that the reader feels should have been included. Their absence here does not infer their ineffectiveness, nor does the inclusion of a drug signify its endorsement. Being a compilation of my own and others' research, the reader may find discrepancies with his own evidence. If so, I welcome any comments and criticisms which will enlighten both our boundaries of knowledge.

N.H.

ACKNOWLEDGMENTS

I WOULD LIKE to extend my heartfelt thanks to Mr. Felix Saucedo, graphics illustrator at the San Antonio Zoo, who in his spare time with just a few deft strokes of his pen reproduced all the chemical formulae and graphs contained herein, which had defied my own best efforts for years.

Also, thanks go to Mr. Joseph Noto, commercial artist, who stepped in at the last minute with some essential additions and corrections when Felix was indisposed with a broken leg.

N.H.

CONTENTS

HANDBOOK OF DRUGS AND CHEMICALS USED IN THE TREATMENT OF FISH DISEASES

PART I
FISH PHARMACOLOGY

Chapter 1

THERAPEUTICS IN FISH DISEASES

TYPES OF THERAPY OTHER THAN DRUG THERAPY

E VEN THOUGH THIS BOOK DEALS in detail only with drugs, other forms of therapy are just as important and ofttimes may be even more important than medication. My failure to consider these methods in detail here should in no way be regarded as an indication of their lack of usefulness in practice.

Regulation of Activity as Therapy

Regulation of activity by increasing or decreasing a fish's movements by physical restraint, expansion or reduction of swimming area, removal or addition of objects or decorations in tanks, and increasing water flow, thereby forcing swimming movements, may all be at times considered as forms of treatment. However, these methods are little used as a form of treatment other than to provide stimulation of blood circulation, remove noxious or toxic substances from the body through increased respiration, or prevent parasites from becoming attached. Therefore, no further consideration of these methods will be given in this text.

Physiotherapy

Physiotherapy of fish diseases is obtained primarily through the use of heat, i.e. raising the temperature to speed up the life cycle of pathogenic organisms so that a drug may act on a particular stage of its life cycle. Conversely, lowering the temperature to slow down the life cycle of a pathogenic agent until more appropriate treatment can take effect may also be an important type of therapy. Massage of the body parts is generally never attempted in fishes and should probably be discouraged at all times, with the possible exception of stripping in the case of an egg-bound female. Ice may be floated in plastic bags in overheated aquaria to prevent anoxia or brain damage caused by heat stroke. There is evidence to indicate that some disorders—forms of exophthalmus, for instance—may be alleviated by placing a sick fish under long wave ultraviolet light for several hours each day (Bevan and Zeiller, 1960).

Psychotherapy

Psychotherapy is usually not thought of as being possible or is of limited concern in treatment; however, provisions for the psychological needs of a fish may be therapeutic (Gr. *therapeutikos*—healing, curative, alleviative) or prophylactic in nature. Providing suitable hiding places or specific types of plants may be exceedingly important, preventing both anaphylactic shock and/or tissue trauma caused by the fish fleeing into solid objects or glass walls. It is also possible that some types of drugs may affect or alter a fish's normal behavior patterns. Careful observation is indicated when treating fish diseases. Turning off the lights and allowing a fish to rest in the dark or putting an opaque screen around a tank may be all that is required for recovery from acute shock.

Surgery

Surgery of fishes is at present confined to the body surfaces. Removal of external parasites with forceps or clipping a diseased or injured fin is pretty much the extent to which surgery can at present be carried out safely. However, internal surgery of the visceral cavity has been successfully performed experimentally, and the time is soon coming when rare or endangered fishes will be able to undergo extensive abdominal surgery. Tumor removal by surgical means is not now uncommon. Nodules produced by the viral disease lymphocystis may be surgically excised, which is the only effective treatment known in this case.

Diet or Nutritional Therapy

Diet or nutritional therapy is yet another aspect of treatment that is often not regarded as a ways and means of preventing or correcting disease conditions. Yet nutritional diseases and disorders, particularly the avitaminoses, are a major reason for the lowered resistance leading to the outbreak of diseases by pathological organisms, as well as being debilitating or fatal in their own right. An entire encyclopedia could be written on this facet of diseases and therapeutics of fishes. Technically, the vitamins themselves are drugs. They are not included in this work because of their intricate interrelationship with food and nutrition, and it is felt that other sources can provide more of the essential detail necessary for their thorough coverage. However, a study of nutritional disorders, particularly in diseases of the liver, should not be neglected.

Regulation of Environment

The regulation of environment as therapy primarily entails water quality and its management by physical, chemical, or mechanical means. Adequate and well-managed filtration systems either with or without carbon or charcoal would fall under this heading. Its importance in preventing the occurrence or inhibiting the spread of disease cannot be overemphasized. A diatomaceous earth filter in aquaria can remove bacteria, provided a proper grade of filter media is used (*see* Fig. 1-1a and 1-1b), and some types of bacteria will adsorb to activated carbon granules. Another form of environmental regulation therapy would include the planting of reeds in a pond or of sticking bamboo stakes in the bottom for the fish to scratch themselves against in order to remove parasites (Hoffman and Meyer, 1974). All are forms of therapy utilizing the physical environment. Water pollution and toxins can also be placed here as a major source of disease and disorders of fishes, and their elimination or control can be considered a form of treatment. Toxicology (Gr. *toxikos*—poison; *logos*—knowledge of) of fishes is still in its infancy, but it is a rapidly growing area of study by environmental ecologists. I have for the most part arbitrarily placed it outside the scope of this book, although it will be discussed briefly in a later section.

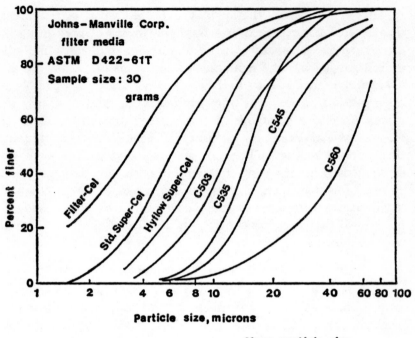

Figure 1-1a.

Product	Mean particle size, microns
Johns-Manville	
Celite 560	50
Celite 545	21.0
Celite 535	16.2
Celite 503	12.8
Hyflo Super-Cel	9.5

Immunization

Immunization is a very complex aspect of fish medicine. The natural production of antigens and antibodies and their induced production through the use of vaccines and serums is an interesting study. Much has been done in this area, particularly in the viral diseases of Salmonidae used as food. The methods and pro-

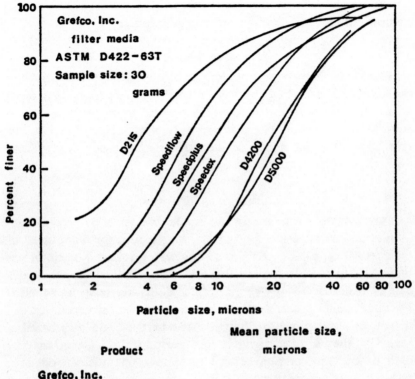

Figure 1-1b.

Diatomaceous earth filters are frequently reported in the literature as being capable of removing particles as small as bacteria from the water. What is not generally stated is that only the very finest grades are reliable in this respect. Most grades available to the aquarist are the coarser grades which will not remove the majority of bacteria from the water. Those grades that will remove most bacteria have very short filter runs and are more expensive. Figure 1-1a (opposite) courtesy of Johns-Mansville Corporation, Denver, Colorado. Figure 1-1b (above) courtesy of Grefco, Inc., Los Angeles, California.

cedures are slowly trickling into other areas of fish keeping, and immunization holds much promise for the future.

Hormone Therapy

Hormone therapy is another type of treatment that technically can be classified as drug therapy. However, there was not enough apparent evidence of its use in fish medicine to warrant its inclusion in this text. There is certainly work being done in this area, but I am not aware of hormones being used for anything other than fish breeding at present.

Prophylaxis As Therapy

Prophylaxis is the single most valuable form of "treatment" known, and overtones of prevention can be seen throughout all of the preceeding topics. By preventing water quality deterioration, toxicants and pollutants are thereby eliminated as sources of disease or disorder. Many carcinogenic agents may also be repelled by these same procedures. Viruses, bacteria, protozoa, fungal spores, and larval forms of helminths and crustaceans *may* be eliminated by the use of ultraviolet sterilization units. Ozone may be used to kill both pathogens and to remove phenols, nitrogenous wastes, and other organic toxins in the water.

Conclusion

Therapeutics in the broadest sense includes any and all remedial agents or measures that will promote the relief of pain, restore health, or prolong the life of a fish. By far and above the method most often employed to achieve this aim is drug therapy; although not always the most prudent action, this is certainly the one most commonly used. The primary purpose of this book is to explore this subject of drug therapy and is therefore our next topic of discussion.

Chapter 2

DRUG THERAPY

ORIGINAL SOURCES OF DRUGS

THE WORD DRUG comes from the Dutch word *droog,* which means dry. This apparently stems from medieval times when drugs were obtained from dried plants. Today a drug is simply a medicinal agent, regardless of its source, that has been found to be of therapeutic value in combatting disease. Antibiotic therapy and chemotherapy are considered to come under this heading also and are very important and specialized aspects of drug therapy. The broad study of drugs, or medicines, and their actions is called Pharmacology (Gr. *pharmakon*—drugs; *logos*—knowledge of), or in our case, Fish Pharmacology. It places primary emphasis on the actions of drugs on etiologic agents, as well as how they are removed or excreted from the fish's system and what effect they might have on the fish while in, on, or in contact with its body. Also included in this study are a number of agents which, while not necessarily used directly as fish medicants, are nonetheless of great benefit in keeping the fish's environment pest- and parasite-free. This would include such chemicals as disinfectants, antiseptics, algicides, and insecticides.

Drugs may be obtained from many different sources. Many foods may serve under some conditions as both sources of nutrition and of medication simultaneously. Vitamins, amino acids, glucose, and some blood products would be included in this category, but, stated previously, these types of drugs and their actions have been excluded from this study.

Animal Origins

Specific substances may be taken from animals and used as drugs. Hormones and other endocrine products such as epineph-

11

rine and insulin may be taken as examples, although they are not presently being used in the treatment of fish diseases. Animals as drug sources for fish medications are extremely rare; very few animal-derived fish drugs have been developed and even fewer are in use.

Plant Origins

Parts of plants and their extracts are a prime source of drugs and always have been. Antibiotics are derived for the most part from bacteria, molds, or *Actinomyces*. Plants often contain preparations concentrated in specific areas of the plant. The root, bulb, wood, bark, leaves, fruit, flowers, or seeds of higher plants often contain concentrations of drugs which may or may not need further refinement in the laboratory before being ready for use. Oftentimes a medication may be prepared simply by infusing leaves from the plant in water. Other times, when the drug in question may be a potent toxin, a purified extract of known concentration is necessary before it can be used safely. Crude drug preparations from plant sources are generally either ineffective or extremely dangerous to use. The refined products, such as antibiotics, are among the most powerful weapons available with which to combat diseases—so much so that further discussion regarding antibiotic therapy and chemotherapy has been set up as a separate section of this book.

Chemical Substances

Technically, all drugs are chemical substances, but what is intended here is to include those chemicals used as drugs that are not obtained from living sources. Some, such as the inorganic acids, bases, salts, and oxides, are extremely simple compounds owing their action to the presence of a single atom or ion. Many are of mineral origin, in which a rock or its pulverized equivalent is used as is. Still others are extremely complex chemicals, synthesized entirely in the laboratory with absolutely no counterpart in nature, e.g. the sulfonamides. Petroleum and coal furnish the hydrocarbon bases for many of these drugs, regardless of whether they are finalized through distillation or chemical synthesis. One building block of special note, from which a great many organic compounds are obtained by chemical substitution, are those, both occurring and synthesized, that utilize the benzene ring.

Synthetic Drugs

Knowing the chemical structure of an antibiotic may enable chemists to synthesize it and thus stay ahead of the development of resistant strains of bacteria by altering the drug's structure slightly without affecting its action. This allows the bacteria to be seemingly more versatile—getting another compound useful in its metabolism—which in the end contributes to its destruction.

ACTIVE PRINCIPLES OF DRUGS (ACTIVE INGREDIENTS)

From a crude form in a plant or animal source, a drug of highly refined purity may be extracted which is much more potent and reliable than the original form. The extraction is termed the active principle of the drug. Such drugs may be roughly classified into various groups or families according to their chemical structures.

Alkaloids

Alkaloids (literally—alkali-like) are organic-based, nitrogenous compounds obtained almost exclusively from plants, although they may also be found in animals. They are bitter to the human taste, and probably to fish as well, and are usually active and effective in small doses. The pure bases are relatively insoluble, but their salts are normally very readily soluble in water. Most often they are sold as the hydrochloride salt of the drug, e.g. quinine hydrochloride. An alkaloid can most often be identified by the "-ine" suffix in its base name.

As a group alkaloids are the most important medicinal agents derived from any source other than inorganic chemicals. Chemically they are like alkalies in that they unite with acids to form salts. The salts have the same activity as the pure alkaloids but are much more soluble and therefore of much greater value in treating fish. Alkaloids are safe when used in small to moderate dosages, but they become powerful toxins to the fishes themselves when used in excessive amounts. Both alkaloids and their salts may be precipitated in the presence of tannic acid or oxidized by potassium permanganate. These chemicals may be used to neutralize alkaloid poisoning in the water in the event of an accidental overdose. They cannot be used in conjunction with alkaloids otherwise. Alkaloids have very complex chemical formulas, but nonetheless many have been synthesized in the laboratory. In addition, a number of substances that are either not found in nature at all or else are found in such minute quantities that their extraction would make the cost of their use prohibitive can be prepared artificially in the laboratory. These are termed artificial alkaloids and resemble natural alkaloids completely in their actions.

Glycosides

Glycosides (glucosides) are plant derivatives containing a sugar and one or more other substances, which are usually steroids. They may be broken down by hydrolysis, and the nonessential carbohydrates (sugar) may be discarded to liberate the most active ingredient, which is termed an *aglycone* or *aglucone*. This, however, may relieve the drug of some of its potency which is present in the parent glycoside molecule. The glycosides are usually colorless and are extracted from the plant with water and alcohol. They are named so that they should end in "-im." *Steroids* are similar to sterols, which are solids at room temperatures. Thus they may need to be dissolved in a transport medium of some sort or else administered orally. Glycosides exert a strong stimulant action on the heart and other areas of the body.

Sterols

Sterols, complex aromatic alcohols, which chemically are phenanthrene derivatives, are obtained from both plant and animal sources and contain such substances as sex hormones, bile salts, and certain vitamins. They are little used as fish medicants, although they are found in a number of foodstuffs. Some carcinogenic agents which are steroid in nature have been found to cause cancer in fishes when they were present in the food.

Plant Organic Acids

Plant organic acids have many similarities in actions to inorganic acids. They are obtained naturally from the fruits of higher plants and are the cause of sour taste in fruits. Limes, lemons, grapefruits, oranges, and other citrus plants contain citric acid. Tartaric acid occurs chiefly in grapes and is made from cream of tartar deposits which coat the sides of wine vats during the fermentation process. If the fermentation process is allowed to extend too long, another plant acid, acetic acid, may be produced. They are all characterized by the presence in their chemical structure of the -COOH radical. They are not extensively used in fish therapeutics, although they may be very effective when application is made as antiseptics or disinfectants.

Tannins

Tannins are complex phenol derivatives, of which tannic acid is the primary active principle. While their chemical structures are not well known, they are widely distributed in nature with practically every family of plants having a number of representatives. Tannins form insoluble precipitates with alkaloids and proteins, so extra caution must be exercised in their use on living fishes. Alkaloid derivatives cannot be used in the presence of tannins as they will be rendered ineffective. Tannins are best used as pond disinfectants or antiseptics.

Saponins

Saponins are a special group of plant glycosides which are nonabsorbable irritants to fishes and their external parasites. They form emulsions when shaken or stirred in water, even in concentrations as low as 1/1000 part of a saponin. They are used as local irritants for the disinfection of external parasites prior to a fish being released into a pond or stream.

Balsams and Resins

Resins are solid or semisolid gummy exudates of vegetable origin. They are obtained from the sap of various trees. They are limited in their composition to the elements carbon, hydrogen, and oxygen, but are in highly complex and confusing combinations. Typically, resins are insoluble in water but can be administered in a solution of alcohol or as a gummy protective ointment. At ordinary room temperatures they are solid, translucent, for the most part colored, and occasionally aromatic compounds which melt easily and are inflammable. In solution they are generally acidic in nature, so the pH should be watched closely when used on pH-sensitive fish.

Gum resins containing resins in a specialized form may result in a class of compounds known as balsams. These are resins, which are liquid or semisolid, containing benzoic or cinnamic acid. Balsam of Peru is used in fish medicine, while benzoic acid may be used as another example to further familiarize the reader with this class of compounds.

Balsams are used as irritants in a short bath to combat crustacean ectoparasites of fishes.

Other Organic Chemical Classes

There are a great many classes of organic chemical compounds widely used in veterinary and human medicine which have not yet found their way into fish medicine. Many never will because either their application does not apply to fish or else they just cannot be successfully used within the aquatic parameters of fishes. Several will be mentioned which may or may not be currently in use in the treatment of fish diseases. They are enumerated to assist the serious researcher in pharmacology who may be searching for new sources of fish medications. This entire section therefore provides a brief glimpse at a subject that can best be termed comparative pharmacology.

Enzymes, while not widely used at present, hold great promise for the future. Their limiting factor seems to be their ease of destruction in the presence of moist heat. *Hormones* are glandular secretions of animal origin which will be used more extensively in the future for medical applications. *Oleoresins* are a special type of resin consisting of volatile oils and resins obtained from vegetable resins. The only one of medical importance that may someday be utilized in fishes is the oleoresin of male fern *(Aspidium oleoresin)*, a very old helminthic. *Carbohydrates,* a broad classification to which glycosides and saponins belong, include a number of *starches, sugars, celluloses,* and *gums* which are, to my knowledge, not used at all in the treatment of fish diseases. Gums may be further broken down into *acacias, tragacanths,* and *mucilages* (including *pectins*), on the basis of their reaction or solubility in water. *Gelatin* is occasionally used as a solidifying medium or transport for alkaline drugs mixed into foods. Gelatin will not solidify in the presence of an acidic medium, but will remain liquid. *Fixed oils, volatile* or *aromatic oils* (also called *essential oils*), *fats,* and *waxes* are little used as fish medicaments due to their immiscibility in water and difficulty in getting either on or into a fish's body. They are lipid derivatives of both plant and animal origin. *Vitamins,* as has been stated previously, are important drugs but will not be considered in this text. The reader is referred to a standard reference work on fish foods and diets such as *Fish Nutrition,* edited by Halver (1972). *Proteins* are complex organic amino acid compounds. Those used in veterinary and human medicine are derived primarily from animal sources, but are not used as medications in fishes for the most part. Proteins are basically used as foodstuffs.

In closing this section, one last group of compounds must be mentioned which really belong to no group at all. These are the *neutral principles* and/or *bitter principles.* One example used in humans is picrotoxin. They are neutral yet active plant products that cannot be placed in any definite chemical category and are not often used as fish medicines.

FORMS OF MEDICATION
(PHARMACEUTIC PREPARATIONS)

The forms of drugs available are many and varied. Most of the more common types will be covered in this section. Often the form in which a drug is compounded is merely a matter of convenience to the manufacturer or user. Other times it is a necessary form for administration. Knowing the difference and limitations of various types of formulations may mean the difference between success or failure in the treatment of a fish or of an epizootic. The art and science of preparing drugs for medicinal use is called *Pharmacy,* thus a pharmaceutic preparation is the form in which a drug is made ready for use. Preparations may occur in the form of solids, liquids, or gases. They may be intended for internal (systemic) or external use in water. The form in which a medication is prepared may serve as an indication of the manner in which it may be used. For instance, capsules are generally (but not always) intended for internal use, while aqueous solutions are intended for introduction into the water for external use.

Formerly, as far back as Roman times, pharmaceutic preparations were prepared and/or dispensed by either the individual or a physician. Later, with greater quality and additional preparations available, pharmacy came into being, and the pharmacist was called on to suitably prepare and dispense the appropriate form and dosage. Today, by the time that fish medicine has come upon the scene, the manufacturers themselves prepare the forms of medication in more or less predetermined dosages and in a variety of forms. This has simplified pharmacy to the extent that only the proper dosage needs to be weighed or counted out and dispensed. This makes the administration of drugs a great deal simpler and much more reliable than it was in the last century. It has led to greater uniformity and better quality with less danger of under- or overdosage.

Types of Solutions

The aquatic nature of the fish's environment and the universal use of baths as a form of treatment makes solutions the *prime* form of medication in fish therapeutics. Injectants are also virtually all composed of solutions. Yet, actually, chemists find difficulty in both defining and classifying solutions. In fish pharmacology, we will use as a working definition the understanding that a true solution is an aqueous preparation of a nonvolatile drug. Thus a nonaqueous substance must be dissolved in another substance which is in turn dissolved in water before there is a true solution. Krug and McGuigan give as a practical definition of a solution the following: "A solution is a homogenous mixture of a substance (or substances) in a liquid which appears clear in ordinary daylight and which cannot be separated into its constituent parts by ordinary mechanical processes of filtration through paper or by decantation after settling."

Solutions consist of two parts: (1) the solute, which is the substance that is to be dissolved, and (2) the solvent, which is the substance into which the solute is dissolved and is the base, aqueous or otherwise, of the solution. Both solutes and solvents may be either solids, liquids, or gases. The solubility of a substance—that is, the extent or degree to which a solute may be dissolved in a solvent—is determined by a number of chemical and physical factors. Temperature exerts a tremendous influence on how much of a substance may be dissolved in any given solvent. In aqueous solutions, the pH frequently is a limiting factor in how much, if at all, a solvent will dissolve a solute. Under some conditions a supersaturated solution may be obtained, but this has no application in fish therapeutics.

Aqueous Preparations

While virtually every drug or medicament used in fish therapeutics must be an aqueous preparation in its final analysis, not all aqueous preparations are used in fish medicine. The most important preparations in this grouping are the *liquores* or, as they are more commonly called, *solutions*. Solutions are merely nonvolatile substances dissolved in water. They constitute the vast majority of fish preparations available. Other solid or powdered forms used in baths are ultimately solutions in the pond or aquarium into which the fish is placed. Every type of medication application depends upon its ability to go into aqueous solution, either in the watery environment or into fish tissues and body fluids which are themselves composed primarily of water, the only exception being those substances within the fish which are composed of fats or fatty acids. [Vitamins (A,B,D, and K) and some other nutrients would be included in this category, and as such are not included in this book.]

An insoluble, or nearly insoluble, substance, such as many of the salts, oxides, and hydroxides of calcium and other compounds, may form collodial suspensions called *magmas*. Their use is limited primarily to disinfection of pond bottoms and for sterilization procedures.

Infusions are obtained by boiling or steeping vegetable material such as bark, roots, or seeds in water to obtain an aqueous raw extract of a medicinal agent. They are generally unreliable insofar as obtaining a proper dosage is concerned, but they are used extensively in a number of the underdeveloped nations where they are the only treatment available.

The use of a volatile substance dissolved in an aqueous medium is termed a *waters* or *aquae*. Ammonia or chlorine solutions are examples. Their primary use is for short-term treatments of ponds and tanks where reduction of the drug from the water is accomplished by evaporation. They are never used internally.

A *syrup* is an aqueous solution containing sugar or a flavoring agent to disguise the taste of a drug. Syrups have no application in the treatment of fishes, and the sugars contained may produce a bacterial bloom in a small tank or aquarium if they are used in lieu of a more proper form.

Another type of collodial suspension or solution exists but is currently not used in the treatment of fishes. This is a *mucilage*, which is a collodial solution of starches, gums, or other similar collodial bodies. They may find use eventually to bind insoluble drugs that occur in the form of powders or tablets so that they may be taken orally or applied adhesively to the skin. At present they are not being used.

Alcoholic Preparations

There are a number of different types of alcohols. In general, ethyl alcohol is the one understood when an alcoholic preparation is mentioned. Other types of alcohols are usually stated in the drug title if one of them is used. Other alcohols commonly employed as solvents for alcoholic preparations include methyl and isopropyl.

Tinctures are alcoholic or partially alcoholic solutions of non-volatile extracts of vegetable or animal origin drugs or of pure chemical compounds. Tinctures vary in strength but usually do not exceed 10% active principle in strength. In general they are used topically as bacteriostats and disinfectants. They usually are somewhat unstable solutions, and many will precipitate in strong light. Dark bottles for storage are advised. Tincture of iodine is used frequently and may serve as an example, but as a group, tinctures are little used in fish therapeutics. *Fluid extracts* are concentrated liquid alcoholic solutions, sometimes reaching 100% in active strength. They are obtained by percolation of a vegetable drug so that one milliliter of fluid extract contains one gram of drug.

Spirits or *essences* are alcoholic solutions of volatile substances. Most contain from 5% to 20% of the active principle. There are virtually none used on fish. *Elixirs* are flavored alcoholic solutions, and to my knowledge are not used at all on fish. Thus we find that tinctures, spirits, and elixirs are the direct alcoholic counterparts of aqueous solutions, waters, and syrups.

Glycerin is used at times as a solvent for medicinal substances termed *glycerites*. Because of their immiscibility in water they are not used to treat fishes. A substitute for glycerin may occaionally be propylene glycol.

Acetone is used to produce a solution of quinaldine for anesthetization of fishes, however its use is not condoned because of its extreme irritating properties on sensitive membranes, i.e. fish gills. A much more rational substitute is ethyl alcohol or even vodka, both of which have anesthetizing properties of their own. Oleic acid produces *oleates*, but these are not used on fish. *Ether* may also occasionally be used as a solvent for a drug, but again they are not used on fish. Ether may, however, be used as a fish anesthetic.

Fatty and Oily Preparations

These preparations are rarely encountered in treating fish and are included more as an attempt at thoroughness than as an indication of their value as fish medicaments. *Emulsions* are suspensions of oils, fats, or petroleum products in water, held together by an emulsifying agent such as gum acacia. They are homogenous liquids that should hold together for six months or longer if well made. A few emulsions are used to treat pond waters, mostly as insecticides.

A *liniment* (L. *linere*—to smear) is a mixture of a drug with an oil or soap but may also be an alcohol or water. They are intended to be used externally or rubbed into the skin, thus they have no application in fish medicine.

An *ointment* is a soft fatty mass as a base to which a drug has been added. The fatty base may consist of lard, cholesterol, wool fat (lanolin), or other heavy fat. They are intended primarily to provide protective coatings or introduce drugs systemically through the skin. As they have a strong tendency to wash off or float away in water, they are not used on fish. The only exception of which I am aware is Volan A adhesive ointment which is used in Europe and is not available in the United States. A *cerate* is an ointment that has been made firm by the addition of wax or paraffin.

Suppositories are mixtures of drugs with some firm oily base such as cocoa butter or glycerinated gelatin. They are intended to be inserted into the body orifices where the body temperature will cause them to melt and thus medicate the system. Of course, such a form of medication has no application in a poikilothermic animal.

Solid Preparations

The most basic solid preparation is a crystalline or powdery substance of either synthetic or natural origin which is usually of very high quality and purity. Such drug substances or mixture of substances, when finely ground to a more or less uniform grade, are termed *powders* and constitute the base of all solid drug preparations. They are most economical when dispensed in bulk but may come in a variety of forms, either with or without filler substances. Powders form the most suitable medium for transporting large volumes of a drug. They are then simply mixed with water to produce an aqueous solution that is ready for use. An exact measured quantity of powdered drug in a sealed sterile container, to which a suitable solvent, usually water, can be added through a rubber seal by means of a hypodermic needle, is termed a *sterile powder.* Many injectible antibiotic drugs which do not have a stable shelf life after being mixed (reconstituted) are marketed in this fashion. Ampicillin is an example of a drug that occurs primarily as a sterile powder.

A powder, when mixed with an inert, cohesive substance, usually a gummy or gelatinous substance, and rolled into a small oval or flattened solid body suitable for being swallowed by a fish is termed a *pill.* When large they are termed a *bolus,* and when extremely small they are termed *granules.* Medicated food pellets may be regarded as pills. Powders may be placed in combination with lactose or some other inert binder, moistened with alcohol or some other volatile liquid to form a wet mass, and then placed into a suitable mold and compressed into a *tablet.* While powdered drug forms are more suitable as well as more economical for use in treating fishes, tablets come in more exact premeasured doses ready for use without the necessity of being weighed out, which is an important consideration when scales are not at hand or technical expertise is lacking. Most drugs which can be taken internally will have a tablet or capsule form.

Tablets have largely been replaced by drug manufacturers with *capsules.* Capsules are exact premeasured quantities of a drug enclosed in a gelatin capsule. They may be either hard or soft but are usually soluble in water after only a few minutes immersion. Capsules are more or less commercial formulations of pills. Sometimes the capsule is coated with an indigestible substance like salol or steric acid or else may be made with a substance that is indigestible in the acid medium of the stomach but will dissolve for release and absorption into the system in the intestine. These are *enteric capsules* and are not yet practical for use in fishes. Capsules are usually available in either 50, 100, 250, or 500 milligram (mg) sizes.

Antimycin A is a drug which is applied as a coating on sand particles. Distributed on the surface of a pond, it dissolves as the sand grain sinks to the bottom of the pond, thus insuring relatively even distribution from top to bottom of the pond. This is a rather unique approach to solid drug preparations for use on fish.

Gaseous Preparations

The extent to which gaseous preparations can be utilized in treating fishes is very slight and depends ultimately on the solubility of the gas in water to produce an aqueous solution. Ozone in the aquarium might be considered an exception, however, as its usefulness as a powerful oxidizing agent has long been recognized. Its ability to "burn up" a pathogen can be a valuable aid as long as it is recognized that at the same time it is eliminating a pathogen it is also destroying a fish's gills. This chemical, therefore, must be used both intermittently and sparingly, if not completely reserved for handling by an expert.

Gaseous preparations of ammonia and chlorine are also used to destroy pathogens and to sterilize and disinfect ponds and raceways. Most application is by means of large tanks mounted on boats or tractors, and the gas is either released directly into the water or else mixed with water and then sprayed or poured into the pond. The solubility of the gas in the water and its action on fish and/or parasites are the prime considerations when contemplating the use of a gaseous preparation. Temperature and pH along with the volatility of the gas must also be considered. Generally, removal from the water is accomplished by simply allowing time for the substance to completely evaporate out due to its volatile nature. In the case of chlorine, sodium thiosulfate can be used to neutralize the elemental ion. Incidentally, an overdose of sodium thiosulfate in marine aquaria may produce a milky white colloidal substance in the water that is lethal to fish life.

METHODS OF ADMINISTRATION

The fundamental principles of treating fishes is the same as for any other animal, including man. However, the variable nature of the fluid habitat of fishes introduces some special problems and considerations into their therapeutics. Their poikilothermic nature must also be considered when searching for the proper drug and its route of administration. Many otherwise desirable drugs may be rendered inactive or otherwise unsuitable for use because of these considerations.

Topical Applications

The simplest and most direct method of treating fishes is to apply the drug directly to the body surface. Wounds, skin ulcerations, and other localized infections or traumas may be treated by this method by using a concentrated solution of a suitable chemical, usually an oxidizing agent, disinfectant, or antiseptic. A great many drugs in the form of emulsions, linaments, ointments, and lotions, which would otherwise be highly useful agents, are unsuitable for use on fishes because they will either wash off, dissolve, or float to the water surface because of their lighter specific gravity. In order to be useful topically, a drug must be insoluble in water, act immediately upon contact, be denser than water, or be adhesive enough to adhere to the body of a fish that will in all likelihood do its best to scrape it off.

In the use of this method of treatment, the individual fish must be caught and raised to the surface in order for the drug to be applied. A wet towel thrown over the fish will allow both a firm grip to hold the fish steady and also reduce dehydration or drying out if the fish must be kept out of water for any length of time. Application can be made by pouring the drug directly onto the body surface or from a squeeze drop bottle, or it can be applied with a cotton swab on the end of a small dowel. Of course, this is not an economically desirable method of treating large groups of fishes because of the time and effort involved.

Administration by Baths

Virtually every drug available to the hobbyist is a water-soluble compound designed to be added to the aquarium. The commercial fish farmer or hatchery operator has a somewhat wider range of choice with oral medications and some injectants, but he is still bound to the ease of administration and generally lower costs of administering baths to the fish. Only the veterinarian, research scientist, and some public aquariums have the full range of techniques and drugs available to them, yet here, too, the most commonly used form of treatment is a bath of some sort. Baths are equally applicable whether for one fish in a small aquarium or a full fish farm. It does not matter if one is a novice or a veteran fish keeper, the method is just as easy for either to use. The enormous numbers of fish pathogens, either external parasites or bacterial infective agents, which can best be approached for treatment by this technique is not the only reason for the popularity of the administration of baths. Ease of absorption into the fish's system also plays a part in the popularity of this type of treatment. Absorption through the fish's gills, mucous membranes, or the integument for treatment in cases of internal bacterial disease is a rather inefficient method of treatment, but there are exceptions, e.g. Furanace®.

Baths as treatments may be divided into a variety of types depending on the concentration of the drug or chemical used and the type of pathogen being combatted. Technically, baths may be considered as an extended form of topical application. They are classified according to time duration, ranging from a momentary dip to an indefinite period in which the drug is applied and then simply left in the water. The latter is usually attended by a gradual decline in efficacy until either none or only a residual effect remains.

Some precautions and considerations must be taken when using drugs in baths. The use of carbon filtration in aquaria usually must be discontinued, as most dyes and antibiotics as well as many other types of compounds can be filtered out by it. Various combinations of drugs and chemicals must be avoided as they might not only nullify good effects of each but may become toxic to fish in their combined effect. This is a process called drug antagonism, which is covered more fully under the antibiotic therapy section. The pH of the water must also be considered as some drugs become more, or less, powerful or lose their effect entirely at different pHs, while others may simply precipitate out of solution, notably the various sulfonamides. Some drugs may be inactivited by light, and hence must be used in darkened aquaria. Temperature has a drastic effect on the activity of a great many drugs. Still others simply will not work at a concentration that is nontoxic to fish but lethal to pathogens and so must be stepped up in concentration while the duration of exposure is shortened.

Water hardness may affect the activity of a drug or chemical adversely.

The methods of administering baths to fishes are covered separately according to their classification by time duration in the following sections.

Dips

A dip may vary in duration from a few seconds in an extremely high concentration of a very powerful substance to several minutes in a slightly less active solution. For purposes of establishing definition, a dip will herein be regarded as a bath having a maximum time duration of three minutes or less. (This time duration may differ from other authors, some of whom place the limit at one minute and others at five.) Due to the strength of the solutions used in dips, some can produce tremendous stress on a fish. An already sick or weak fish may be unable to tolerate it and may die as a result of treatment. In general, however, it is an effective method of treating external conditions or of combatting ectoparasites. Dips are frequently used to disinfect fish when transferring them from one aquarium or pond to another.

Administration is accomplished by placing the fish in a small, previously prepared container of a well-mixed concentrated solution of medication. The fish is usually left in a dip net and just suspended in the solution. Immediately upon removal the fish is rinsed off by being either sprayed or dipped in a separate unmedicated water bath. This is intended to remove traces of concentrated medication and to prevent residual contact that may burn or otherwise damage sensitive tissues, particularly the gills. It also prevents buildup of medication in the tank or aquaria to which the fish are being transferred following treatment.

Short Baths

Some authors describe a short bath as being no longer than fifteen minutes, others say one hour, and still others extend it to twenty-four hours. On closer examination, it is apparent that each is describing a somewhat different method or type of fish keeping, based on the concentration of drug being used and/or the availability of oxygen during treatment. The longest duration is an aquarium situation in which a separate tank is used with a significantly lower drug concentration than is found in a dip. The fish in this instance is released into this solution and allowed to remain until the next day. Here an air pump with an air stone can be used to supply oxygen for respiration during treatment. The fish is then removed and returned to another aquaria of unmedicated water. The time may be any duration shorter than 24 hours, but a longer duration leads either to degradation of the medication or toxicity to the fish, at least at the relatively high concentrations of the short bath.

The commercial fish farmer can rarely provide an amount of oxygen on the scale necessary to prevent oxygen depletion for an extended time when the water flow is stopped in a raceway. Consequently the fish farmers dosage is a little higher and the time much shorter than twenty-four hours. An hour is probably an optimum limit if a proper dosage is used. The method of the short bath in this type of fish farming is to turn off the flow of water in a raceway or similar swift-flowing facility and to add a relatively high concentration of medication, being sure that sufficient mixing occurs to avoid "dead" areas that might go unmedicated. The removal of medication after treatment is accomplished by turning on the flow of water and allowing it to flow out of the raceway.

The shortest period of time still within the limits of definition of a short bath is three to fifteen minutes. Here oxygen starvation is not normally a consideration, but just as in a dip, the concentration itself may be so high that a weak fish will succumb to treatment rather than to disease. The short bath is often more advantageous than a dip when stress factors are of paramount concern. In fish farming operations, the fact that the fish do not have to be handled is also a significant feature of the short bath. It is suitable for use with a wide range of aqueous preparations, including suitable antibiotics, inorganic acids, bases, salts, oxides, and various insecticide preparations used in the treatment of ectoparasites.

Flush

Although there have been a few experimental setups devised whereby a flush could be used in a closed system such as an aquarium, this must be considered as an exclusively open water system method of treatment. Essentially a flush is nothing more than a modified short bath which overcomes the disadvantage of having to run the risk of anoxia in a high density fish population. Its effectiveness as a treatment is not quite as good, however. The drug or medication is added in concentrated form to the water at the inlet and simply allowed to carry through the system and out the effluent pipe. Its duration is regulated by controlling the rate of flow at the water inlet, both of the water and the amount of drug. It significantly reduces the stress of treatment on weak fish, particularly those which might be suffering from gill parasites or disorders. Care must be taken to see that the flow patterns are such that proper mixing and distribution of the medication occurs; otherwise, "dead" areas may occur where sick fish may go untreated or reservoirs of infection may persist. Dosages may then be repeated periodically.

Long Baths (Indefinite)

The long or indefinite baths are the most commonly used methods of treatment available to the fish keeper, on whatever level he is working. Although the long bath is the most simple method to use, unfortunately, because of the low concentrations used, it is also one of the most inefficient methods of treating fish diseases. The long bath is the method most often responsible for development of new antibiotic-resistant strains of bacteria, but to the average home hobbyist, it is virtually the only method of treatment available. It is no mystery then why the home aquarist is the least successful in coping with diseases of fishes.

Some forms of medication, such as Dylox®, work fairly well using this procedure. Larger parasites, such as monogenetic trematodes and crustaceans, may be completely eradicated by this method. Microbial agents may wipe out a fish population before the low concentrations have time to take effect. Acute or advanced cases may not be amenable to treatment, however, as it works slowly over an extended period of time, and most fish do not even show symptoms of illness until it has become quite severe.

In ponds or waterways where fish cannot be easily caught or relocated, and water exchange is very slow, the indefinite bath may be utilized quite well for ectoparasites and external protozoan diseases. Very few drugs can be sufficiently absorbed into a fish's system by this method to be of therapeutic value in cases of internal or systemic disorder. Internal diseases and disorders are rarely controlled, much less cured, by the low concentrations of the long duration bath.

Despite its drawbacks, the ease of application of the long bath will continue to make it popular, as all that one is required to know is how much water is present and how much drug to apply (sometimes only an approximation is needed), then the drug is mixed into the water. About the only consideration that must be given is whether an activated carbon filter, if present, will remove the drug being used. If so, then the filter should be disconnected during treatment. Safe dosages have been worked out for the majority of drugs that are amenable to this method, so the possibility of drug toxicity is minimal. In fact, the contrary may be true, as the addition of more drug may be necessary each day in order to maintain even a very low concentration; some drugs are biodegradeable, while others may induce a tolerance buildup in both fish and pathogen.

Constant Flow

The constant flow method is one available large-scale method to be found in fish therapeutics. Perforated pipes stretching across a flowing stream or river are used to discharge medication at a constant rate for as long as desired. A metering pump or siphoning arrangement is used to regulate the amount of drug being dispensed, and a few readings are taken periodically downstream until the dispersion rate can be worked out. Sometimes an adjustment upwards or downwards on the metering device is necessary, but when the desired parts per million (ppm) are indicated in downstream analysis, the barrels of medication should be kept flowing. Such a massive scale is useful when there is no control over the water flow or the volume of water being treated is exceedingly large. TFM (Trifluromethyl nitrophenol) has been successfully used to control lampreys and hagfishes ascending rivers from the Great Lakes.

Concentrations may vary according to whether a cure is being sought or merely a prophylaxis when pathogens are known to be present but do not pose an immediate threat to fish life. In general, concentrations are somewhat low in order to avoid the possibility of allowing an eddy somewhere to build up a lethal concentration of chemical.

A modification of the technique has been developed for use in large scale, closed, recirculating systems such as might occur in some of the larger public aquariums. The chemical level is carefully monitored, sometimes automatically, to sustain a constant level of medication throughout the entire system. Here it is normally used as a standard prophylaxis rather than as a form of treatment, such as by maintaining a copper level in a marine aquarium system to prevent an outbreak of *Oodinium*. Grave consideration must be given to the type of medication being used. Destruction of biological filters may occur if antibiotics are used, and many chemicals will build up in the system and then overload it if there is a sudden change in pH or temperature. Long-term effects of toxic buildups in the fish themselves must also be considered, particularly the accumulative poisoning effects which can occur when heavy metal compounds containing such elements as zinc, copper, and mercury are used.

Oral Administration

The oral administration of medications can save much time and effort when utilized in treatment, but there are some major drawbacks which must not be overlooked or underestimated. In hatcheries and in pond culture, where large volumes of fish are involved, medicated foods are used extensively to combat systemic infections, as a prophylaxis, and to stimulate growth in food fishes.

On a smaller scale, or individually, a rubber tube catheter can be used to tube-feed and/or give exact dosages to sick fishes that no longer have any appetite. This limited method is used primarily on larger, expensive aquarium fish and on breeders in pond culture. Because of the stress of handling an already sick or starved fish, the catheter method of treatment must be considered as a last resort. When successful, however, the results can be quite dramatic.

In most applications, a commercial, medicated food is used to dose large numbers of fishes, although medicated preparations can be made up at the hatchery as they are needed. Usually, an antibiotic such as one of the tetracyclines or a sulfonamide is used. A number of years ago it was discovered that chickens being given certain antibiotics in their drinking water as a disease prophylactic gained weight more rapidly and reached marketable size much sooner than those that were unmedicated. Soon it became standard practice in poultry farming, and now it has overlapped into fish farming, even though there is little evidence to indicate its usefulness as a weight-gaining aid in fish. Apparently, weight gain in poultry is due to the depression of the normal intestinal bacterial flora, leaving more nutrients available for absorption by the bird. Since fish are notoriously lacking in normal intestinal bacteria, no appreciable nutrient saving is accomplished, thus there is no appreciable weight-gaining advantage to feeding antibiotics to fish as part of their normal diet.

The wisdom of this practice is now in serious question on other grounds as well, as new and more virulent strains of bacteria are appearing which are resistant to antibiotics that formerly would have made the recovery of the fish routine. These new strains are far more devastating upon a fish population which no longer has any natural immunity to them; in addition, treatment is made exceedingly difficult because of bacterial drug resistance. Another disastrous side effect of this practice is that many human antibiotic-resistant pathogenic strains are beginning to appear in ponds and rivers in various parts of the world.

Medicated foods in pelletal form, either of the floating or sinking variety, are thrown upon the surface of the water, a process termed *broadcast feeding*. This results in an uneven distribution of the feed among the fishes as the feeding habits of the fish override any intent or purpose of the fish farmer or hobbyist. Those fish that are weaker or less aggressive receive little or no medication, while the healthy, aggressive ones probably obtain an overdose of the drug being applied. This may be all right when using a nontoxic anthelminthic, but it is not good practice when using an antibiotic. One of the first symptoms of serious systemic infection is a loss of appetite, so those most seriously ill may receive no medication whatsoever. In addition, the social hierarchy or pecking order allows only those at the top to obtain the bulk of any food available, while those on the bottom must settle for the leftovers. Thus those with the greatest need are the ones most deprived, while those with the least need run the risk of being poisoned by an overdose of what would have been a lifesaving medication in a more moderate dose. It is generally conceded that feeding medications to fish is most useful as a prophylaxis rather than as a treatment, yet, as we have seen, this may be even more damaging in the long run. Still, there are occasions when it may be the only way to save any appreciable number of fish at all in a complement of valuable stock that is difficult to catch out of an area for treatment, i.e. when for some reason a pond cannot be drained or during an acute attack of bacterial hemorrhagic septicemia, where speed of administering a drug over an extensive area to an extensive population may be the only workable solution.

The possibility of giving to one fish an individual dose of medicine orally, while not out of the question, may become a battle of wits on occasion. After starving a fish for several days beforehand in order to make it desperate for food, a capsule or tablet dropped into the water will be immediately engulfed, and just as quickly spat out. Disguising it in the center of a chunk of shrimp or some such other delicacy has no more success, although it may stay in the mouth for a few seconds longer. Very seldom can a fish be enticed into eating of its own free will enough pure unadulterated medication to be of therapeutic value.

One other method of medicating fish orally, especially marine fish, is to administer the drug in the form of a bath of high salinity. Then, because of the natural osmotic forces, which cause a marine fish to lose body fluids to its environment, it must drink seawater to replenish its losses. In doing so the fish takes in and utilizes the drugs in the water as well. A point to remember is that this is also how copper toxicity in marine aquaria can occur when using copper sulfate as a treatment. Freshwater fish are constantly absorbing water through a selective membrane in their skin and gills which excludes most drugs and salts, so they never drink water, thus reducing the danger of drug toxicity when using baths in fresh water.

Parenteral Administration (Injections)

The metabolic processes of fish are geared to their poikilothermic nature. Their heart muscles and associated chambers do not pump blood as reliably or strongly as do the hearts of more advanced vertebrates. Their muscle tissue is poorly vascularized, making diffusion into the system slow or very poor at best. All of these reasons speak against the use of injections in fish, but nonetheless it works wonders when it works. It is the most effective and direct route of administering the majority of the newer antibiotics as long as consideration is given to the action the drug will take on the fish, its absorption rate into various tissues, and its exsorption route. The method of administration must be chosen carefully, based upon an understanding of the drug being used.

Further adverse considerations are the amount of time and effort involved in catching and injecting large numbers of fish as well as the tremendous stress that handling can place upon them. Parenteral injection is best suited for small numbers of valuable fish, such as the routine injection of breeder *Cyprinidae* in the spring to prevent the occurrence of bacterial haemorrhagic septicemia or to prevent furunculosis in *Salmonidae*. The treatment of valuable aquarium display fishes is admirably suited to this approach, provided the correct drug is used.

Some types of injections of special use in higher forms of life, e.g. intrapleural or intrasternal, are impossible in fish because of the absence in fish of associated or comparable structures. Intravenous injections are also both difficult and impractical on any but the largest fishes (Herman, 1972).

Parenteral administration of drugs may be accomplished in a variety of ways, depending upon the drug to be used and its most desirable route of administration. In all cases, however, injection is accomplished through the use of standard medical hypodermic syringes with hollow needles attached. The size of the syringe is determined by the amount of drugs to be used, and the bore and length of the needle are determined by the size of the fish it is to be used upon. Generally doses are extremely small even in larger fish, and a tuberculin syringe with about a 24 to 26 gauge needle is probably the most commonly employed size (although a 30 gauge needle can be used on extremely small fish).

Intramuscular Injection

Subcutaneous injection, which means that the drug is placed under the skin, has little to recommend it in the application of most antibiotics. The skin of a fish apparently does not have a great deal of contractibility, and once a needle hole is punched into it, it does not seal itself as well as most animal tissues. Therefore, leakage of the medication back out of the injection site occurs frequently enough to be considered a significant problem.

Many drugs injected intramuscularly (I.M.) are not absorbed into the fish's system rapidly enough to be effective, and the fish can die before the drug starts to take effect. This is primarily due to the poikilothermic nature of the fish and the metabolic activity of its muscles rather than to any fault of the drug. Still other drugs are not absorbed at all and become pockets of localized overdoses. This causes the cells in the vicinity of the injection site to die from antibiotic toxicity, resulting in a sterile abscess. Injectable oxytetracycline and some of the sulfonamides fall into this category. On the other hand, gentamycin works best when injected intramuscularly.

Intramuscular injections may be administered into any large muscle; however, on the shoulder, midway between the eye and the first dorsal spine, or in the space just posterior to the dorsal fin and above the midline of the body have been found to be the most easily accessible sites. On smooth-skinned or small-scaled fish, insertion of the needle is little or no problem, but on large-scaled fish, such as carp or other *Cyprinidae,* a needle may bend or break before it will penetrate those large, tough scales. The needle must be glided underneath a scale somewhat posterior to the actual injection point at a definite, low angle. After penetrating the integument, but before entering the muscle layer itself, the needle should be raised to a more erect angle and inserted deeply into the muscle. Caution must be exercised at all times in restraining the fish to be injected, because a sudden thrust of the fish can cause an inserted needle to either break off or rip a gash in its side.

Intravenous Injection

Intravenous injection (I.V.) affords the most rapid dispersal and the most effective route by which an antibiotic can be administered. Unfortunately, it can only be used on the largest of specimens, as a fish's body is composed primarily of extensive capillary networks rather than major vessels.

Two primary sites lend themselves to the introduction of drugs into the circulatory system. One is into the heart itself, by direct cardiac puncture. Located underneath the pectoral girdle, it can be reached by inserting a needle squarely through the girdle itself if it is cartilaginous enough, or by angling forward into the heart from just posterior to the pectoral girdle, being careful not to penetrate the peritoneum. The other injection site would be into the caudal artery which is located against and just ventral to the vertebral column. It can be reached by turning the fish belly up and sticking the needle straight in, toward the vertebral column from the ventral midline, at a point just anterior to the caudal origin. By drawing back on the plunger slightly after placement of the needle, entrance into the circulatory system is indicated by blood entering the syringe. The presence of vacuum in the syringe indicates placement in muscle or interstitial tissue. These sites can also be employed for the removal of blood samples to be used in blood studies.

Intraperitoneal Injection

The most commonly employed method of injecting fish is intraperitoneally (I.P.), which eliminates most of the difficulties encountered in I.M. or I.V. injections by making it necessary only to insert the needle into the visceral cavity and squeeze the plunger. Widely used in all phases of fish keeping, from public aquariums to fish farming, it has as its only drawback the absorptive ability of the drug being used. The drug must be highly absorbable and able to pass through either the intestinal wall or some other membrane and absorbed into the fish's system. Merely squirting a drug into the body cavity is not enough. Fortunately some of the most powerful antibiotics, e.g. chloramphenicol or streptomycin, will work in this fashion. It is therefore very probable that this method will continue to be highly popular and widely used for some time to come.

The method of I.P. administration is quite simple. A loaded syringe is inserted into the belly of a fish until it penetrates all of the dermal layers and the peritoneum. Then the proper amount of drug is dispensed, and the needle is withdrawn. A team of workers, set up in assembly line fashion, can treat a fairly large number of fish in a relatively short time. One man sits and injects the fish while his co-workers keep catching, weighing, and then directing new fish to him to treat, while others release the treated ones into a separate holding tank. In practice the needle is not even changed between injections. Although I am personally somewhat wary of this procedure, it is accepted practice around the world.

CALCULATION OF DOSAGES AND SOLUTIONS

Dosages and solutions can often be a confusing and perplexing aspect of medicating fishes. However, the problem can be fairly easily rectified with a little basic algebraic math involving ratios and proportions and the ability to convert one system of weights and measures into another more convenient or appropriate for our purposes. Once a basic understanding of ratios and proportions is aquired, then conversions are of minor consequence, and a quick glance at a table of equivalents will give the correct figures to use. This section on dosages and solutions is adapted for the most part from Blume (1969).

Systems of Measurement

In this text we will consider three basic systems of measurement, which are, unfortunately, all in common use in this country. The first, simplest, and most exact is the *scientific* or *metric system*. It is the one most often used by veterinarians and fish pathologists. Its basic units are (1) the gram (weight), (2) the liter (volume), and (3) the meter (linear). When these units are multiplied by ten or its multiples we need only add a Latin prefix to obtain the new values. For instance, 1 gram multiplied by 1000 becomes 1 kilogram (kilo = 1000). A table of metric units is contained in Table 2-I.

Table 2-I. METRIC UNITS OF MEASURE			
LATIN PREFIX	**WEIGHT** *Basic Unit is Gram (gm)*	**VOLUME** *Basic Unit is Liter (l)*	**LINEAR** *Basic Unit is Meter (m)*
Kilo (= 1000X)	Kilogram (kg)	Kiloliter (kl)	Kilometer (km)
Hecto (= 100X)	Hectogram (Hg)	Hectoliter (Hl)	Hectometer (Hm)
Deka (= 10X)	Dekagram (Dg)	Dekaliter (Dl)	Dekameter (Dm)
Deci (= 1/10X)	Decigram (dg)	Deciliter (dl)	Decimeter (dm)
Centi (= 1/100X)	Centigram (cg)	Centiliter (cl)	Centimeter (cm)
Milli (= 1/1000X)	Milligram (mg)	Milliliter (ml)	Millimeter (mm)

There is also a relationship between the units themselves, which is revealed in their definitions. The gram is equal to the weight of 1 milliliter (1/1000 liter) of pure distilled water at 4°C. The metric volume unit, the liter, is equal to the contents of 1 decimeter (10 centimeters) cube. Even though a liter contains 1000 milliliters and was intended to contain 1000 cubic centimeters, in actuality it contains 1000.028 cubic centimeters (cc). The difference is negligible, and for all practical purposes they are considered equivalent. Therefore 1 gm = 1 ml = 1 cc of distilled water at 4°C.

The meter, the linear metric measurement, does not concern us directly at this point in a discussion of weight and volume, but is included for the sake of thoroughness. Centimeters, millimeters, and microns (1/1000 of a millimeter) are the units most commonly encountered in fish therapeutics. The metric system is the system of choice in 98 percent of the countries of the world. Only the United States and two or three other countries still persist in the other less functional systems. Its use, especially in drug administration, is being phased into common usage in this country.

The official system in the United States has been the *apothecaries' system,* our second method of measurement. It was brought to this country from England by the early American colonists and is still in use here, although its use has long been abandoned in England. While the system is still fairly accurate, it is not nearly so straightforward and easy to work with as is the metric. Rather than attempt to define all of the units, a table of apothecary equivalents is given in Table 2-II.

The third system of measurement is noteworthy in that it only contains measures of volume. Known as the *household system,*

Table 2-II. APOTHECARIES' EQUIVALENT		
WEIGHT UNITS	**FLUID UNITS**	
20 grains (gr) = 1 scruple 3 scruples = 60 grains 60 grains = 1 dram (dr) 8 drams or 480 grains = 1 ounce (oz) 12 ounces = 1 pound (lb)	60 minims (m) = 1 fluid dram 8 fluid drams of 480 minims = 1 fluid ounce 16 fluid ounces = 1 pint (pt) 2 pints = 1 quart (qt) 4 quarts = 1 gallon (gal)	
WEIGHT UNITS*	**=**	**FLUID UNITS***
1 grain	=	1 minim (1 drop)
60 grains	=	1 fluid dram or 60 minims
480 grains	=	1 fluid ounce or 480 minims

*Approximate equivalents only, but when needed are acceptable for the preparation and administration of solutions and drugs.

it is an approximate measure only and should never be substituted for one of the other systems when accuracy is demanded. All measurements and equivalents are, of necessity, approximate and can be likened to a pinch of salt or a dash of pepper. Approximate household equivalents are listed in Table 2-III.

TABLE 2-III. APPROXIMATE HOUSEHOLD EQUIVALENTS		
VOLUME UNITS		
60 drops (gtt) (L. *gutta* — gtt)	=	1 teaspoon (tsp)
2 teaspoons	=	1 dessertspoon
2 dessertspoons (4 tsp)*	=	1 tablespoon (tbsp)
2 tablespoons	=	1 fluid ounce (oz)
6 fluid ounces	=	1 teacup
8 fluid ounces	=	1 glass or 1 measuring cup
*Approximately 3 tsp = 1 tbsp in practice.		

Incidentally, many of the dosages expressed in this book are in ppm (parts per million), which simply means milligrams per liter. For instance, 15 ppm = 15 mg/1.

Ratios and Proportions

Here is where the actual calculation of values comes into being, where we go from a known equivalent to an unknown. A ratio is simply a fraction; that is, $\frac{1}{4}$ when written as a proportion becomes 1:4, or 1 part in 4. A proportion is two fractions or ratios that are equivalent. For instance, $2/4 = \frac{1}{2}$ or, written as a proportion, 2:4 :: 1:2. The first and fourth terms are called the extremes. The second and third terms are called the means. By multiplying them together we obtain the equation, the product of the means equals the product of the extremes, i.e.:

(means) 4 × 4 = 16

(extremes) 2 × 8 = 16

Since the product of the means (16) equals the product of the extremes (16), we know our equation is balanced and therefore correct.

When writing proportions, care must be taken to keep terms in their proper order. Small (numerator a) is to large (denominator A) as small (numerator b) is to large (denominator B), or small units to small units as large units are to large units (a/A = b/B; a:A :: b:B; a/b = A/B; or a:b :: A:B) ; all express the same thought, and therefore all are correct.

While this may be mildly confusing when using only numerical values, it may become even more so when numerical values and two different units of measure are involved as they are in equivalent dosage situations. For example, there are approximately 15 gr in 1 gm (known equivalents). How many grains do 2 grams contain?

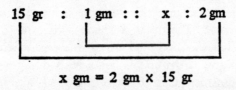

$$x \text{ gm} = 2 \text{ gm} \times 15 \text{ gr}$$

By multiplying and cancelling terms common to both sides our answer is:

$$x = 30 \text{ gr}$$

Unless the proportion is stated properly, using the numerical values *and* the equivalents in their proper order, the product of the means *may not* equal the product of the extremes, and the dosage will be wrong. For instance, in the known equivalents 15 gr = 1 gm, grains are smaller *equivalent units* than grams, so the proportion may be written 15 gr:1 gm; but 1 is a smaller *numerical unit* than 15, so the proportion may also be written *1* gm:*15* gr. Both ways are correct. What is important to remember is that whichever way it is written, the unknown half of the equation must be written in the same manner as the known half.

right	15 gr : 1 gm :: 30 gr : 2 gm	15/1 = 30/2
	1 gm : 15 gr :: 2 gm : 30 gr	1/15 = 2/30
wrong	15 gr : 2 gm :: 30 gr : 1 gm	15/2 = 30/1
	1 gm : 30 gr :: 2 gm : 15 gr	1/30 = 2/15

To avoid confusion we must adopt a consistent method of setting up our problem. Start every proportion with a ratio of two known values, i.e. 250 mg/1, or 5 gr/tablet, or 250 mg/10 gal, etc. Place this on the left-hand side of the equation. Next make certain that the unit of measure of the first term is the same as that of the third, and the second is the same as that of the fourth. If they are in different systems, they should be converted to be consistent.

The only exception is when we are dealing with known strengths of solutions, in which case the first and second terms must be the same and the third and fourth terms must be in another unit of measure. As an example, 10% : 100% :: 100 ml : 1000 ml.

This system of determining unknown values from known values may be used to solve almost any medication or dosage problem found in fish medicine. It may be divided into three categories or formulas. Formula A deals with the conversion of known equivalents to obtain an unknown equivalent, i.e. 15 gr: 1 gm :: x gr:0.5 gm. Formula B deals with dosages known to be available for administration into required (unknown) dosages, i.e.:

$$5 \text{ gr} : 1 \text{ tablet} :: 15 \text{ gr} : x \text{ tablets}$$
$$5x = 15$$
$$x = 3 \text{ tablets}$$

Formula C deals with the known strengths of solutions to obtain unknown quantities to be used, i.e.:

$$5\% : 100\% :: x \text{ ml} : 1000 \text{ ml}$$
$$100x = 5000$$
$$x = 50 \text{ ml}$$

All of the above formulas are essentially the same one—simple ratios and proportions—used for different applications. In all dosage and solution problems there may be two, but no more than two, different units of measure in addition to numerical values. All dosage problems can be solved using formulas A and B. All solution problems can be solved using formula C.

Since many of our conversions are only approximate, we must allow a little room for error. No more than a 10 percent margin of difference between prescribed and administered dosages may be considered safe. For example, if 100 mg of a drug is prescribed, then no more than 110 mg nor less than 90 mg may be given safely.

Determining Dosages

A few problems commonly encountered in administering drugs will be exposed in the following sections, and a few rules and guidelines will be offered which will make the problems simpler. First to be considered is the form in which the drug to be used presently exists. Is it in the form of a tablet, a powder, a capsule, or some other form? Is it already in a solution? If so, what strength? Secondly, how much and in what fashion, or manner, is it to be administered?

Tablets

Tablets cannot be divided accurately unless they are scored or marked for breaking along lines of cleavage, so, if at all possible, they should be obtained in the desired dosage. One common exception occasionally encountered is the fractional dosage of tablets intended to be dissolved in a sterile solution and then administered hypodermically. After determining the fractional portion of the tablet necessary, it is next necessary to determine the amount of solvent that will make the dosage easier to measure out. Here, minims may be a very convenient measure. If at all possible, the volume of solvent should be kept within an upper range of 10-24 minims, provided, of course, that the drugs or tablets will dissolve in that amount of solvent and that the fish is large enough to withstand such a large dose. Therefore, at least 10 minims should be used to dissolve 1 tablet, and 20 minims to dissolve 2 tablets, and so on. There should be, however, at least 10 minims left to administer to the fish unless it is a very small specimen. Normally, sterile saline or sterile distilled water is used as a solvent.

Solving dosage problems to give tablets parenterally may require three steps. It may be necessary to first convert the prescribed and available dosages into the same system of measure; second, determine how many of the available tablets must be used;

and third, reduce improper fractions if a fractional part of a tablet is used. As an example, suppose 0.5 mg of a drug is to be administered parenterally which is available in 1/200 gr tablets. First, units of measure must be converted:

$$1 \, mg \, : \, 1/60 \, gr \, :: \, x \, mg \, : \, 1/200 \, gr$$
$$1/60x \, = \, 1/200$$
$$x \, = \, 0.33 \, mg$$

Then, the second step is to determine how many tablets are necessary:

$$0.3 \, mg \, : \, 1 \, tablet \, :: \, 0.5 \, mg \, : \, x \, tablets$$
$$0.3 \, x \, = \, 0.5$$
$$(x \, = \, 5/10 \, \div \, 3/10 \, = \, 5/10 \, \times \, 10/3 \, = \, 5/3 \, = \, 1\tfrac{2}{3})$$
$$x \, = \, 1\tfrac{2}{3} \, tablets$$

Finally, it must be determined how much solvent to use and how much of the resultant mixture to use:

$$1 \, 2/3 \, tablets \, / \, 2 \, tablets \, = \, 5/3 \, / \, 2 \, = \, 5/3 \, \div \, 2/1 \, =$$
$$5/3 \, \times \, \tfrac{1}{2} \, = \, 5/6 \, of \, 2 \, full \, tablets$$

Dissolving each tablet in 12 minims of solvent yields 24 minims of diluent. By expelling 4 minims, or 1/6 of the total, the correct dosage is then ready to be administered.

Administering larger than necessary amounts of solution increases the possibility of tissue trauma. It is advisable to use as small an amount of solvent as possible, which should never exceed 24 minims. Also, if one uses more than this amount, there would be too little space left in a 2 ml syringe to permit agitation of the solvent and tablet. Most drugs are now available in solution which were formerly available only in tablet form, so this method is presented to assist in those rare occasions which do sometimes arise and can be most perplexing.

Capsules, Powders, and Crystals

An easy task to accomplish is the administration of capsules and powders, as the extent of one's knowledge need not go beyond knowing how much drug is required, and then to weigh it out and administer it. Capsules cannot be divided accurately; therefore, when a fractional dose is required, it must be broken up and weighed out or dissolved in a solution and treated as a fraction of a solution. Capsules are usually prescribed in terms of complete units, such as 1-250 mg capsule per 10 gal of water. Occasionally one may encounter a case where a fractional part of a capsule is required, but this is the exception rather than the rule. Powders pose no difficulty at all as long as an accurate scale is available.

A few drugs are measured in other systems of measurement, sometimes their very own unique system. The ones most commonly found are *milliequivalents* and *units*. Milliequivalents (mEq) are equal to 1/1000 of an equivalent and refer to the number of ionic charges of an element or compound. Milliequivalents are a measure of the chemical combining power of a substance. Potassium chloride (KCl) is an example of a drug measured in milliequivalents. A unit of a drug means something different for every drug measured in those terms. Penicillin is the drug most frequently referred to in units. The penicillin unit is equivalent to the antibiotic activity of 0.6 micrograms (mcg) of USP Penicillin Sodium Reference Standard. One milligram of this kind of penicillin equals 1667 units. Still other types of penicillin have different milligram-to-units equivalents. For example, one milligram of benzathine penicillin equals 1211 USP units. When a drug is prescribed in units or milliequivalents it is necessary to know the number of units or milliequivalents in a particular volume or capacity measure, e.g. 400,000 units/ml or 20 mEq/15 ml.

Tables and Conversions

Volume Equivalent Units

1:1000 solution	= 3.8 gm/gal
	= 0.1 gm/100 ml
	= 0.13 oz/gal
	= 1 ml/l
1 cubic centimeter (cm^3 or cc)	= 1 ml
	= 1 gm of H_2O at 4°C
	= 0.061 in^3
	= 0.001 qt
	= 0.002 pt
	= 0.034 fl oz

1 cubic inch (in³)

$= 16.387$ cm³
$= 0.0043$ gal
$= 0.017$ qt
$= 0.035$ pt
$= 0.036$ lb
$= 0.576$ oz
$= 0.554$ fl oz
$= 0.00058$ ft³
$= 0.0164$ l
$= 16.39$ gm

1 cubic foot (ft³)

$= 28.31$ l
$= 7.481$ gal
$= 62.426$ lb of fresh water
$= 28,355$ gm of water
$= 29.992$ qt
$= 59.844$ pt
$= 998.816$ oz
$= 957.5$ fl oz
$= 1728$ in³
$= 28,316$ cc
$= 28,316$ ml
$= 28,316$ gm
$= 28.316$ l

1 cup

$= 48$ tsp
$= 16$ tbsp
$= 8$ oz
$= 237$ ml

1 fluid (or liquid) ounce (fl oz)

$= 6$ tsp
$= 2$ tbsp
$= 0.0078$ gal
$= 0.031$ qt
$= 29.57$ gm
$= 0.062$ pt
$= 0.065$ lb
$= 1.04$ oz
$= 1.8$ in³

                   = 29.57 cc
                   = 29.57 ml
                   = 0.0296 l

1 gallon, U.S. (gal.)*

= 3.785 l
= 0.1339 ft^3
= 231 in^3
= 8.345 lb of water
= 3785.4 gm of water
= 4 qt
= 8 pt
= 135.52 oz
= 128 fl oz
= 3785.4 cc
= 3785.4 ml

1 grain/gallon (gr/gal)

= 19.12 ppm
= 142.9 lb/million gal

1 Imperial gallon (Imp gal)

= 4.5459 l
= 0.1605 ft^3
= 277.42 in^3
= 4.845 qt

1 kiloliter (kl)

= 1000 l
= 264.18 gal
= 35.315 ft^3

1 liter (l)

= 1000 ml
= 1000 cm^3
= 1.7598 liquid pt
= 1.057 liquid qt
= 0.264 gal
= 203 tsp
= 67.6 tbsp
= 35.28 oz
= 33.8 fl oz
= 4.23 cup

---

*To obtain volume of a rectangular or square aquarium in U.S. gallons = L × W × H (all in inches) /231 cubic inches.

$= 2.1134 \text{ pt}$
$= 2.205 \text{ lb}$
$= 61.025 \text{ in}^3$
$= 0.0353 \text{ ft}^3$
$= 1000 \text{ gm}$
$= 1 \text{ kg of water}$

1 part per million (ppm)

$= 1 \text{ mg/l}$
$= 3.8 \text{ mg/gal}$
$= 2.7 \text{ lb/acre foot}$
$= 0.0038 \text{ gm/gal}$
$= 0.0283 \text{ gm/ft}^3$
$= 0.0000623 \text{ lb/ft}^3$
$= 1233 \text{ gr/acre foot}$
$= 0.0586 \text{ gr/gal}$
$= 8.34 \text{ lb/million gal of water}$
$= 1 \text{ unit of weight in 1 million}$
  units of weight (1 lb/999,999
  lb of water)
$= 1 \text{ oz/1000 ft}^3 \text{ of water}$
$= 1 \text{ gm/264 gal of water}$
$= 1 \text{ gm/m}^3 \text{ of water}$

1 milliliter (ml)

$= 1 \text{ cm}^3$
$= 1 \text{ cc}$
$= 20 \text{ drops (approx.)}$
$= 0.20 \text{ tsp}$
$= 0.061 \text{ in}^3$
$= 0.001 \text{ l}$
$= 1 \text{ gm of water}$
$= 0.002 \text{ lb of water}$
$= 0.0003 \text{ gal (U.S.)}$

1 percent solution (1%)

$= 38 \text{ gm/gal}$
$= 1.3 \text{ oz/gal}$
$= 10 \text{ gm/1000 ml}$
$= 10 \text{ ml/1000 ml}$
$= 10 \text{ ml/l}$
$= 38 \text{ ml/gal}$

	= 1 gm/100 ml
	= 1 oz/0.75 gal (U.S.)
	= 4.53 gm/lb.
	= 0.624 lb/ft³
1 pint (pt)	= 0.5679 l
	= 0.125 gal
	= 0.5 qt
	= 1.043 lb
	= 16.69 oz
	= 16 fl oz
	= 28.875 in³
	= 0.0167 ft³
	= 473.18 cc
	= 473.18 ml
	= 0.473 l
	= 473.18 gm
1 pound/million gallons	= 0.1199 ppm
1 quart (qt)	= 946.35 ml
	= 946.35 cc
	= 946.35 gm of water
	= 0.95 l
	= 0.25 gal
	= 2.0 pt
	= 2.085 lb of water
	= 33.36 oz
	= 32 fl oz
	= 57.75 in³
	= 0.0334 ft³
1 tablespoon (tbsp)	= 3 tsp
	= 15 ml
1 teaspoon (tsp)	= 5 ml
	= 5 cc
	= 5 cm³

Weight Equivalent Units

1 centner (1 zentner)	= 50 kg
1 cubic inch (in^3)	= 16.39 gm
1 cubic foot (ft^3)	= 28,316 gm
1 doppel zentner (dz—a European weight)	= 100 kg
1 dram (dr)	= 1.772 gm
1 grain (gr)	= 64.8 mg
	= 0.065 gm
	= 0.35 oz
1 grain/gallon (gr /gal)	= 142.9 lb/million gal
1 gram (gm)	= 15.432 gr
	= 0.0353 oz
	= 0.034 fl oz
	= 0.0022 lb
	= 0.002 pt
	= 0.001 l
	= 1000 mg
	= 0.001 kg
1 hundredweight (cwt)	= 100 lb
	= 45.3592 kg
1 kilogram (kg)	= 2.205 lb
	= 1000 gm
1 microgram (mcg or μg)	= 0.001 mg
1 milligram (mg)	= 1000 mcg
	= 0.001 gm
	= 0.0154 gr
1 ounce (oz)	= 480 gr
	= 28.35 gm
	= 0.0075 gal
	= 0.03 qt
	= 0.06 pt
	= 0.0625 lb
	= 0.96 fl oz
1 part per million (ppm)	= 0.134 oz/1000 gal
	= 0.0283 gm/ft^3
	= 1 oz/1000 ft^3

	= 2.7 lb/acre foot
	= 1 unit of weight in 1 million units of weight
1 percent in food (1%)	= 4.5 gm/lb
	= 0.2 oz/lb
	= 83 gr/lb
	= 10,000 ppm in food
1 pound (lb)	= 5760 gr
	= 373.24 gm
1 pound, avoirdupois (lb)	= 7000 gr
	= 453.6 gm
	= 16 oz
	= 0.12 gal
	= 0.016 ft^3 of water
	= 0.48 qt
	= 0.96 pt
	= 15.35 fl oz
	= 27.68 in^3
	= 453.59 cc or cm^3
	= 453.59 ml
	= 453.59 gm
	= 0.454 l
1 pound/million gallons	= 0.1199 ppm
1 stone	= 14 lb
1 ton, metric	= 1000 kg
	= 2,204.6 lb
1 ton, U.S. (T)	= 2000 lb
	= 906 kg

Linear Equivalent Units

1 acre (A)	= 43,560 ft^2
	= 0.405 hectare
	= a square, 208.71 ft/side
	= a circle with a diameter of 235.4 ft
1 acre foot (1 acre of surface	= 43,560 ft^3
area covered by 1 ft of water)	= 2,718,144 lb of water (approx.)

	= 325,850 gal of water (approx.)
	= 1,233,342 l
1 centimeter (cm)	= 0.3937 in
1 cubic centimeter (cm³)	= 0.0610 in³
1 cubic foot (ft³)	= 7.481 gal
	= 29.922 qt
	= 59.844 pt
	= 62.426 lb
	= 998.816 oz
	= 957.51 fl oz
	= 1728 in³
	= 28.32 l
1 cubic inch (in³)	= 16.387 cc or cm³
	= 0.0043 gal
	= 0.017 qt
	= 0.035 pt
	= 0.036 lb
	= 0.576 oz
	= 0.554 fl oz
1 cubic meter (m³)	= 35.314 ft³
	= 61,024 in³
	= 1000 l
	= a cube, 1 m/side
1 foot (ft)	= 12 in
	= 30.48 cm
	= 0.305 m
1 hectare (ha)	= 2.47 acres
	= 10,000 m²
1 inch (in)	= 2.54 cm
1 kilometer (km)	= 0.62 miles
1 meter (m)	= 3.28 ft
	= 39.37 in
	= 100 cm
1 mile	= 1.61 km
1 millimeter (mm)	= 0.04 in

1 square foot (ft² or sq ft)	= 930 cm²
	= a square, 12 in/side
1 square meter (m²)	= a square, 100 cm/side
	= 10.764 ft²
	= 1550 in²
	= 10,000 cm²
1 yard (yd)	= 3 ft
	= 36 in
	= 91.44 cm
	= 0.914 m

Temperature Conversions

Centigrade (C°) = (Fahrenheit −32) × 5/9
Fahrenheit (F°) = (Centigrade × 9/5) + 32

Other Useful Equivalents and Conversions

RATE OF FLOW
1 ft³/sec = 646, 300 gal/24 hours
          = 449 gal/minute
1 million gal/24 hours (1 day) = 1.547 ft³/second
                               = 694 gal/minute

SALINE CONCENTRATIONS
1.0% salt solution = 0.622 lb salt (9.9 oz) /ft³ of water
                   = 0.083 lb salt/gal of water

OXYGEN AND CARBON DIOXIDE
Oxygen in ppm × 0.7 = O_2 in cc or ml/l
Oxygen in cc or ml/l × 1.429 = O_2 in ppm
Carbon dioxide in ppm × 0.509 = CO_2 in cc or ml/l
Carbon dioxide in cc or ml/l × 1.964 = CO_2 in ppm

HOW TO CALCULATE THE CALORIC CONTENT OF ANY FOOD
There must first be available an analysis of the food which
contains at least the following: percent moisture, percent
protein, percent fat, percent ash, and percent fiber. With this
information at hand, the following procedure should be used:
  1. Calculate the percent dry matter (100% − the moisture
     content).

2. Calculate the percent nitrogen-free extract or carbohydrate (subtract the total of the % protein, % fat, % ash, and % fiber from 100%).
3. Multiply the percent nitrogen-free extract (NFE) by 4 to obtain the number of carbohydrate calories/100 gr.
4. Multiply the percent protein by 4 to obtain the number of protein calories/100 gr.
5. Multiply the percent fat by 9 to obtain the number of fat calories/100 gr.
6. Add 3, 4, and 5 together to obtain the total calories/100 gr.
7. Multiply 6 by 4.54 to get the calories/lb.
   (We use 4 and 9 as factors rounded off to the nearest whole unit, but actually the caloric values of 4 for NFE, 4 for protein, and 9 for fat are physiological fuel values and account for digestibility and urinary loss or urea calories. For gross calories use 4.15 for NFE, 4.4 for proteins, and 9.4 for fats.)

MISCELLANEOUS
1 kilohertz (kHz) = 100 cycles/second
1 microwatt second (mws) = microwatt seconds/cm^2
1 minute = 60 seconds

ENGLISH TO METRIC CONVERSIONS

To Convert:	Multiply by:	To Obtain:
Inches	25.4	Millimeters
Millimeters	0.03937	Inches
Grams	0.03527	Ounces
Pounds	0.4536	Kilograms
Pounds/Acre	1.121	Kilograms/hectare
Number/100 cm^2	9.29	Number/ft^2
Acres	0.4047	Hectares

TABLE 2-IV
TREATMENT CONVERSION CHART

(Amounts listed are for active ingredients or a trade name preparation, depending on the recommendations)

parts per million (ppm)	dilution	% solution	mg/l	gm/l	mg/gal	oz/gal	oz/1,000 gal	gm/ft²	oz/1,000 ft²	lbs/acre foot
0.1	1:10,000,000	0.00001	0.1	0.0001	0.38	0.000013	0.013	0.0028	0.1	0.27
1	1:1,000,000	0.0001	1	0.001	3.8	0.00013	0.134	0.0283	1	2.7
2	1:500,000	0.0002	2	0.002	7.6	0.00029	0.268	0.0567	2	5.4
3	1:333,333	0.0003	3	0.003	11.4	0.00040	0.402	0.0851	3	8.1
4	1:250,000	0.0004	4	0.004	15.2	0.00053	0.536	0.1134	3.99	10.8
5	1:200,000	0.0005	5	0.005	19.0	0.00067	0.670	0.1418	4.99	13.5
6	1:161,600	0.0006	6	0.006	22.8	0.00080	0.804	0.1701	5.99	16.2
7	1:142,900	0.0007	7	0.007	26.6	0.00093	0.938	0.1985	6.99	18.9
8	1:125,000	0.0008	8	0.008	30.4	0.00117	1.072	0.2268	7.99	21.6
9	1:111,000	0.0009	9	0.009	34.1	0.00120	1.206	0.2552	8.98	24.3
10	1:100,000	0.0010	10	0.010	38.0	0.0013	1.340	0.2835	9.98	27.0
11	1:90,909	0.0011	11	0.011	41.8	0.0014	1.474	0.3118	10.98	29.7
12	1:83,333	0.0012	12	0.012	45.6	0.0016	1.608	0.3401	11.98	32.4
13	1:76,923	0.0013	13	0.013	49.4	0.0017	1.742	0.3684	12.97	35.1
14	1:71,429	0.0014	14	0.014	53.2	0.0018	1.876	0.3967	13.97	37.8
15	1:66,667	0.0015	15	0.015	57.0	0.00195	2.010	0.4250	14.98	40.5
16	1:62,500	0.0016	16	0.016	60.8	0.0021	2.144	0.4533	15.97	43.2
17	1:59,235	0.0017	17	0.017	64.6	0.0022	2.278	0.4816	16.97	45.9
18	1:55,555	0.0018	18	0.018	68.4	0.0023	2.412	0.5099	17.96	48.6
19	1:52,632	0.0019	19	0.019	72.2	0.0025	2.546	0.5382	18.96	51.3
20	1:50,000	0.0020	20	0.020	76.0	0.0026	2.680	0.5620	19.97	54.0
100	1:10,000	0.0100	100	0.100	380.0	0.013	13.400	2.8350	99.84	270.0
125	1:8000	0.0125	125	0.125	475.0	0.016	16.750	3.5338	134.80	337.5
250	1:4000	0.025	250	0.25	950.0	0.03	33.500	7.0875	249.60	675.0

TABLE 2-IV—(continued)

parts per million (ppm)	dilution	% solution	mg/l	gm/l	mg/gal	oz/gal	oz/1,000 gal	gm/ft²	oz/1,000 ft²	lbs/acre foot
500	1:2000	0.05	500	0.5	1,900.0	0.07	67.000	14.1750	499.20	1,350.0
750	1:1333	0.075	750	0.75	2,950.0	0.10	100.500	21.2625	748.80	2,025.0
1,000	1:1000	0.1	1,000	1	3,800.0	0.13	134.000	28.3500	998.4	2,700.0
2,000	1:500	0.2	2,000	2	7,600.0	0.27	268.000	56.7000	2,000.0	5,400.0
3,000	1:333	0.3	3,000	3	11,400.0	0.40	402.000	85.1000	3,000.0	8,100.0
4,000	1:250	0.4	4,000	4	15,200.0	0.53	536.000	113.4000	3,990.0	10,800.0
5,000	1:200	0.5	5,000	5	19,000.0	0.67	670.000	141.8000	4,990.0	13,500.0
6,000	1:166.6	0.6	6,000	6	22,800.0	0.80	804.000	170.1000	5,990.0	16,200.0
7,000	1:142.9	0.7	7,000	7	26,600.0	0.93	938.000	198.5000	6,990.0	18,900.0
8,000	1:125	0.8	8,000	8	30,400	1.07	1,072	226.8	7,990	21,600
9,000	1:111	0.9	9,000	9	34,100	1.20	1,206	255.2	8,980	24,300
10,000	1:100	1	10,000	10	38,000	1.34	1,340	283.5	9,984	27,000
20,000	1:50	2	20,000	20	76,000	2.67	2,680	567.0	20,000	54,000
25,000	1:40	2.5	25,000	25	95,000	3.34	3,350	709.0	25,000	67,500
30,000	1:33.33	3	30,000	30	114,000	4.01	4,020	851.0	30,000	81,000
40,000	1:25	4	40,000	40	152,000	5.34	5,360	1,134.0	39,900	108,000
50,000	1:20	5	50,000	50	190,000	6.68	6,700	1,418.0	49,900	135,000
60,000	1:16.16	6	60,000	60	228,000	8.01	8,040	1,701.0	59,900	162,000
70,000	1:14.29	7	70,000	70	266,000	9.35	9,380	1,985.0	69,900	189,000
75,000	1:13.33	7.5	75,000	75	295,000	10.01	10,500	2,127.0	74,900	202,500
80,000	1:12.50	8	80,000	80	304,000	10.68	10,720	2,268.0	79,900	216,000
90,000	1:111.1	9	90,000	90	341,000	12.02	12,060	2,552.0	89,800	243,000
100,000	1:10	10	100,000	100	380,000	13.35	13,400	2,835.0	99,840	270,000

Chapter 3

ACTIONS AND USES OF DRUGS

DRUGS DO NOT CURE DISEASE in fish, but they can materially enhance or alter "natural processes." Drugs cannot make tissues perform functions for which they are not physiologically adapted, but at times they may be used to inhibit natural processes, thereby effecting a cure. Drugs may act on fish to alter physiological processes by causing tissues to perform their normal functions more or less swiftly, intensely, or efficiently. They may serve to stimulate activities as diverse as cellular respiration or antibody formation to produce immunity. They may serve to replace deficiencies, thus bringing about a state of "normalcy" or health. Still other drugs may act on foreign bodies, usually in an attempt to bring about their destruction without harming the fish. For instance, alkalies may be used to neutralize acids, or antibiotics may be used to inhibit or distort the mechanisms of infectious agents. Thus drug action may be broken down into two very broad, sometimes overlapping, categories: (1) those which act to produce a physiological response, usually upon the host fish and (2) those which act to destroy or overcome the agent responsible for the disease condition. Some drugs may work in both categories simultaneously. Those drugs which act on foreign agents are called chemotherapeutic drugs and include antibiotics. Each of these categories will be covered separately in subsequent sections.

The manner of prescribing drugs as therapeutic agents may be approached from three primary standpoints. Each is dependent upon the degree of understanding of the drug being used and the agent being acted upon. First is the case in which no attempt is made to remove the basic underlying cause of the disease or dis-

57

order, and only the fish's symptoms are treated. Indeed, in a number of such instances, the causative factor or factors are unknown. This is the approach known as *symptomatic therapeutics.* Second, a medicine may be used which experience has shown to be of benefit, but about which the mode of action or the active principle of the drug being used is unknown or little understood. Again it may not even be necessary to know the etiologic agent involved, but just that if procedure "A" is followed, disease "X" will probably be eradicated. This is *empirical therapeutics.* The scientific basis of any drug therapy follows a known, established course, using known, established methods and modes of action to produce known, established results. This third method is called *rational therapy,* and as it is the ideal sought, the next few paragraphs will discuss this method in greater detail.

The purpose of a course of any therapeutic measure, drug or otherwise, is to relieve symptoms, restore normal metabolism (healthy condition), drive out or destroy the causative agent, and produce a balance such that anabolism and catabolism are in direct proportion to the metabolic requirements of the organism being treated. To accomplish this end a regimen has been worked out that allows for the systematic understanding of the action(s) a drug may take and the use(s) to which it may be applied.

When a substance is known or suspected to effect a beneficial therapeutic effect upon a fish, a name—both scientific and popular—is first derived or determined. The drug source, whether animal, vegetable, mineral, or synthetic chemical origin, must be derived or determined. A purified extract must be obtained by various chemical processes. Then it must be determined how or if the drug enters a fish's body, how it accomplishes its beneficial action, what harm it might do, both to the fish and to the environment, and how it is eliminated or destroyed after accomplishing its purpose and what aftereffects, if any, remain. A determination as to how the substance may be administered is made experimentally by giving the drug to a group of test fishes, orally, parenterally, and by baths. Its effect in all cases is studied for its acute effects on various physiological functions of the fish. Functions such as blood pressure, respiration rate, muscular contractions, secretions (such as mucous or urine), and oxygen consumption under the effects of the drug are all studied in minute detail.

The fatal dose of the drug (the *lethal concentration* or LC_n) must be determined to find the maximum dose the fish can tolerate. Physio-psychological effects, such as excitation, coma, or convulsions, are studied, as well as urine and respiratory excretions. The chronic effects of prolonged exposure at various dosage levels are studied to determine the effects on growth, reproduction, and other essential body functions. Pathological changes in body tissues and blood cells are examined. If a drug substance can pass all of the above tests, then it is ready to be tried on sick fish.

All of the above mentioned tests are made on "normal" healthy fish. Once the normal is known for a drug, then reliable tests can be made in pathological circumstances. All of the tests are then repeated to determine the effects on sick fish as well as the pathogen it will hopefully attack or drive out. It is thus understandable that the adequate testing of any drug takes many years.

CLASSIFICATION BY ACTION OR ACTIVITY ON FISH

Drugs and chemicals may be grouped according to the physiological effect they produce or by the site of their activity on the fish's body. Those acting on the skin or other body surfaces at the point of application are known as drugs with *local actions*, while those acting inside the body, remote from the point of application, either through absorption or entrance into the bloodstream, are considered to have a *systemic action*.

Drug actions may be *selective*, in which case the drug may single out a certain tissue or type of cell and act only upon those cells. Anesthetics, for instance, depress nerve cell function. This action is due to a marked chemical affinity by the drug towards certain specific characteristics of those cells and no others. Or, drug actions may have a *general* effect, in which they act upon or affect all protoplasm with which they come in contact. Antiseptics, acids, alkalies, and the heavy metals may be included in this group.

Local Effects

Among those drugs which produce a local effect, there may be a loose arrangement initiated, describing these drugs according to their direct uses. Thus, *antiseptics* are used to treat infections, while *anthelminthics* are used to destroy or expel various types of worms. Tissues may be destroyed entirely by a *caustic* but induced to heal by a *vulnerary*. *Irritants* may be used to stimulate tissues by providing a mild irritation, while *counter-irritants* may be used to expel or neutralize other undesirable external irritants. *Acids* may be used to supply a deficiency or neutralize an overalkaline water condition, while *alkalies* may be used for counteracting the opposite or acid condition. An *astringent* may be used to contract or harden tissues to stop bleeding or serum loss, while a *stimulant* is used to increase the flow of blood or increase activity in the affected part. *Anodynes* relieve pain (of very little or no use in fish), while *anesthetics* may be used to produce anesthesia. As may be noted, these actions may be either general or selective, although the preponderance of drugs used on fish which produce a local effect are general in their actions. For every drug action there is a counteraction which will oppose it or neutralize its effects.

Systemic Effects

Systemic drugs produce many of the same effects as local drugs, as well as producing a few special effects of their own. Types of systemic drug actions include the *physiologic action,* which is the drug action upon normal healthy tissues, and *therapeutic action,* which is its action on a diseased tissue (the action of the same drug in the same dosage might be quite different when used on normal healthy tissues than it would be when used on diseased tissues).

A systemic drug may serve to increase the activity of a tissue through *stimulation,* but it is well to note that overstimulation of cells, either through overdose or prolonged use of a drug, will result in tissue or cell depression. *Depressive actions* occur when the use of a drug results in a decrease in the ability of cells to continue their function. This may be accomplished in a variety of ways. The site of the drug action may even be remote from the tissues affected, such as when a drug acting on the brain lowers blood pressure or respiration. Sometimes drugs depress by preventing or promoting the action of some other chemical substance, such as by inhibiting enzyme production or other chemical regulators. They may also serve to exert an internal or external direct action on the effector cells.

Drugs may act systemically by *irritation*. Normally an irritant produces slight temporary damage to some cells. Caustics are very weak concentrations of irritants. Mild irritation will usually stimulate the cell to repair this damage, thus affecting a cure of the diseased condition at the same time. Prolonged irritation will cause depression of this cellular activity, while marked irritation will cause disintegration and death of the cell.

A *side action* occurs when a drug action is produced other than the one for which the drug was given or intended. It becomes an *untoward action* if its side action is harmful or toxic to the fish. *Antagonistic action* occurs when two or more drugs have an opposite or contradictory effect. Antagonism is discussed further under the heading of antibiotic therapy.

Synergistic action occurs when the action of two or more drugs becomes additive in their effect on a cell or tissue. Each drug exerts its own influence as well as enhancing the action of the others, resulting in a combined effect greater than that which could be achieved with each separately. The point to be made here is that both antagonism and synergism (which is also discussed further under antibiotic therapy) are not exclusively properties of antibiotic therapy but may occur with many other types of drugs as well.

Cumulative action occurs when one dose of a drug has not been eliminated before another is given. This may cause an accumulation in the fish's body and, if prolonged, may produce toxic symptoms. If there is no accumulation, then a *tolerance action* may develop, and then the dosage must be progressively increased in order to maintain what was formerly a therapeutic level. In a similar manner, bacterial tolerance may be built up to a drug until the drug no longer has any effect on the microorganism. It has then become resistant to that drug.

Occasionally, a drug may produce an effect contrary to normal, or for which there is no explainable mechanism. This results in drug *idiosyncracy* and may involve an overresponse or an under-response, both of which may be abnormal to the expected reaction.

Drug *habituation* and *addiction* are drug actions which are entirely feasible in fishes but about which little or nothing is known.

ANTISEPTICS AND DISINFECTANTS

A discussion of the properties of antiseptics and disinfectants or the chemicals included in these categories may be considered in the same section, because in many instances the only difference is in the concentration and consequent strength of the solution. Literally, antiseptic means *against sepsis*, and since sepsis is the contamination of a fish's system by the introduction of toxic substances or pathogenic organisms into the blood stream, an antiseptic may be defined as a substance which prevents or inhibits this occurrence (Krug and McGuigan, 1955). A disinfectant is merely a stronger solution, but it goes one step further by destroying the cell and rendering sterile objects, places, or surfaces which might be harboring pathogens.

The strength and activity of a disinfectant is such that it will kill almost *any* living cell, including that of a fish or a person, should one's skin remain in contact with it for any length of time. Therefore, disinfectants should never be used upon the bodies of living fishes or in situations where fishes might be returned to the water before the disinfectant is thoroughly removed or flushed out of the system. Disinfectants are also known as *germicides* and are characterized by their strong concentrations. The activity of the chemical is due to its degree of ionization (ionic activity), the temperature of the solution, and the length of time it is in contact with the tissue or materials it is being called upon to act against. Most disinfectants and antiseptics are hindered in their actions by the amount of extraneous organic matter present, and the same strength solution will have different effects when varying degrees of organic matter are present.

Disinfectants and their dilutions, known as *antiseptic strengths,* are among the most dangerous chemicals to use on or around fishes, yet some of the most respectable and time-tested chemical treatments of fish diseases are contained in this group. They owe their action to a direct and positive reaction with the protoplasm of the cell they come in contact with and are nonselective to the tissue or species of organism they act upon.

Some antiseptic strengths, including potassium permanganate and hydrogen peroxide, release oxygen upon contact with protoplasm, oxidizing it and burning up the cell. The salts of heavy metals, e.g. copper, zinc, mercury, or arsenic compounds, combine chemically with the cell constituents, altering their composition and producing erratic, terminal cell function. Some compounds, e.g. acids or alkalies, simply dissolve or destroy the protein of the cell, while others such as phenol and its derivatives produce coagulation or precipitation of the cell proteins. Chemicals such as formalin or sodium chloride dehydrate the cell, while still other chemicals may cause them to be hydrated.

All of the old standard dyes such as acriflavine, methylene blue, and malachite green are included in this category. Alcohol, chlorine, iodine, and silver compounds are placed here also. Perhaps most surprisingly, nitrofurazone and the other nitrofuran derivatives, generally regarded as antibiotics, are antiseptics at low dilutions and become disinfectants at higher concentrations, but are not antibiotics at all, even though they are quite effective against a wide range of gram-positive and gram-negative bacteria and may be given orally for systemic use.

In general, antiseptics and disinfectants are used as topical applications, dips, and baths. Some, however, may be used internally or systemically. Many of those used in the latter fashion also have anthelminthic properties.

Another class of chemicals, related to or included in the category of disinfectants, are those that can alter surfaces or interfaces of cells, causing their destruction. These are called *detergents,* but they may act as antiseptics or disinfectants when applied in the treatment of fish diseases. The most notable detergent in use in fish medicine is benzalkonium chloride (Roccal®). Lysol, another detergent, is a mixture of phenol and linseed oil soap.

CHEMOTHERAPY

Modern chemotherapeutic agents are defined as those chemicals that, when used in the treatment of infectious diseases, will effectively kill the causative microorganisms but will produce little or no injury to the fish or its tissues. Technically, this ideal definition includes antibiotics, but because of their special nature they will be considered separately. Although all antibiotics are chemotherapeutic agents, not all chemotherapeutic agents are antibiotics. Today, most chemotherapeutic agents are thought of as well-defined chemical substances, usually prepared synthetically, which are not derived from microbial growths. In addition, there are a number of drugs which can be included either in the previous section or as chemotherapeutic agents, depending upon their concentration, dosage, or applications, e.g. antiseptics and disinfectants.

Apart from the above, chemotherapy may be broken down into three slightly overlapping divisions: (1) antibacterial agents other than antibiotics, including primarily the exclusively synthetic sulfonamide drugs, (2) the antiprotozoal agents which contain a number of alkaloids, essential oils, iodides, and metallic compounds (essential oils are not used in the treatment of fish diseases and will not be discussed), and (3) metazoan parasiticides composed of insecticides and numerous other chemicals used in the control or elimination of parasitic worms and crustaceans or their intermediate hosts, i.e mollusks. All of these classes will be considered in the following sections.

Antibacterial Agents (Sulfonamides)

In 1932, a completely synthetic drug was patented in Germany as an antibacterial agent. That drug, Prontosil®, marked the beginning of a new age in the treatment of diseases, human or otherwise, as it was the first really effective chemical agent active against systemic bacterial diseases, and further, it was completely synthetic and manufactured entirely in the laboratory, having absolutely no counterpart in nature. In 1935, chemists synthesized Neoprontosil®, a more soluble and therefore more versatile compound which was marketed as a bright red dye. It was shortly thereafter shown that the active principle at work in both of these drugs was an amino-benzene-sulfonamide radical (H_2N-C_6H_4-SO_2NH-), now known as the sufonamide group.

In retrospect, the sulfonamide sulfanilamide was discovered to have been synthesized from benzene in 1908, but was never tested for its antibacterial activity and was merely a chemical curiosity. By splitting off the last hydrogen atom on the sulfanilamide compound, which is the simplest possible sulfonamide, and adding a variety of other radicals in its place, a large number of products can be obtained, all of which have the same sulfonamide activity, but possess otherwise differing characteristics of solubility, pH response, and disease specificity, according to what other chemical radical is attached.

One radical that leads to a special group of drugs in itself is the pyrimidine radical. This gives rise to the sulfapyrimidines—sulfadiazine, sulfamerazine, and sulfamethazine. These drugs are widely used as oral medications in trout and salmon culture and were probably the first sulfa drugs to be used on fishes, their history going back to the 1940s.

While it is not yet possible to state with definite certainty exactly how sulfa drugs work, it is known that they interfere with the normal metabolism of the bacterial cell in some fashion to produce a bacteriostatic effect. It is believed that bacteria mistakenly substitute the sulfonamide radical for para-aminobenzoic acid (both chemicals closely resemble each other in their chemical structure). Para-aminobenzoic acid is a bacterial vitamin and is vital to enzyme systems within its structure. Where large amounts of para-aminobenzoic acid are present naturally, such as in pus pockets and necrotic areas, sulfonamides have little effect and must be present in extra large quantities in order to be effective. If the sulfonamide is there first, however, no infection is likely to be able to form.

$$\overset{\displaystyle H}{\underset{\displaystyle H}{N}} - \langle\!\!\!\bigcirc\!\!\!\rangle - COOH$$

PARA — AMINOBENZOIC ACID

Normally sulfonamides are given orally, and this is the first choice as a route of administration. They are rapidly absorbed from the fish's intestinal tract into the bloodstream and are extremely effective against gram-positive bacteria, particularly the streptococcus, staphylococcus, and other related coccus forms. They reach therapeutic levels in the blood and *all* body tissues very rapidly. Just as rapidly, however, the fish's body begins to act to eliminate them. A good bit of the drug is filtered out by the liver, and through a process termed acetylation the sulfonamide is inactivated. Acetylated sulfas are nontherapeutic against bacteria but *may* be toxic to fish if a sufficient quantity is produced.

Sulfonamides in solution are very alkaline, which is all right in the bloodstream and body tissues and fluids, but when they are filtered out by the kidneys they enter the acidic medium of urine. This drastic alteration in pH frequently causes the sulfonamides to precipitate out of solution as insoluble crystals or powders. In some cases of impaired renal sufficiency it may prove fatal, and even with normal renal function large doses may produce total kidney failure due to the presence of impacted sulfa drugs in the glomeruli. Sulfonamides should never be used in cases of known or suspected kidney disease.

There is a method, however, whereby the risk of renal damage is reduced to a minimum or else eliminated entirely. This is through the use of combinations of sulfonamides, such as the triple sulfa combination of sulfadiazine, sulfamethazine, and sulfamerazine. All of these drugs have the same degree of activity against the same types of microbes, yet have different rates of absorption from the intestine into the bloodstream and slightly different precipitation points in an acidic pH. Thus one drug is already into the bloodstream at a therapeutic level while the other two are still being absorbed. Then when the first drug reaches the kidneys, even though there may be some insoluble precipitates formed, they are not enough to clog the renal passages and are excreted. Also at this same time the other drugs are now reaching therapeutic levels in the blood and each will in its turn be eliminated by the kidneys without undue stress to the fish's system. The overall effect is one of prolonged drug activity at therapeutic levels with a lessened possibility of toxic untoward effects on the fish.

In the final analysis, the effectiveness of sulfonamide therapy is based on each individual case or fish, as theoretically is the proper dosage. If the fish's liver is particularly efficient, toxic acetylation may occur. If its kidneys are weak or damaged, or if the drug is slightly overdosed, renal damage ranging from mild to severe may occur. If there are extensive necrotic areas, the drug may simply be ineffective in stopping the bacteria, even though the bacteria is susceptible to the drug. Then, too, there is the possibility of bacterial drug resistance developing in cases of prolonged usage or of inadequate doses. There are a number of other possible untoward side effects which have been noted in human and veterinary medicine but which have not yet been detected and/or reported in fishes.

Sulfonamides are poorly absorbed into the fish's system from the surrounding waters. Thus all of the preceding systemic complications are not a consideration when using sulfas as baths for external bacterial invasions (fin and tail rot) and superficial fungus infections (*Saprolegnia*). The sodium salts of the sulfonamides are particularly soluble and therefore fast acting and can be dissolved in waters of almost any pH. Some other forms may be difficult to dissolve in waters from some areas due to pH factors. Sulfonamides have been used as injections, but for some reason there is a higher degree of acetylation when this is done, and it is not recomended.

Antiprotozoal Agents

In most instances of external protozoan diseases or infestation, a variety of antiseptics and disinfectants are available which are quite effective in their control. In addition to this rather large group of chemicals there are a number of protozoan specific drugs which, rather than being general protoplasmic poisons or destroyers, like the antiseptics and disinfectants, act toward the inhibition or destruction of particular groups of protozoans with little or no cellular damage to adjacent fish tissues, either externally or systemically. Some antibiotics in double or triple strength, if they can be tolerated by the fish at those levels, are sometimes effective in the control of protozoans, and, likewise, some antiprotozoal drugs in double or triple strength are effective against bacteria.

Antiprotozoal drugs act by disrupting some vital step in the metabolism of the organism. There are two primary classes of antiprotozoal drugs in use in fish medicine: (1) *alkaloid antiprotozoals,* used primarily against ectoparasitic protozoans, and (2) *metallic antiprotozoal compounds,* used primarily against intestinal and systemic protozoans. There are other classes of drugs in use in veterinary and human medicine that are useful against protozoans, but they are not used on fish and will not be considered here. One of the recent drugs developed which is coming to be used more and more in the treatment of a number of protozoan diseases of fish is metronidazole.

Alkaloid Antiprotozoals

For untold centuries the natives of Peru have combatted malaria and other systemic protozoan maladies by chewing the bitter bark of the Cinchona tree. It was introduced into Europe in 1639 and received its name from the wife of the Spanish viceroy of Peru, the Countess of Chinchón, who was allegedly cured of a malarial fever by its use. In 1820, a German scientist isolated the active principle of the bark, an alkaloid which he called *quinine.* It was not until May, 1944, however, that it was first synthesized by two American scientists. The use of quinine in fishes stems from the mid-1950s when it was discovered that the hydrochloride salt of quinine was effective in the treatment of "Ich."

The use of quinine in either a known or unknown form as a specific chemotherapeutic agent to selectively kill pathogenic microbes precedes by several centuries Paul Ehrlich's "magic bullets" *(see* following section). Today, at least twenty alkaloid derivatives of medical importance have been isolated from Cinchona bark, making it the single most important natural drug source known.

A number of synthetic antiprotozoal drugs are now also available, chief among them being quinacrine hydrochloride (Atabrine®), a derivative obtained from the yellow dye acridine. It is used primarily to effectively control *Cryptocaryon* outbreaks in marine aquaria.

All of the quinine and synthetic alkaloid derivatives are active against the asexual stage of protozoans which undergo multiple stages in their life cycles. They are all effective in small doses and become general protoplasmic poisons if used in large doses, therefore a series of small doses is much safer to use than a single large one. They may produce toxic effects in fishes or may even dye the fish yellow temporarily, but normal coloration will return gradually following the discontinuation of their use. Occasionally some totally unexpected, usually fatal, idiosyncrasy will occur with the use of such alkaloid derivatives in fishes, which indicates that there is much more to be learned regarding the use of these drugs in treatment. They are normally used in the form of baths for the control of external protozoans, and they are rather ineffective against bacteria (although excessively large doses will kill bacteria). They can usually be used safely in marine aquaria with established bacterial filters with little or no damage to the marine minienvironment. Because of their bitter taste it is not likely that these drugs can be used orally, but may be effective vermifuges and systemic antiprotozoals if they can be made palatable to the fish. These alkaloid derivatives are normally fatal if injected parenterally.

Metallic Antiprotozoal Compounds

In 1910, Paul Ehrlich, in Germany, discovered in his now famous experiment 606 an arsenic compound, arsphenamine, which would act to kill trypanosomes in mice and the spirochete of syphilis in man. It was the culmination of a twenty-five-year search for "magic bullets," specific chemical compounds which would attack specific types of cells without appreciably harming other tissues or cells. With this discovery was born the modern day, deliberate, laboratory development of chemotherapeutic agents to combat specific diseases, parasites, or metabolic conditions. The first chemotherapeutic drugs developed were antiprotozoals, and this remained true until effective antibacterial therapy began with the sulfonamides in the 1930s.

Most metal-containing antiprotozoals are effective against protozoans but not against bacteria. Most of them are both toxic and fatal to fish in larger doses and are accumulative poisons in cases of prolonged exposure to minute doses. The metal compounds most often encountered as antiprotozoals in fish therapeutics include, but are not limited to, salts and oxides of arsenic, mercury, antimony, cooper, silver, and bismuth. The exact mechanism by which they act on protozoans is at present unknown. The arsphenamides are believed to exert their effects through liberation of arsenoxide. Arsenicals such as carbarsone and acetarsone have been used for years in fish medicine for control of the intestinal parasite *Hexamita* (hole-in-the-head disease). The use of many others have been explored as possible controls for *Myxosoma*, the "whirling disease" of salmonids, but to no avail.

In general, these compounds are fed to fish in their food in order for them to act systemically on internal protozoan disorders. The same compounds could conceivably be used as antiseptics or disinfectants at greater strengths when used as baths. Many are also the bases for effective anthelminthics. All metallic compounds are poisons in large doses and are safe to fish only to a moderate degree, so dosage recommendations should not be exceeded.

Metazoan Parasiticides and Pesticides

Anthelminthics

In principal, a *vermifuge* is a drug which will irritate or anesthetize a worm, causing it to release its hold and be expelled from its host, while a *vermicide* is a drug which will kill the worm outright and then be expelled by the normal elimination processes of the host fish. In practice, however, the difference is generally one of dosage and/or type of worm being treated, so the broad term *anthelminthic (anti*—against; Gr. *helminthos*—worms) is used to mean any agent intended for, or useful in, the control or elimination of worms in fishes. There are metazoan parasites of fishes other than worms, of course, and they will either be included in the discussion of insecticides or rather arbitrarily excluded from discussion at all, as the metazoan parasites not covered in these two categories are of relatively minor importance anyway. Further, our overview of anthelminthics will exclude those worms found in the gills or on the external body surfaces of fish as well as those found internally in the bloodstream or in muscle tissues.

Our discussion of anthelminthics will thus be focused on the numerous digenetic termatodes, cestodes, nematodes, and acanthocephalans found mostly within the intestinal tract. A good many may also be found in other organs of the viscera or else free in the visceral cavity. They constitute what is perhaps the most difficult group of parasites of fishes to diagnose and/or treat, because the factors essential for absolute control of worms in fish are difficult to ascertain directly, and most of our knowledge consists of statistical probabilities. For instance, if 50 percent of a group of necropsied fish from a pond are found to have from one to fifty or more nematodes of a given species, then it is assumed that the remainder are likewise affected in the same proportions and are treated accordingly with an appropriate anthelminthic. Then, following treatment, more fish must be necropsied to determine the effectiveness of the treatment which is then assumed to be successful or unsuccessful based on these findings. Now while this procedure contains or enables us to ascertain the necessary facts for successful treatment—that is, the type of worm(s) present, the appropriate type of medication to be used, and a method for determining the effectiveness of the treatment—it does not work very well if only one or two extremely valuable fish are on hand, nor does it allow for direct knowledge of just how effective the treatment is on any one given fish. Most anthelminthics used on fish have not been properly or completely evaluated as to their worth, and much work remains to be done in this area. Di-*n*-butyl tin oxide is one of the most often recommended products and is presumed to be one of the most successful fish anthelminthics developed thus far, based on experimental and practical applications.

There are occasions when treatment may be of far greater danger and harm to the fish than it is to leave the worms intact and unmedicated. Paradoxically, the successful elimination of some types of worms may be fatal to the fish, particularly in the case of severe infestations. There are a number of ways in which this may occur. For instance, large numbers of nematodes all suddenly being killed or anesthetized may simply produce a mechanical blockage of the fish's intestinal tract due to the worms becoming intertwined into an impacted ball. Or perhaps a large number of acanthocephalans, which embed their heads in the intestinal walls and feed on blood, may die and be released into the intestinal tract. Their former attachment points will bleed freely and may cause the fish to hemorrhage to death. Even in cases where there are only a few worms, the traumatized intestinal lesions are open invitations to bacterial pathogens. Then too, some types of worms, in defensive response to the medication or as a result of their death and decomposition, may release a toxic material. Whether or not it would be fatal to the fish would be determined by the nature of the toxin itself and/or the number of worms present. Many anthelminthics themselves in excessive amounts are toxic to fish, and if medicated food is spread among a group of fishes, the dominant feeders may be poisoned along with their parasites.

Another problem associated with anthelminthics is that they must be given orally to be effective, and sometimes it just is not possible to induce the fish to consume the medication. Also many digenetic trematodes form cysts in various visceral organs and are virtually impervious to treatment of any kind, no matter what drug is used. They are perhaps the most difficult fish pathogens to cope with because of their resistance to treatment. Fortunately, if they are encysted, they will do little or no harm to the fish, unless present in sufficient numbers to produce mechanical blockage of some sort, either in the intestine itself or in some other vital organ. Digenetic trematodes are perhaps best dealt with on a long-term basis by cutting them off from their final or intermediate hosts, such as birds and snails.

Insecticides

Insecticides are used in the treatment of fish diseases to combat ectoparasites such as crustaceans, monogenetic trematodes, and leeches. Insecticides began to be used on fish parasites back in the late 1940s soon after their discovery. There are three main groups into which they may be placed according to their chemical makeups: (1) the DDT group, which is the oldest group of chemical insecticides in use in fish medicine, (2) the BHC, or Benzene hexachloride group, and (3) the organophosphate group, which is also the most recent group to be developed and placed in general use. They are all what is known as contact insecticides and in general owe their action(s) to their ability to penetrate the chitinous cuticle or exoskeleton of arthropods and then paralyze or poison the nervous system. They also possess some lipolytic and carcinocidal properties as well. As a rule they are highly active at extremely low concentrations, often in the parts per billion range.

After two decades or so of usage, it was becoming rather apparent that the DDT and BHC groups had some very serious drawbacks to their usage, and most of them are now either obsolete or unlawful to use, although they are still being recommended in the literature and are used in some parts of the world. Their effectiveness diminished with time and usage as fish parasites developed resistant strains and the use of more and more of the chemical was becoming necessary with less and less effectiveness. In addition, it was discovered that these insecticides were having a deleterious effect on the phytoplankton and zooplankton population of natural waters as well, and there is danger of breaking the food chain at its base with their continued use. The chief concern, however, was and still is that these two groups of chemicals do not break down in nature (nonbiodegradable) and tend to accumulate in fish tissues, particularly the liver. Thus they may be passed along in the food chain until they reach man, where their accumulative nature may eventually reach toxic levels. They have been detected in the livers of animals far removed from where they have ever been used, such as in fish-eating polar bears in the Arctic.

Initially it was believed that this last drawback had been eliminated with the development of the biodegradable organophosphates. Now it is being discovered that many of these chemicals may be carcinogenic to man, particularly among those people associated with their manufacture and/or heavy usage. They are currently the most widely used crustacicides, and Dylox® (Dipterex®) is by far the most frequently recommended chemical for *Argulus* or *Lernaea* infestations. Dylox is lethal to sharks in aquaria in incredibly small dosages. Just a few parts per billion produces disorientation and loss of motor control.

On the whole, the margin of safety for insecticides is less than for any other group of drugs or chemicals used in fish medicine. The amount that is lethal to parasites is so close to the amount that is lethal to fishes that extremely careful dosage determinations and administrations must be made, and treatments should be observed closely for indications of fish toxicity reactions. There is no room for error when using insecticides to treat fish.

Stammer, in 1959, characterized the progressive stages of poisoning a fish goes through when exposed to overdoses or prolonged exposure to insecticides and is here quoted from Kabata (1970):

1. Initial stage, characterized by increased activity and marked irritability of the fish.
2. Stage of excitation. Harmful effects become obvious. The fish begins to lose its balance, from time to time turning over on its side. It becomes even more irritable. The operculum movements become faster, denoting increase in respiration rate.
3. Convulsive stage. Loss of balance becomes severe. The fish remains on its side longer and attempts to swim in this position, often in circles. Periods during which the fish remains motionless alternate with periods of rapid movements, convulsive spasms, and jerks.
4. Lethal stage. Most movements have ceased. Convulsive twitching of fins, progressive diminution of eye reflexes. Depending on the concentration of the toxic solution, death ensues in a few hours to several days.

The first two stages are reversible by removing the toxin and placing the fish eventually in clean water. A steady diminution of the toxic levels is more preferable than a direct transfer to nontoxic waters, and the survival rate among fish is enhanced by this procedure. The third stage will appear to improve at first, when placed in clean water, but then the fish's condition will reverse itself and deteriorate, and it will most likely die. The fourth stage is of course fatal and irreversible once attained.

ANTIBIOTIC THERAPY

Defining the term literally, antibiotics are substances that can destroy living matter. In practice it is restricted to mean antibacterial agents derived from microbial origins. Thus antibiotics are bactericidal or bacteriostatic agents derived originally from other microbes, chiefly bacteria, molds, and *Actinomyces*. They are chemotherapeutic agents with special properties.

The concept of antibiotics originated with Pasteur, but it was hardly more than the germ of an ideal until Alexander Fleming described the actions of penicillin in 1929. Even then, the idea was very nearly allowed to drop into obscurity because of the discovery of synthetic sulfa drugs and the advent of modern chemotherapy in the early 1930s. In 1944, streptomycin was developed in the laboratory, and in 1947, from a soil sample collected in a farmers mulched field near Caracas, Venezuela, Chloromycetin® was obtained. Since that time the use and development of antibiotics has grown at an enormous pace. Today thousands of laboratories all over the world are searching for new types of antibiotics, and they are finding them, too. Most bacterial diseases can now be treated successfully with at least one or more of the antibiotics now available, although bacterial resistance to antibiotic therapy is becoming a matter of growing concern. The indiscriminate use of antibiotics and their use for trivial ailments is unjustifiable and can in no way be condoned.

Antibiotics selectively inhibit or destroy pathogenic organisms without doing any appreciable harm to the host organism being treated. Generally this constitutes a bacterial organism invading the body of a vertebrate animal, i.e. fishes. They may impose either a bacteriostatic (detected by checking microbial growth) or a bactericidal (kills the microbial agent) action on the microbe, depending on their activity or dosage concentration. If the action is bacteriostatic, the supposition is that microbial cell division or reproduction is somehow being interfered with, thus slowing down the disease process so that natural body defenses may keep from being overwhelmed and to give them time to wall off or destroy the invading microbe. The bactericidal antibiotics go to work chemically on the pathogen itself and actively cause it to be destroyed. The ability of an antibiotic to interfere with the development of life processes of bacteria without seriously damaging vertebrate cells depends upon the interference with or inhibition of metabolic functions essential to the microorganism but not to the host.

The mechanisms by which antibiotics achieve their success have been slow in becoming understood. These mechanisms and their actions are in many instances still poorly understood, but considerable progress has been made in this area in recent years. This knowledge is necessary to provide the basis for a course in rational therapy with these drugs. Thus the drugs currently available may be broken down into various classes according to the anatomical or biochemical sites on the microorganism at which they exert their primary effect.

First to be considered are those antibiotics that affect the bacterial cell wall. These antibiotics include such drugs as bacitracin, cycloserine, cephalothin, the penicillins, ristocetin, and vancomycin.

The cell wall of plants (bacteria), as opposed to the cell membrane surrounding animal cells, is a rigid supporting structure which protects the cell both from environmental trauma and bursting from its own high internal osmotic pressure and is, therefore, essential to the life of a bacterium. The bacterium contains an essential structural component, N-acetyl muramic acid, which is kept from being incorporated into the cell wall structure by the inhibitory effect of these antibiotics. Without it the cell wall does not form properly when the growing cell divides, so it swells and bursts due to excessive internal osmotic pressures. Thus these antibiotics serve as bactericides. In order for these drugs to work, the bacteria must be actively engaged in growing and reproducing, and only at this time is it vulnerable to this class of antibiotics.

This group of drugs affecting the bacteria cell wall may be relatively ineffective against bacteria in abscesses and areas of necrotic tissues. The probable reason for this is that, even though the bacteria are susceptible to the antibiotic, the conditions in an abscess or necrotic area are less than optimum for the growth of bacteria, and thus they are not multiplying at a sufficiently rapid rate for the drug to work properly. The drug is being excreted or neutralized by the fish before it can do its job.

A second major group of antibiotics are those that affect the bacterial cell membrane. This group includes, among others, amphotericin B, colistin, gentamicin, kanamycin, neomycin, novobiocin, nystatin, polymyxin, and streptomycin.

The cell membrane in both plants and animal cells serves very much the same function. Therefore, when using this second group of drugs, the margin of safety is not so great as in those drugs affecting the cell wall, which has no exact counterpart in animal cells. Most of these drugs have a relatively low safety threshold, may produce toxic reactions in fishes if overdosed, and may produce kidney or nerve damage.

These membrane-affecting drugs produce their effect by interfering with the biochemical characteristics of the cell membrane, which is a very delicate structure. It is biochemically distinct from the cell wall and serves to maintain the integrity of the cell by controlling the permeability characteristics of the cell, actively transporting nutrients into, and waste products out of, the cell, and probably storing the enzymes used in the synthesis of the bacterial cell wall. Antibiotics of this group produce a bactericidal effect by disrupting these vital functions.

A third major grouping consists of those antibiotic agents which affect or inhibit protein synthesis in bacteria, including chloramphenicol, kanamycin, lincomycin, the macrolide group (erythromycin, oleandomycin, and tylosin), neomycin, and the tetracylines. It will be noted that some of these are also included in the previous grouping. Apparently, on some bacterial species, they function in one manner, and on others, in another manner. Because protein synthesis is a rather broad category, there are some drugs in this group that are bacteriostatic and some that are bactericidal in their effect, depending upon their specific route of action.

Some of the bacteriostatic agents, such as chloramphenicol and the tetracyclines, do not have a lethal effect on bacteria. They merely act to inhibit protein synthesis in susceptible organisms which is essential to their ability to multiply and reproduce. It is thus necessary for the defense mechanisms of the host to be operative in order to eliminate the infective agent. This is not so critical a consideration when treating with bactericidal agents.

Another group of antibiotics go straight to the heart of the bacteria and affect nucleic acid metabolism. The chief antibiotic in this group is griseofulvin, where again the action is primarily bacteriostatic. Some antibiotic agents affect the intermediary metabolism of bacteria. Isoniazid, *p*-aminosalicylic acid, and the sulfonamides are included in this group.

Considered collectively, these last three groups will all act through the inhibition of natural metabolic processes. Since the biochemical pathways are similar in both microorganisms and fishes, they must be used with caution, and some consideration of the effect they will have on the fish if their use is prolonged or excessive must be exercised. Their selective toxicity appears to be due to the faster rate of metabolism and protein synthesis in microorganisms than in fish, but they will eventually affect the host fish if their use is sustained beyond safe therapeutic limits.

Quite often, antibiotics may be used in combinations, either through deliberate design or through ignorance. Sometimes, when it is felt that one drug is not being productive, therapy will be switched to another, without prior removal of the first. This may be detrimental or advantageous, depending on the drugs being used. One of three possible effects may be anticipated: antagonistic, synergistic, or indifferent.

An *antagonistic effect* is produced when one drug acts to thwart the effectiveness of another so that the total effect of the combination is less than it would have been if only the least powerful drug had been used singly. This is most likely to occur when a protein synthesis inhibitor, such as chloramphenicol, is used in conjunction with a cell wall inhibitor, such as penicillin. In this example, one drug which acts to inhibit cell multiplication thwarts the action of another which requires rapid cell multiplication for its action, with a net effect of slowing the course of the disease only briefly.

Most often, an antagonistic effect is encountered when a bac-

TABLE 3-I
ANTIBIOTIC INCOMPATIBILTIES

ANTIBIOTIC	INCOMPATIBLE WITH
Ampicillin	Do not mix with any drug
Carbenicillin	Chloramphenicol
	Erythromycin
	Gentamycin
	Lincomycin
	Oxytetracycline
Chloramphenicol	Carbenicillin
	Erythromycin
	Nitrofurans
	Oxytetracycline
	Polymyxin B
	Sulfonamides
	Vancomycin
Erythromycin	Carbenicillin
	Chloramphenicol
	Iodides
	Lincomycin
Gentamycin	Do not mix with any drug
Kanamycin	Do not mix with any drug
Lincomycin	Do not mix with any drug
Methicillin	Oxytetracycline
Oxytetracycline	Ampicillin
	Carbenicillin
	Calcium Salts
	Chloramphenicol
	Erythromycin
	Methicillin
	Nitrofurans
	Penicillin G
	Polymyxin B
	Sodium bicarbonate
	Sulfonamides
Penicillin G	Oxytetracycline

teriostatic drug is used in combination with a bactericidal drug; therefore, these types of drugs should never be used in combination. At its worst, an antagonistic action may prove toxic to the fish as well as the bacteria or may even enhance the growth of the organism it is attempting to curtail.

A *synergistic effect* is a decidedly positive reaction in which the action of two or more drugs produces an action which is greater than the sum of the effect each drug could have effected if used singly. As a strictly hypothetical example, if drug X can kill 10 percent of a particular microorganism, and drug Y can kill 15 percent of the same organism when used singly, then if 80 percent of the microorganisms are killed when they are used in combination, we have a synergistic effect.

Unfortunately, only a few such synergistic combinations exist. They occur more frequently and may be more often anticipated when a cell wall inhibitor is used in conjunction with a cell membrane inhibitor, such as the effect produced by the combination of penicillin and streptomycin. Penicillin, used by itself, is virtually worthless in the treatment of fish diseases.

The *indifferent response* is simply no interaction one way or the other. The predominate action is roughly equal to that of the most powerful agent being used, with any others being overshadowed. The indifferent response is the most common type of response encountered.

Ideally, an antibiotic will exhibit a number of exclusively beneficial characteristics, with no undesirable ones. It should be stable, with a long shelf life in storage, not easily destroyed by the natural enzymes of fish tissues when used, nor inhibited by the presence of blood, serum, or pus, and not easily filtered out and excreted by the kidneys. It should be easy to administer, preferably by several routes, and should diffuse readily and rapidly in the fish without any undue toxic or adverse side effects. It must remain a viable drug in the body tissues without breaking down for a relatively long period of time, as well as being neutral to fish tissues, especially the kidneys, liver, and blood, even if the dosage is built up over a period of time through absorption from the water or repeated doses. In short, it must be absolutely safe in fish while being decidedly lethal to a wide range of both gram-negative and gram-positive pathogens. It should be swift and powerful in its action without inducing resistance on the part of bacterial pathogens. This stated ideal is, unfortunately, still being sought.

Chapter 4

TOXICOLOGY

TOXICOLOGY IS AN INTEGRAL PART of the study of drugs and their possible or actual toxic effects on fishes. It is a subject that must be taken into consideration with each and every drug used for treatment. Because of its considerable impact on fishes, it will be discussed here, but only briefly. What is desired in this work is an understanding of the therapeutic effects of drugs, not necessarily their toxic side effects, but they must be acknowledged nonetheless. Toxicology, a large and serious study itself, will be given only a cursory review, but the interested reader is advised to seek out the United States Fish and Wildlife Service's *Investigations in Fish Control* series for an in-depth understanding of what is being done in this area of fisheries research.

Toxic substances, or poisons, are those which when introduced into a fish's body, usually in very small doses, produce a deadly or extremely noxious effect. Poisons may have an acute or chronic course in their action on fish. Some drugs may be toxic or therapeutic, depending upon the dosage. Others may be toxic in combination with other drugs, according to water conditions, temperature, or other conditions. Because a toxic substance may enter the body by various routes, it may be toxic when administered by one route and harmless by another. For instance, lionfish venom is lethal to other fishes if injected, yet a larger fish may swallow an entire lionfish with all its venom with no ill effects (a bit of expensive first-hand knowledge there). Sometimes a fish's age or its disease may alter a fish's tolerance to what is normally a safe dosage, thus producing a toxic reaction.

The mode of action may be local, as when an acidosis or alkalosis develops in the water and a breakdown of mucous or oxi-

82

dation of the skin or gills occurs; or the action might be systemic, such as might occur with cyanide poisoning, heavy metal poisoning, or bacterial toxins.

Toxins may be grouped or classified according to the physiological action they have upon the system. (1) *Corrosives* act locally to bring about active tissue destruction and disintegration. Strong acids and caustic alkalies (bases) as well as some oxides and phenol are the chief offenders in this group. (2) *Irritants* also produce destruction of tissue, but the effect is usually of a somewhat milder nature and more gradual over a longer period of time. They are chiefly inorganic metal salts, such as copper, arsenic, or lead, or they may be nonmetallic poisons such as cyanide, chlorine, or iodine. Gaseous products are also offenders in this group. (3) *Neurotoxins* or *neurotropic poisons* act chiefly upon the nervous system. They are almost always organic poisons, mostly of vegetable origins (here we are referring to drug toxicity, not environmental or industrial waste pollutants). Many alkaloids and glycosides are included in this group. Nerve poisons as a rule produce no overt tissue destruction. Each has its own characteristic symptoms, and sometimes these are very difficult to detect.

Any attempt to overcome the effects of poisoning in fishes should follow a rather commonsense-type approach. First, further poisoning is prevented by removing the source of the poisoning, if possible. This may be as simple as placing the fish in another container, or it may involve dilution to a nontoxic level by adding fresh water. When a poison cannot be easily removed for some reason, an attempt should be made to chemically or physically neutralize its effect. The next step is to attempt to reduce the effect of the toxin and work to support the life of the fish by symptomatic treatment of the fish and to further reduce the physiological antagonism of the toxin. For instance, the addition of methylene blue serves as a temporary oxygen donor when a state of methemoglobinemia exists which may have come about as a result of nitrite or cyanide toxicity.

PART II
MATERIA MEDICA

Chapter 5

ANNOTATED DOSAGES AND TREATMENTS

A LL OF THE PRECEDING TEXT has dealt with background material
useful to the in-depth understanding of that which is to follow. We are now to the point of taking what we have learned
regarding drugs and chemicals and using it in the treatment of fish
diseases. The following materia medica (L. *materia*—matter;
medica—medical) is the heart and core of this work.

Growing governmental concern about the possible unknown
effects drugs and chemicals might be having on the environment
resulted in enactment of the Federal Environmental Pesticide
Control Act (FEPCA), which has been in effect since 1972. It requires that all drugs and chemicals in use in fish culture and fishery management receive approved registration by either the Environmental Protection Agency (EPA) or the Food and Drug
Administration (FDA). These agencies thus constitute both the
governing and limiting forces in the use of fish medicines in the
United States. By February, 1976, only eighteen products had
such approved registration (Meyer and Schnick, 1976). Thus all
other medications are being used in violation of regulations, since
nonapproved drugs can still be obtained. Those approved, along
with any restrictions placed on their use, are indicated in the
following drug catalog. The legislation on this matter is still in a
state of flux, and undoubtedly many more drugs will be registered
as required data are submitted and evaluated by the appropriate
agency. In the meantime, the reader must use his own discretion
when treating his fish.

INTRODUCTION

The medicine cabinet of the fish culturist or hobbyist is rather bare in comparison to the other fields of human and veterinary pharmacy. Sources of information on fish drugs are sometimes difficult to obtain, so a great deal of the drug information in this book has come from other related sources. The chemistry of each drug is the same regardless of its use. The actual dosages and treatment uses, however, have in all instances been taken from the literature on fish diseases.

Standard textbooks on pharmacology have proved to be of inestimable value in establishing the interrelationships between drugs and their actions on fishes. The *United States Pharmacopeia* (USP) has been used in cases where it could provide information on a drug used in treating both fish and human diseases. The *National Formulary* has been consulted on still other drugs. *New and Nonofficial Remedies* has been consulted, but each year brings forth a new volume, and information is too scattered through it over the years to be a reliable reference. The *Physicians' Desk Reference* (PDR) is highly useful, both for drug information and also as an aid in knowing what drugs are currently available on the market. Another newer, fairly technical work is the AMA's *Drug Evaluations*. A somewhat briefer, more concise treatment is contained in the old *The Epitome of the United States Pharmacopeia and National Formulary*. Another standard, which was not available during the writing of this work, but which would be invaluable to serious, competent workers in this field, would be the *Pharmacopeia Internationalis*, prepared by the World Health Organization. The Food and Drug Administration puts out the *National Drug Code Directory* each year, which lists currently available drugs, their manufacturers, their synonyms, and the forms in which they are available.

All of the above reference sources are intended for use in human medicine, so it is only when a drug is useful for both humans and fish that these sources can be used. They are technical, highly reliable sources of drug information when they are applicable, but still some comparative medicine must be used when adapting their information to use in fish.

Somewhat closer to our actual needs, and covering a great many drugs and chemicals not covered in the preceding references, are the veterinary drug information sources, the *Veterinary Red Book,* and the journalistic veterinary "blue books." Rossoff's *Handbook of Veterinary Drugs* has become an invaluable source for cross-referencing drugs available to veterinarians with those of physicians.

The *Farm Chemicals Handbook,* by Berg, is a guide to agricultural products, primarily insecticides, some of which are of value in fish medicine. *The Pesticide Index,* by Frear, also serves the same purpose. *Chemical Synonyms and Trade Names,* by Gardner and Cooke, serves as a cross-reference guide to chemical names as opposed to their trade names (generic versus proprietary). *The American Drug Index,* by Wilson and Jones, is a useful compendium to check for those drugs available in this country.

It is here, when seeking references for drugs used to treat fish, that the supply of sources of drug information begins to falter. The survey of drugs and chemicals by Hoffman and Meyer, *Parasites of Freshwater Fishes,* is about the most comprehensive single source heretofore available to the fish practitioner. It does not cover antibiotics and microbial agents, however, so it is therefore limited in scope to metazoan and protozoan parasites. The *Progressive Fish-Culturist,* a quarterly journal published by the U.S. Government Printing Office, consistently provides more information than any other single U.S. source, but this information is random and scattered from issue to issue and is not always readily available to the average fish keeper. Van Duijn's excellent work, *Diseases of Fishes,* contains only a short chapter and scattered brief references to useful drugs and is again not a thoroughly comprehensive review. In short, there is no single comprehensive source of drug information for the fish keeper. It is the intention of this book to fill that void.

After all of the above reference sources have been consulted, there still remains a handful of drugs that are included in this text which have not previously been covered. These may be just simple unproven remedies, but most likely they are foreign drugs not available in the United States. They may also be drugs which have been banned by a U.S. governmental agency and whose manufacture and distribution have been discontinued in this country. This group of drugs has been included not only for the sake of thoroughness (and because the reader will still find them used and/or recommended in the literature) but because a good percentage of the drugs banned in this country are available and being used safely and successfully in foreign countries. Since this work will be distributed outside as well as in the United States, the information on this group of drugs will be valid and useful elsewhere. Any drug selected for use in the treatment of any fish disease is of course in the final analysis dependent upon its availability.

The drugs and chemicals listed here, their dosages and applications, and any remarks regarding them have been gleaned from the literature over a number of years. The amount of literature available on fish diseases is vast, although most of this information is diffused and scattered. Because of this impressive amount of knowledge available, some prior knowledge by the reader is therefore assumed regarding fish pathogens. It is assumed that the reader knows the difference between a protozoan and a trematode, or perhaps the difference between *Cryptocaryon* and *Benedenia,* or *Trichodina* and *Gyrodactylus.* Hopefully, if the reader can provide an accurate diagnosis, this book will serve to provide an appropriate drug and dosage to be used in the treatment of a particular ailment. To find drugs used to treat the various classes or phyla of pathogens, the reader should consult the appendices, which will list the drugs under the heading that they are covered in the text, but which do not cover the names of drugs that are cross-referenced to those particular drugs. If a preferred medication is not listed in the appendices, the reader is directed to the alphabetical listing in the text to find under which name the drug is described. Ideally, all of the drugs would have been listed according to their generic names, and their trade names would be cross-referenced. This has proven to be a difficult task, however, and so some are not listed in such detail. Any drug not listed in this text is an oversight on my part and not a deliberate attempt to void recognition of a useful product. I would appreciate hearing of any additional knowledge of the reader about any other drugs available that could possibly be included in future revisions or editions of this work. As stated before the inclusion of a drug or manufacturer is not an endorsement or a recommendation for its use, nor is the exclusion of a drug or manufacturer a denial of its value or worth.

ANNOTATED ALPHABETICAL LISTING
OF DRUGS AND SYNONYMS*

ACETARSOL—See Acetarsone.

ACETARSONE

Composition: N-acetyl-4-hydroxy-*m*-arsanilic acid.

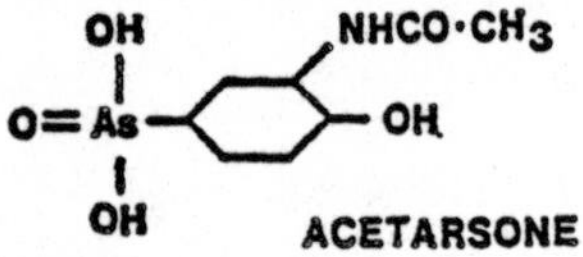

$$O=As\begin{matrix}OH\\ \\OH\end{matrix}\text{---}\bigcirc\begin{matrix}NHCO\cdot CH_3\\ \\OH\end{matrix}$$

ACETARSONE

Synonyms: Acetarsol; Stovarsol.

Uses or Treatment for: Protozoacide [internal protozoans; coccidiosis *(Eimeria)*].

Dosage: (1) 1 mg/gm of food; (2) 10 mg/kg of fish in food for 3 to 4 days.

Remarks: An effective medication.

References: Hoffman & Meyer (1974); Naumova & Kanaev (1962); Reichenbach-Klinke (1966).

ACETIC ACID, glacial—See Acetic acid, commercial grade.

ACETIC ACID, commercial grade

Composition: CH_3COOH.

Synonyms: Vinegar.

Uses or Treatment for: External Protozoa [*Ambiphyra pyriformis, Costia, Trichodina (= Cyclochaeta)*]; Turbellaria *(Planaria)*; Monogenea *(Gyrodactylus)*; Hirudinea (leeches); crustaceans *(Argulus, Salmincola)*.

Dosage: (1) 10% solution; (2) 2 tablespoons in 25 liters of water; (3) 1000 ppm; (4) 1500 ppm of glacial acetic acid as a dip for 5 to 10 minutes; (5) 2000 ppm as a dip for 45 to 60 seconds; (6) 10,000 ppm; (7) 1:500 (glacial acetic acid diluted in water) as a 30 to 60 second dip; (8) 1:2000 (500 ppm) glacial acetic acid diluted in water) as a bath for 30 minutes.

Remarks: 629 ppm for 1 hour and 15.8 ppm for 72 hours did

---

*Please note that many of the drug names listed are trade names and as such are registered trademarks.

not reach a lethal concentration in *Ictalurus sp.*

References: Clemens & Sneed (1959) ; Davis (1953) ; Embody (1924) ; Fasten (1912) ; Herman (1972) ; Hoffman & Meyer (1974) ; Hora & Pillay (1962) ; Kabata (1970) ; Khan (1944); Reichenbach-Klinke & Elkan (1965) ; Reichenbach-Klinke & Landolt (1973) ; Tripathi (1954) ; Van Roekel (1929).

ACHROMYCIN—See Oxytetracycline.

ACINITRAZOLE
Composition: 2-acetamido-5-nitrothiazole.
Synonyms: None.
Uses or Treatment for: Protozoacide (hexamitiasis).
Dosage: (1) 40 mg /kg of feed for 4 days.
Remarks: Used in Norway.
References: Snieszko (1975).

ACRALDEHYDE—See Acrolein.

ACRIFLAVINE, hydrochloride
Composition: Acid salt of Acriflavine.
Synonyms: Trypaflavine.
Uses or Treatment for: Dye; egg disinfection; bacteriostatic agent; fungicide; external protozoacide *(Chilodonella, Ichthyophthirius multifiliis).*
Dosage: (1) 10 ppm for 2 hours.
Remarks: Reportedly not effective in preventing fungus on fish eggs; 100 ppm at 20°C is toxic to guppies in 48 hours; not as safe for use as Acriflavine neutral.
References: Hoffman & Meyer (1974) ; Schäperclaus (1954).

ACRIFLAVINE, neutral
Composition: Mixture of 3,6-diamino-10-methylacridinum chloride and 3,6-diaminoacridine.
Synonyms: Trypaflavine.
Uses or Treatment for: Dye; egg disinfection; antiseptic; infected wounds; ulcers; skin parasites (ectoparasites) ; bacteria *(Columnaris);* fungicide *(Saprolegnia);* external protozoacide *[Ambiphrya, Chilodonella, Cryptocaryon irritans, Hexamita; Ichthyophthirius multifiliis* (Ich), *Oodinium ocellatum, O. pillularis, Scyphidia];* Monogenea *(Cleidodiscus).*

Dosage: (1) 1 gm/100 l of water; (2) 2 mg/gal of water; (3) 1 gm/100 l of water for 2 to 12 hours; (4) 0.1% solution added to food; (5) 3-10 ppm in water as a prolonged bath; (6) 20 ppm is inhibitory to *Saprolegnia;* (7) 10 ppm for 10 hours; (8) 0.2-0.6 ppm in 2 applications at 2-day intervals; (9) 5-10 ppm added to water for from several hours to several days; (10) 500 ppm as a bath for 30 minutes.

Remarks: Normally used as a long duration bath; will kill live plants; may reduce fecundity in guppies; 100 ppm = LC_{100} to guppies; 13 ppm = LC_{15} in *Roccus saxitilis;* may damage slime coating of skin and create vulnerability to bacterial disease in marine fish; available as a powder or solution; manufactured by Pfaltz & Bauer, Inc.[*]

References: Amlacher (1970); Bauer (1958); Bureau of Sport Fish and Wildlife (1968); Clemens & Sneed (1959); De Graaf (1962); Ergens (1962); Herman (1972); Hoffman & Meyer (1974); Kingsford (1975); Loader (1963); Patterson (1950); Reichenbach-Klinke (1966); Reichenbach-Klinke & Elkan (1965); Reichenbach-Klinke & Landolt (1973); Schäperclaus (1954); Smith (1942); Snieszko (1975); Wellborn (1971); Willford (1967a); Yousuf-Ali (1968).

ACROLEIN

Composition: 2-propenal.

Synonyms: Acraldehyde; Aqualin.

Uses or Treatment for: Herbicide; molluscicide *(Australorbis glabratus).*

Dosage: 3 ppm in water.

Remarks: 0.046-0.079 ppm = LC_{50} in *Lepomis macrochirus* and *Salmo trutta;* manufactured by Webster; (Theophylline).

References: Ferguson et al. (1961); Hoffman & Meyer (1974); Johnson (1968).

ACTAMER—See Bithional.

AEROSPORIN—See Polymyxin B, sulphate.

AIVET—See Nifurprazine.

---

[*]For a complete listing of drug companies referred to in the text and their addresses, see Appendix II.

ALBAMYCIN—See Novobiocin.

ALBUCID, Sodium
Composition: N-acetylsulfanilamide.
Synonyms: Sulfacetamide; Sulfacyl; Sulfacetamide sodium.
Uses or Treatment for: Antimicrobial (bacterial fin rot); protozoacide *(Cyclocheata)*.
Dosage: (1) 1 gm/10 l of water; (2) 2000 ppm.
Remarks: 2000 ppm toxic in 96 hours at 20°C; see also Globucid, Sulfonamides; available as ointment or solution; manufactured by Jenkins, Pharmaderm, Zemmer.
References: Amlacher (1970); Hoffman & Meyer (1974); Schäperclaus (1954).

ALBUCIDNATRIUM—See Globucid.

ALCOHOL, Absolute—See Alcohol, Ethyl.

ALCOHOL, Ethyl
Composition: Ethyl alcohol.
Synonyms: Absolute alcohol; drinking alcohol; Everclear; vodka.
Uses or Treatment for: Anesthesia; tranquilizer.
Dosage: Add until fish becomes unsteady or lethargic.
Remarks: Occasionally used to collect marine tropicals; vodka, gin, whiskey, etc., may be substituted.
References: None.

ALCOHOL, Iodated
Composition: Iodine in an alcohol solution (7-10%).
Synonyms: Tincture of iodine.
Uses or Treatment for: Disinfection; skin wounds; injuries; goiter; bacteria *(Acinetobacter,* corynebacterial kidney disease) ; Crustacea *(Argulus)*.
Dosage: (1) 10% solution painted on wounds with an artist's paint brush; (2) 10-minute bath at 100 ppm iodine; (3) in the form of a Lugol's solution or iodine (for goiter) ; (4) touched to parasite at full strength *(Argulus)*.
Remarks: May cause irritation and burns on some marine fishes *(Platax sp.);* available as tinctures; manufactured by Barre, Bates, BBC, CLI, FTP, Humco, Lannet, Lilly, Purepac

Pharm, PD, Rondex.
References: Amlacher (1970); Berg & Gorbman (1954); Berg & Gordon (1953) ; Snieszko (1975) ; Van Duijn (1973) .

ALKYL-DIMETHYL-BENZYL-AMMONIUM   CHLORIDE — See Benzalkonium chloride.

ALPEN—See Ampicillin trihydrate.

ALUM—See Aluminum sulfate.

ALUMINUM SULFATE, commercial grade
Composition: $Al_2(SO_4)_3 \cdot nH_2O$.
Synonyms: Alum.
Uses or Treatment for: Flocculent; Protozoa [*Ichthyophthirius multifiliis* (Ich)].
Dosage: 50,000 ppm as a dip for 1 minute.
Remarks: None.
References: Gopalakrishnan (1966) ; Hoffman & Meyer (1974) ; Prytherch (In Mellen, 1928) .

AMCILL—See Ampicillin trihydrate.

AMEBACILIN—See Fumagillin.

AMMINOSIDINE—See Emtrysidina.

AMMONIA, 28% in water
Composition: NH_3 or NH_4OH.
Synonyms: Ammonium hydroxide.
Uses or Treatment for: Monogenetic trematodes *(Gyrodactylus, Dactylogyrus).*
Dosage: (1) 10-25 cc/l of water for 10 to 15 minutes;   (2) NH_4OH (25 ppm) + $CuSO_4$ (0.5 ppm) in fresh water only.
Remarks: See also Ammonium hydroxide.
References: Hoffman & Meyer (1974) ; Reichenbach-Klinke & Landolt (1973) .

AMMONIUM CARBONATE
Composition: A mixture of Ammonium bicarbonate and Ammonium carbonate.
Synonyms: Hartshorn.
Uses or Treatment for: Protozoa *(Myxosoma cerebralis).*
Dosage: 1000 ppm applied to water.

Remarks: Reportedly was not effective.

References: Hoffman & Hoffman (1972); Hoffman & Meyer (1974).

AMMONIUM CHLORIDE, Commercial grade

Composition: NH_4Cl.

Synonyms: AM-CH, AMC-7½, Ammoneric, BP-82, Darammon, Prochlor.

Uses or Treatment for: Protozoa *(Myxosoma cerebralis);* Monogenea *(Gyrodactylus);* Crustacea *(Argulus).*

Dosage: (1) 10-25 gm/l of water in the form of a bath (for 10 to 15 minutes); (2) 1:2000 (500 ppm) solution for 24 hours; (3) 1:1000 solution for 4 hours; (4) 1:500 solution for 30 minutes; (5) 1000 ppm indefinitely; (6) 25,000 ppm as a dip for 10 to 15 minutes.

Remarks: Dosage No. 5 not effective against *Myxosoma sp.;* manufactured by Artaco, Bowman Pharm, Brunswick, Cutter Labs, Hartford, MacEslin, Progress, Schlicksup, Scripp, Scruggs, Sutliff & Case; available as tablets.

References: Chen (1933); Hoffman & Hoffman (1972); Hoffman & Meyer (1974); Kabata (1970); Reichenbach-Klinke (1966); Reichenbach-Klinke & Elkan (1965); Roth (In Mellen, 1928); Schäperclaus (1954); Van Duijn (1973).

AMMONIUM HYDROXIDE

Composition: NH_4OH.

Synonyms: None.

Uses or Treatment for: Monogenea *(Dactylogyrus sp.).*

Dosage: (1) 2000 ppm as a dip for 10 minutes; (2) Acriflavine + Ammonium hydroxide (0.25 gm of Acriflavine/l of 10% NH_4OH) used at 100 ppm as a dip for 60 to 90 seconds; (3) 500 ppm as a dip for 5 to 15 minutes; (4) NH_4OH (25 ppm) + $CuSO_4$ (0.4-0.5) added to water.

Remarks: See also Ammonia, 28% in water.

References: Bauer (1958); Ergens (1962); Hoffman & Meyer (1974); Ivasik et al. (1967); Lavroskii & Uspenskaya (1959); Pasovskii (1953); Reichenbach-Klinke (1966); Van Duijn (1973).

AMMONIUM NITRATE, commercial grade
Composition: NH_4NO_3.
Synonyms: None.
Uses or Treatment for: Cnidaria (hydras); Turbellaria *(Planaria sp.).*
Dosage: (1) 0.5 gm/10 l of water, repeat after 2 days—long duration bath; (2) 0.005 gm/l of water; (3) 1 gm/20 cc of water; (4) 50,000 ppm as a dip; (5) 1200 ppm at 4-8°C.
Remarks: 800 ppm = LC_{100} to *Lepomis macrochirus* in 3.9 hours; 4545 ppm = LC_{100} to *Carassius auratus* in 90 hours.
References: Amlacher (1970); Hoffman & Meyer (1974); McKee & Wolf (1963); Reichenbach-Klinke & Elkan (1965); Reichenbach-Klinke & Landolt (1973); Schäperclaus (1954).

AMMONIUM SULFATE
Composition: $(NH_4)_2SO_4$.
Synonyms: None.
Uses or Treatment for: Algae *(Pyrmnesium).*
Dosage: 10 ppm.
Remarks: Effectiveness determined by pH and temperature.
References: Sarig (1971); Shilo & Shilo (1953).

AM-PEN—See Ampicillin trihydrate.

AMPHICOL—See Chloramphenicol.

AMPICILLEX—See Ampicillin trihydrate.

AMPICILLIN—See Ampicillin trihydrate.

AMPICILLIN, SODIUM
Composition: A semisynthetic form of penicillin.
Synonyms: Polycillin.
Uses or Treatment for: Bacteria (gram-positive and gram-negative bacteria).
Dosage: Undetermined.
Remarks: Has a shelf life when mixed of only a few hours; use immediately; not effective in salt water; available as capsules, sterile powder; manufactured by Bristol Labs.
References: Kingford (1975).

AMPICILLIN TRIHYDRATE

Composition: A semisynthetic form of penicillin.

Synonyms: Acillin, Alpen, Amcil, Am-Pen, Amphikin, Ampicillex, Ampi-Co, Ampillin, Amplin, Divercillin, Norcillin, Omnipen, Penbritin, Principen, Ponecil, Rancillin, Ro-Ampen, SK-Ampicillin, Supen, Tabocillin, Totacillin.

Uses or Treatment for: Bacteria (gram-positive and many gram-negative bacteria).

Dosage: Undetermined.

Remarks: Has a shelf life of 1 to 2 weeks; not effective in salt water; available as powder, sterile powder, capsules (250 and 500 mg); forms most often used manufactured by Aberdeen, Amer Quinine, APC, Ascher, Ayerst, Belkins, BBC, Beech-Mass Phar, Berla, BT, Carchem, Coastal, Columbia Medic, FTP, Nortex, PD, Purepac Pharm, Rondex, Rowell, RPL, SCA, SKF, Squibb, Stayner, Tablroc, Tutag, West-Ward, Winston, Wyeth, Ulmer-Pharcal, Zenith.

References: Kingsford (1975).

AMPI-CO—See Ampicillin trihydrate.

AMPIKIN—See Ampicillin trihydrate.

AMPLIN—See Ampicillin trihydrate.

AMPROL—See Amprolium.

AMPROLIUM

Composition: 1-[(4-amino-2-propyl-5-pyrimidinyl) methyl]-2-picolinium chloride hydrochloride.

Synonyms: Amprol.

Uses or Treatment for: Protozoacide *(Ichthyophthirius multifiliis).*

Dosage: 1 ppm.

Remarks: None.

References: Hoffman & Meyer (1974).

AMPYROQUIN

Composition: 4-(7-chloro-4-quinolylamino)-1-pyrrolidyl-*o*-cresol dihydrochloride.

Synonyms: Propoquin.

Uses or Treatment for: Protozoacide (*Ichthyophthirius mul-tifiliis*).
Dosage: 0.5 ppm.
Remarks: Reportedly not effective; product of Parke, Davis & Company.
References: Hoffman & Meyer (1974).

ANILINE GREEN—See Malachite green.

ANTHIUM DIOXIDE

Composition: 5% chlorine dioxide.
Synonyms: Microcide.
Uses or Treatment for: Crustacea (copepods in salt water).
Dosage: 0.2 ppm.
Remarks: None.
References: Hoffman & Meyer (1974); Zeiller (1966).

ANTIMONY POTASSIUM TARTRATE

Composition: Antimony potassium tartrate.
Synonyms: None.
Uses or Treatment for: Skin worms; trematodes; nematodes.
Dosage: 1.5 mg/l of water.
Remarks: None.
References: Reichenbach-Klinke & Elkan (1965).

ANTIMYCIN A

Composition: Antibiotic derived from *Streptomyces sp.*
Synonyms: Fintrol.
Uses or Treatment for: Fish toxicant; Protozoa [*Trichodina* (= *Cyclochaeta*)]; Monogenea (*Cleidodiscus*); Crustacea (*Lernaea cyprinacea*).
Dosage: 0.005 ppm.
Remarks: Reportedly not effective against Protozoa; toxic to small fish; 1-2 ppm of potassium permanganate will neutralize or detoxify this drug; manufactured by Ayerst.
References: Berger, Lennon, and Hogan (1969); Burress & Luhning (1969a, 1969b); Foye (1968); Gilderhus et al. (1969); Hoffman & Meyer (1974); Howland (1969); Lennon & Berger (1970); Schneider (1974); Schoettger & Svendson (1970); Walker et al. (1964).

AQUA-AID

Composition: Ingredients listed on package (commercial formulation).

Synonyms: None.

Uses or Treatment for: Protozoa *(Ichthyophthirius multifiliis)*.

Dosage: Twice the recommended dosage on label.

Remarks: Recommended dosage not effective; tablets available from Bates.

References: Hoffman & Meyer (1974).

AQUA-AMMONIA

Composition: Ammonia in water (exact composition unknown).

Synonyms None.

Uses or Treatment for: Algae *(Pyrmnesium)*.

Dosage: 10-15 ppm.

Remarks: Causes rise in pH; do not use if pH is above 9.

References: Beresky & Sarig (1965); Sarig (1971); Sarig, Lahav, and Vardina (1960).

AQUALIN—See Acrolein.

AQUARI-SOL—See Collargol.

AQUAROL

Composition: Unknown commercial formulation.

Synonyms: None.

Uses or Treatment for: Bacteria (bacterial fin rot); fungi *(Saprolegnia);* Protozoa *(Chilodonella, Cosia, Ichthyophthirius);* Cnidaria, Hydrozoa *(Hydra)*.

Dosage: (1) 2 gm/25 l of water; (2) 80 ppm as a dip at 3-day intervals (for fungi); (3) 80 ppm daily for 3 days (Protozoa).

Remarks: As a long duration bath—repeat every 3 days for 3 weeks.

References: Amlacher (1961b, 1970); Hoffman & Meyer (1974); Reichenbach-Klinke (1966); Reichenbach-Klinke & Elkan (1965): Reichenbach-Klinke & Landolt (1973).

ARALEN PHOSPHATE—See Chloroquine phosphate.

ARASAN—See Thiram.

ARGENTUM CREDE—See Collargol.

ARTEMISIN—See Santonin.

ARTHINOL—See Carbarsone.

ARYCIL

Composition: Arsenical preparation with a 36.4% arsenic content.
Synonyms: None.
Uses or Treatment for: Bacteria (carp pox) .
Dosage: 3 intraperitoneal injections of 1 cc of a 1% solution, and then of a 5% solution, repeated 3 times.
Remarks: None.
References: Amlacher (1970) .

ARGYROL—See Silvol.

ASPIRIN

Composition: Acetylsalicylic acid.

COOH

OCOCH₃

ACETYLSALICYLIC ACID

Synonyms: Various trade names.
Uses or Treatment for: Reduces shock and stress in newly transported fish.
Dosage: 1-50 gr tablet/10 gal of water (fresh or salt) .
Remarks: Over 31 manufacturers in U.S.; see NDCD (1972) .
References: NDCD (1972) .

ATABRINE, hydrochloride

Composition: 3-chloro-7-methoxy-9-(1-methyl-4-diethyl-amino-butylamino) acridine.

CH₃

HN—CH

CH₃O   CH₂CH₂CH₂N(C₂H₅)₂

N   CL   **QUINACRINE**

Synonyms: Atebrine; Chinacrine; Mepacrine; Quinacrine; Quinacrine hydrochloride.

Uses or Treatment for: Skin parasites; Protozoa *(Crypto-caryon irritans, Henneguaya, Ichthyophthirius, Oodinium ocellatum,* many sporozoans) .

Dosage: (1) 1 gm/100 l of water; (2) 0.01 gm/l of water in the form of a long duration bath; (3) 1.6-10 ppm in water; (4) 8-12 mg/gal in salt water.

Remarks: Keep treatment tank dark, as strong light will inactivate this drug; 10 ppm toxic to *Lebistes* (guppies) ; 0.2-0.8 ppm = LC_{100} to Centrachidae; 38 ppm = LC_1 to *Ictalurus* in 48 hours at 17°C; 119 ppm = LC_1 to *Salmo* in 48 hours at 12°C; 80 ppm = LC_1 to *Salvelinus fontanalis;* manufactured by Winthrop.

References: Amlacher (1961b, 1970) ; Berrios-Duran et al. (1964) ; Chang (1960) ; Clemens & Sneed (1959) ; Hoffman & Meyer (1974) ; Kingsford (1975) ; Pfeiffer (1952) ; Reichenbach-Klinke (1966) ; Reichenbach-Klinke & Elkan (1965); Reichenbach-Klinke & Landolt (1973) ; Schäperclaus (1954); Slater (1952) ; Van Duijn (1973) ; Willford (1967a) .

ATEBRINE—See Atabrine, hydrochloride.

AUREOMYCIN

Composition: 7-chloro-4-dimethylamino-1,4,4a,5,5a,6,11,12a-octahydro-3,6,10,12,12a-pentahydroxy-6-methyl-1,11 dioxo-2-naphthacenecarboxamide.

Synonyms: Biomitsin; Biomycin; Chlortetracycline.

Uses or Treatment for: Antibiotic; bacteria [Columnaris *(Chondrococcus columnaris),* cold-water disease *(Cytophaga psychrophila),* eel disease in Japan *(Vibrio)];* fungi *(Saprolegnia); Protozoa (Chilodonella, Costia, Hexamita, Ichthyophthirius, Oodinium).*

Dosage: (1) 13 mg/l of water in the form of a long duration bath; (2) 10-20 ppm in water; (3) 0.13 ppm; (4) 0.001-0.0015 ppm in food for 1 to 4 days; (5) 1000 ppm in food for 1 to 4 days; (6) 10,000 ppm in food; (7) added to food at a rate of 10-20 mg/kg of food.

Remarks: Has a shelf life in solution of only a few hours, use immediately after mixing; available in capsules and powders; manufactured by Lederle.

References: Amlacher (1961b, 1970); Borshosh & Illesh (1962); Hoffman & Meyer (1974); Kingsford (1975); Reichenbach-Klinke (1966); Reichenbach-Klinke & Elkan (1965); Reichenbach-Klinke & Landolt (1973); Sneiszko (1975); Van Duijn (1973).

BACITRACIN

Composition: A mixture of polypeptide antibiotics produced by a strain of *Bacillus subtilis.*

Synonyms: None.

Uses or Treatment for: Bacteria (gram-positive bacteria); fungi (marine fungus).

Dosage: 250-300 mg/gal of water.

Remarks: Especially valuable for treatment of eye fungus on jawfish; has a shelf life of one week; 33 manufacturers produce it as an ointment, only 3 produce a tablet or powder, i.e. National Drug, Premo, and Upjohn; avoid the use of Zinc Bacitracin and Bacitracin formulations containing zinc as they are toxic to fish.

References: Deufel (1967); Noyes (1974).

BALSAM OF PERU—See Balsam of Peru oil.

BALSAM OF PERU OIL

Composition: Benzyl cinnamate—extract from *Myroxylon pereirae*—oleoresin containing cinnamic acid.

Synonyms: Balsam of Peru; China oil; Peru oil.

Uses or Treatment for: Crustacea *(Argulus);* insecticide.

Dosage: 40 ppm for 3 hours.

Remarks: None.

References: Hoffman & Meyer (1974); Kabata (1970); Kelly (1962).

BARIUM CARBONATE
Composition: BaCO$_3$.
Synonyms: None.
Uses or Treatment for: Molluscicide (snails).
Dosage: According to recommendations on label.
Remarks: Do Not Use—Toxic to Fish! Presence identifiable for several months.
References: Deschiens (1961) ; Hoffman & Meyer (1974).

BARIUM CHLORIDE
Composition: BaCl$_2$ · 2H$_2$O.
Synonyms: None.
Uses or Treatment for: Molluscicide (snails).
Dosage: Safe dosage undetermined.
Remarks: Do Not Use—Toxic to Fish!
References: Hoffman & Meyer (1974).

BASIC BRIGHT GREEN, oxalate
Composition: Tetra-ethyl-diamino-triphenyl carbinol.
Synonyms: Brilliant green.
Uses or Treatment for: Dye; fungi (mycosis) ; Protozoa *(Ichthyophthirius)*.
Dosage: (1) 60 mg/l in the form of a bath of 45 seconds duration; (2) 0.12-1 ppm for 2.5 to 5 hours.
Remarks: Trophs killed subepithelially; 18 times less expensive than Malachite green.
References: Hoffman & Meyer (1974) ; Musselius & Flippova (1968) ; Reichenbach-Klinke & Elkan (1965).

BASIC VIOLET
Composition: Unknown.
Synonyms: None.
Uses or Treatment for: Protozoa *(Ichthyophthirius)*.
Dosage: 0.12-0.5 ppm for 2 to 5.5 hours.
Remarks: Kills trophs subepithelially.
References: Hoffman & Meyer (1974) ; Musselius & Flippova (1968).

BAYER 73—See Bayluscide
BAYER 2353—See Niclosamide.

BAYER 29493—See Baytex.

BAYER 9015

Composition: Unknown.

Synonyms: Unknown.

Uses or Treatment for: Unknown.

Remarks: 1.0 ppm toxic to *Ictalurus* in 96 hours.

References: R. Allison (1969) ; Hoffman & Meyer (1974) .

BAYGON, 50% wettable powder

Composition: o-isopropoxyphenyl N-methylcarbamate.

Synonyms: Propoxur; Uden.

Uses or Treatment for: Hirudinea (leeches, *Erpobdella punctata, Illinobdella moorei, Piscicola salmositica, Placobdella parasitica, Theromyzon sp.*); Crustacea *(Lernaea cyprinacea).*

Dosage: (1) 0.5-1.0 ppm; (2) 1 ppm applied weekly for 4 weeks.

Remarks: Fish should not be present during treatment; 5.0 ppm toxic to *Ictalurus;* not effective against *Lernaea.*

References: R. Allison (1969) ; Hoffman & Meyer (1974) ; F. Meyer (1969a) .

BAYLUSCID—See Bayluscide.

BAYLUSCIDE

Composition: Aminoethanol dichloronitro-salicylanilide (ethanolamine salt of niclosamide) or 3-trifluoromethyl-4'-nitrosalicylanilide.

Synonyms: Bayer 73; Bayluscid.

Uses or Treatment for: Molluscicide (snails) .

Dosage: 0.5-1.0 ppm in water.

Remarks: Toxic to fish for 3 weeks after treatment; 0.04-0.24 = LC_{50} to many species of fish (trout and minnows) ; 0.78-0.8 ppm = LC_{16} to *Roccus* and *Tilapia.*

References: Berrios-Duran et al. (1964) ; Bills & Marking (1976) ; Deufel (1964) ; Hoffman & Meyer (1974) ; Howell et al. (1964) ; Kawatski et al. (1975) ; Marking & Hogan (1967); Reichenbach-Klinke (1966) ; Wellborn (1971) .

BAYTEX

Composition: O,O-dimethyl-O-[4-(methylthio)-m-tolyl] phosphorothioate.

Synonyms: Bayer 29493; Entex; Fenthion; Tiguvon.

Uses or Treatment for: Protozoa *(Ichthyophthirius)*; Hirudinea (leeches, *Erpobdella punctata, Illinobdella moorei, Piscicola salmositica, Placobdella parasitica, Theromyzon sp.);* Crustacea [*Argulus sp., Lernaea cyprinacea* (crayfish)]; insecticide.

Dosage: (1) 0.23 ppm; (2) 0.1 ppm (not effective against *Ichthyophthirius);* (3) 0.5-1 ppm; (4) 0.12 ppm tri-weekly for two weeks *(Argulus);* (5) 0.25 ppm weekly for 4 weeks *(Lernaea);* (6) 0.6% in diet (not effective).

Remarks: 0.23 ppm = LC_{100} in crayfish; 30 ppm = LC_{50} in *Cyprinus carpio;* 0.6 ppm = LC_{50} in *Esox lucius;* 0.5 ppm = LC_{50} in young trout; 0.4-0.9 ppm was toxic to *Lepomis macrochirus;* 0.9 ppm was nontoxic to *Ictalurus punctatus,* but 2.9 ppm = LC_1 and 5 ppm was toxic; 2.2 ppm = LC_1 in *Salmo gairdneri* in 48 hours at 12°C; 1.8 ppm = LC_1 to *Salmo trutta* in 48 hours at 12°C; 4.3 ppm = LC_1 to *Salvelinus fontinalis* and *S. namaycush* in 48 hours at 12°C; available in capsules or liquid; manufactured by Baylor.

References: R. Allison (1969); Hoffman & Meyer (1974); Lüdeman & Kayser (1962); F. Meyer (1969a); Osborn (1966); Reichenbach-Klinke (1966); Willford (1967a).

BENASEPT—See Benzalkonium chloride.

BENKOSAL—See Benzalkonium chloride.

BENZALKONIUM CHLORIDE

Composition: Benzalkonium chloride; alkyl dimethyl benzyl ammonium chloride.

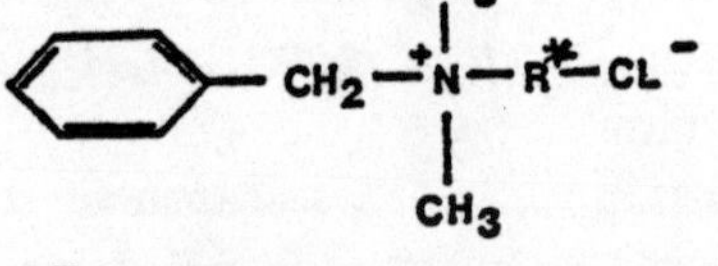

*R represents any Alkyl from $C_8 H_{17}$ to $C_{18} H_{37}$

Benzalkonium Chloride

Synonyms: Aqueous Neobenz-All, Benasept, Benkosal, Germicidal Zalkonium chloride, Phemerol chloride, Phemerol crystals, Roccal, Zephiran, Zephiran chloride, Zephirol, Zonium chloride.

Uses or Treatment for: Disinfectant; viricide; bacteria (bacterial gill disease, fin rot, myxobacterial disease) ; Protozoa *(Costia, Ichthyobodo, Ichthyophthirius, Myxosoma cerebralis,* Trichodinids) ; Monogenea *(Gyrodactylus); * Hirudinea *(Piscicola salmositica).*

Dosage: (1) up to 0.02 gm/l of water; (2) 1:2000 to 1:4000 solution in the form of a 30-minute bath; (3) 1:50,000 solution; (4) 0.5 ppm (not effective against Ich) ; (5) 250-500 ppm for 20 to 30 minutes; (6) 200 ppm (not effective against *Myxosoma cerebralis); * (7) 1-2 ppm for 1 hour (not effective against *Piscicola).*

Remarks: 0.74-2.05 ppm not appreciably toxic to fish; toxic in soft water, less effective and less toxic in hard water; sold as 10-50% solutions of Benzalkonium chloride, a quaternary ammonia compound (germicide) ; available as a solution or manufactured by Barre, Bluline, Canfield, Flar, MCC-M, PD, Progress, Vitarine, Winthrop, Xttrium; see also Hyamine.

References: Earp & Schwab (1954) ; Hoffman & Hoffman (1972) ; Hoffman & Meyer (1974); Reichenbach-Klinke (1966); Reichenbach-Klinke & Elkan (1965) ; Reichenbach-Klinke & Landolt (1973); Rucker & Whipple (1951) ; Schäperclaus (1954) ; Sneiszko (1975) ; Willford (1967a) .

BENZENE HEXACHLORIDE
Composition: 1,2,3,4,5,6-hexachlorocyclohexane — a gamma isomer of benzene hexachloride.

Synonyms: BHC; Gammexane; Lexone; Lindane; 666; Tri-6.

Uses or Treatment for: Hirudinea (leeches, *Hemiclepsis marginate); * Crustacea *(Argulus japonicus, Argulus sp., Lernaea cyprinacea); * insecticide.

Dosage: (1) 0.014 ppm; (2) 7% solution used at 10 ppm; (3) 0.03 mg/l of water for 13 hours; (4) 5% powder in quantities of 8-10 gm/m^3 of water; (5) 2.7 ppm in weekly doses (Lexone); (6) 0.5 ppm; (7) 100 ppm for 30 minutes; (8) 0.12-0.78 ppm *(Argulus); * (9) 0.2 ppm; (10) 0.0013-0.5 ppm (effective range against *Argulus); * (11) 0.0625-2.66 ppm *(Lernaea); * (12) 1:

10,000,000 for 2 to 3 days; (13) prepare a 1% stock solution in absolute alcohol, use at 1 cc/100 l (approx. 20 Imp gal or 25 U.S. gal) *(Argulus)*.

Remarks: CAUTION: Toxic to humans, causing hyper-irritability, convulsions, and death; may be absorbed through the skin; avoid direct contact with solutions containing this chemical; slight milky white precipitate may form when chemical is added to water, disappears with stirring; concentrations of 0.25 ppm were not lethal to carp at 25-27°C with a pH above 8.0; *Argulus* showed rapid development of resistance; 0.25 ppm = LC_{100} to *Notemigonus crysoleucas* in 96 hours at 24°C; 1:5,000,000 solution may kill pike in 24 hours; practically insoluble in water.

References: Clemens & Sneed (1959); De Graaf (1959); Giudice (1950); Gopalakrishnan (1964); Hindle (1949); Hoffman & Meyer (1974); Ivasik & Svirepo (1964); Katz (1961); Kislev & Ivleva (1950, 1953); Lahav & Sarig (1967); Lahav, Sarig, and Shilo (1964, 1966); Lahav, Shilo, and Sarig (1962); Lewis (1961); McNeil (1961); Malacca Research Institute (1963); F. Meyer (1966a, 1967); Putz & Bowen (1964); Reichenbach-Klinke (1966); Saha & Chakraborty (1959); Saha & Sen (1958); Sarig (1966, 1968, 1971); Sarig & Lahav (1959); Schäperclaus (1949, 1950); Sproston (1956); Stammer (1959); Surber (1948); Wellborn (1971); Van Duijn (1973).

BETADINE

Composition: Iodine + polyvinylpyrrolidone complex (1% iodine).

Synonyms: Povidone-Iodine; PVP-I.

Uses or Treatment for: Disinfectant; disinfection of fish eggs; viricide; bacteria [*Acinetobacter*, Furunculosis *(Aeromonas salmonicida)*].

Dosage: (1) 100 ml/l—painted on; (2) 100-200 ml/l—as a bath for 10 minutes; (3) 10-minute bath at 10-100 ppm Iodine.

Remarks: May burn exposed tissue on marine fish or smooth-skinned fish if applied topically; 10 ppm not effective against

Ichthyophthirius; an Iodophor containing 1% Iodine; manufactured by Purdue; see also Povidone-Iodine.
References: Hoffman & Meyer (1974) ; Snieszko (1975) .

BETANAPHTHOL

Composition: β-hydroxynaphthalene.
Synonyms: Isonaphthol; 2-naphthol.
Uses or Treatment for: Antiseptic; parasiticide; Protozoa *(Hexamita).*
Dosage: 5 gm/kg of fish, in food for 4 to 5 days.
Remarks: None.
References: Hoffman & Meyer (1974) ; Reichenbach-Klinke (1966) .

BHC—See Benzene hexachloride.

BIOCIDAL RUBBER—See Di-*n*-butyl tin oxide.

BIOMITSIN—See Aureomycin.

BIOMYCIN—See Aureomycin.

BIPYRIDILIUM—See Diquat and Paraquat.

BISMUTH VIOLET—See Gentian violet.

BIS-OXIDE

Composition: Tri-*n*-butyl tin oxide.
Synonyms: None.
Uses or Treatment for: Anthelminthic.
Dosage: According to recommendations on label.
Remarks: None.
References: Hoffman & Meyer (1974) .

BITHIN—See Bithionol.

BITHIONOL

Composition: 2′,2-thiobis(4,6-dichlorophenol) .
Synonyms: Actamer; Bithin; Cogla; Lorothidol; TBP.
Uses or Treatment for: Antimicrobial; fungi (oral prophylaxis against *Saprolegnia);* Cestoda *(Bothriocephalus);* Acanthocephala *(Echinorhynchus).*
Dosage: (1) 0.2 gm/kg of fish mixed at 2% in food, feed for 2 to 3 days; (2) 10,000 ppm in food daily for 3 days against

cestodes (was not effective and caused hematological disorders).
Remarks: Used in France; a French product.
References: Gerard & de Kinkelin (1971) ; Hoffman & Meyer
(1974) ; Klenov (1970) ; Snieszko (1975).

BLUESTONE—See Copper sulfate.

BORIC ACID
Composition: H_3BO_3.
Synonyms: Neo-flo bufopto.
Uses or Treatment for: Disinfectant.
Dosage: Unknown.
Remarks: Incompatible with quaternaries; 17 manufacturers
market an ointment, only BBC, Rondex, and Prof Pharcal
have medicinal solutions.
References: Hoffman & Meyer (1974).

BRIGHT GREEN—See Malachite green.

BRIDINE—See Iodophors.

BRILLIANT GREEN—See Basic bright green or Malachite
green.

BROMEX-50
Composition: 1,2 dibromo-2,2-dichloro-ethyl dimethyl phosphate.
Synonyms: Dibrom; Naled.
Uses or Treatment for: Protozoa *(Ichthyophthirius);* trematodes; Monogenea *(Benedenia, Cleidodiscus, Dactylogyrus an-
choratus, D. vastator, Gyrodoctylus sp.);* Crustacea (copepods,
Achtheres, Argulus sp., Ergasilus sp., Lernaea sp., Salmincola);
pesticide; insecticide.
Dosage: (1) 12 ppm; (2) 0.12-0.15 ppm added to (pond) water
for an indefinite time; (3) 0.3 ppm; (4) 0.18 ppm in
ponds; (5) 1-1.5 ppm daily (as needed to inhibit Ich).
Remarks: 2.0-40 ppm toxic to fish; 2-5 ppm $= LC_{50}$ to *Carassius
auratus;* 1-2 ppm $= LC_{50}$ to *Lebistes reticulatus;* 3.4 ppm $=
LC_{100}$ to both *Lepomis macrochirus* and *Micropterus salmoi-
des;* 0.08 ppm $= LC_{50}$ to *Salmo gairdneri.*
References: Hoffman & Meyer (1974) ; Kabata (1970); Lahav
et al. (1966) ; Lahav & Sarig (1967) ; F. Meyer (1969b) ; Sarig
(1966, 1968, 1969, 1971) ; Snieszko (1975).

BUFFODINE—See Iodophors.

BUTTER OF ZINC—See Zinc chloride.

BUTYL TIN OXIDE—See Di-*n*-butyl tin oxide.

BUTYNORATE—See Dibutyltin dilaurate.

CADMIUM SULFATE
Composition: $CdSO_4 \cdot nH_2O$.
Synonyms: None.
Uses or Treatment for: Molluscicide (snails).
Dosage: 5-15 ppm.
Remarks: 15 ppm nontoxic to *Carassius auratus*.
References: Deschiens (1961); Deschiens & Tahiri (1961); Hoffman & Meyer (1974).

CALCIUM CARBONATE, commercial grade
Composition: $CaCO_3$ (occasionally with $MgCO_3$).
Synonyms: Calaron, Creta, Dolomite, Lime.
Uses or Treatment for: Protozoa *(Chilodonella)*; Mollusca (snails).
Dosage: 195-1135 kg/hectare (700-1000 lb/acre), apply while pond is drained, flush before refilling.
Remarks: Most often obtained and used in bulk; available in tablets of medical purity; manufactured by Invenex, Lilly, Sutliff & Case, Wendt-Bristol.
References: Amlacher (1961b); Hoffman & Meyer (1974).

CALCIUM CHLORIDE
Composition: $CaCl_2$.
Synonyms: Chloride of lime.
Uses or Treatment for: Disinfecting pond bottoms; Protozoa *(Eimeria)*; Cestoda *(Bothriocephalus)*; Crustacea *(Salmincola)*.
Dosage: (1) 85% solution; (2) 5 centner/hectare; (3) 8500 ppm; (4) 0.3-0.5 ton/hectare.
Remarks: 10,000 ppm toxic to fish; manufactured by Bristol Labs, Invenex, Upjohn.
References: Babaev & Shcherbakova (1963); Bauer et al. (1969); Fasten (1912); Hoffman & Meyer (1974); Kabata (1970); Musselius & Strelkov (1968); Reichenbach-Klinke (1966).

CALCIUM CYANAMIDE
Composition: CaNCN.
Synonyms: Cyanamide.
Uses or Treatment for: Disinfection of ponds and tanks; fungi *(Branchiomyces demigrans, B. sanguinis, B. sp.);* Protozoa [*Babesisoma, Ceratomyxa* in salmon, *Cryptobia, Glugea, Henneguya, Hofferulus, Myxobolus,* Myxosporidae, *Nosema, Plistophora, Thelohania, Thelohannelus, Trypanosoma,* whirling disease *(Myxosoma cerebralis)*].
Dosage: (1) 1 kg/m^2; (2) 2000 kg/hectare (1833 lb/acre) to 5000 kg/hectare (4453 lb/acre) applied when wet to drained ponds every 3 to 4 months: (3) 200 gm/m^2, distributed on the bottom and banks of drained but still wet ponds.
Remarks: Destroys spores and eggs in drained pond bottoms.
References: Amlacher (1961b, 1970); Ghittino (1970); Hoffman & Meyer (1974); Schäperclaus (1932); Snieszko (1975); Tack (1951).

CALCIUM HYDROXIDE, commercial grade
Composition: Ca(OH)$_2$
Synonyms: Hydrated lime; Limewater; Slaked lime.
Uses or Treatment for: Protozoa *(Chilodonella sp., Myxosoma cerebralis);* Molluscicide (snails).
Dosage: (1) 5000 ppm; (2) Ca(OH)$_2$ + Ca(OCl)$_2$:(3:1) applied at a rate of 2385 kg/hectare (2100 lb/acre).
Remarks: Will raise pH; 100 ppm may prove toxic to fish in 3 to 7 days; medical quality manufactured by Lilly, BBC.
References: Hoffman & Hoffman (1972); Hoffman & Meyer (1974); McKee & Wolf (1963).

CALCIUM HYPOCHLORITE
Composition: Ca(OCl)$_2$.
Synonyms: Chlorinated lime; HTH; Perchloron.
Uses or Treatment for: Disinfection of tanks; ectoparasites; Protozoa [coccidiosis *(Eimeria)*]; Crustacea *(Lernaea).*
Dosage: (1) 100-200 mg/l of water; (2) 10 mg/l of water; (3) 0.0001% (1 ppm) at temperatures higher than 14°C for 3 days; (4) 500 kg/hectare (466 lb/acre) is used in Russia; (5) 600-1200 ppm (as free Cl) for 16 hours (inhibits *Myxosoma);*

(6) 0.8-0.9 ton/hectare.

Remarks: May be toxic to fish; 300-400 ppm for 16 hours in-effective against *Myxosoma*.

References: Bauer et al. (1969) ; Chechina (1959) ; Hoffman (1972) ; Hoffman & Hoffman (1972) ; Hoffman & Meyer (1974); Kabata (1970) ; Reichenbach-Klinke (1966) ; Reichenbach-Klinke & Elkan (1965); Reichenbach-Klinke & Landolt (1973); Schäperclaus (1954).

CALCIUM NITRATE

Composition: Ca$(NO_3)_2$.

Synonyms: None.

Uses or Treatment for: Pond disinfection.

Dosage: 1 kg/m² of water.

Remarks: None.

References: Reichenbach-Klinke & Elkan (1965) ; Reichen-bach-Klinke & Landolt (1973).

CALCIUM OXIDE

Composition: CaO.

Synonyms: Quicklime; Unslaked lime.

Uses or Treatment for: Disinfection of ponds; fungicide *(Branchiomyces demigrans, B. sanguinis);* Protozoa [*Chilo-donella, Costia, Cryptobia, Babesiosoma, Ceratomyxa* in sal-mon, *Glugea, Henneguya, Hofferulus, Ichthyophthirius, My-xobolus,* Myxosporidae, *Nosema, Plistophora, Thelohania, Thelohannelus, Trichodina, Trypanosoma,* whirling disease *(Myxosoma cerebralis)*]; monogenetic trematodes *(Dactylo-gyrus, Gyrodactylus);* Hirudinea (leeches, *Piscicola geometra);* Crustacea *(Argulus);* molluscicide (snails).

Dosage: (1) 150-200 kg/hectare (2.47 acres) ; (2) 10-15 gm/hectare; (3) 2 gm/l for 5 seconds as a short duration bath; (4) 0.1-0.15 kg/m³ of water; (5) 2000 ppm as a dip for 5 seconds; (6) 3000 kg/hectare on drained ponds; (7) 880-1320 lb/acre (1000-1500 kg/hectare) ; (8) 200 gm/m², distributed on the bottom and banks of drained, but still wet, ponds; (9) 2.5 ton/hectare.

Remarks: Destroys spores and eggs in drained pond bottoms.

References: Amlacher (1961b, 1970) ; Bauer (1958) ; Bauer

et al. (1969) ; Chechina (1959) ; Ghittino (1970) ; Hoffman & Hoffman (1972) ; Hoffman & Meyer (1974) ; Ivasik & Karpenko (1965) ; Kabata (1970) ; Reichenbach-Klinke & Elkan (1965) ; Reichenbach-Klinke & Landolt (1973) ; Rychlicki (1966) ; Sarig (1971) ; Schäperclaus (1954) ; Snieszko (1975) .

CALCIUM PENICILLIN G—See Penicillin.

CALOMEL

Composition: Mercurous chloride.

Synonyms: Calomelol.

Uses or Treatment for: Protozoa [*Hexamita* (= *Octomites*)]; fungicide.

Dosage: (1) 0.2% solution added to food for 2 days; (2) 2 gm/kg in food for 4 days; (3) 2000 ppm in food for 4 days.

Remarks: Inhibitory only; manufactured by FTP.

References: Amlacher (1970) ; Hoffman & Meyer (1974); Reichenbach-Klinke (1966) ; Reichenbach-Klinke & Landolt (1973) ; Smith & Quistorff (1940) .

CALOMELOL—See Calomel.

CANTREX—See Kanamycin.

CARBARSONE

Composition: *N*-carbamoylarsanilic acid, 28% arsenic.

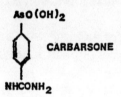

AsO(OH)₂

CARBARSONE

NHCONH₂

Synonyms: Arthinol.

Uses or Treatment for: Protozoacide [*Hexamita* (= *Octomites*)].

Dosage: (1) 0.2% in feed for 4 to 7 days; (2) 2000 ppm in food daily for 3 days.

Remarks: Manufactured by Lilly.

References: Amlacher (1970) ; Hoffman & Meyer (1974); Nelson (1941) ; Reichenbach-Klinke (1966) ; Yasutake et al. (1961) .

CARBARSONE OXIDE

Composition: *p*-carbamidophenyl arsenoxide.
Synonyms: None.
Uses or Treatment for: Protozoacide *(Hexamita (= Octo-mites).*
Dosage: (1) 2000 ppm in food daily for 3 days; (2) 0.2% in food for 3 days.
Remarks: None.
References: Hoffman & Meyer (1974); Snieszko (1975); Yasutake et al. (1961).

CARBENICILLIN DISODIUM

Composition: Carbenicillin disodium.
Synonyms: Geopen.
Uses or Treatment for: Bacteria (gram-positive and gram-negative bacteria, *Pseudomonas*).
Dosage: Undetermined.
Remarks: A very good broad spectrum antibiotic; shelf life when in solution is one day, use immediately; available as sterile powder; manufactured by Roerig.
References: Kingsford (1975).

CASTOR BEAN PLANT

Composition: *Ricinus communis* raw extract.
Synonyms: None.
Uses or Treatment for: Crustacea *(Lernaea cyprinacea).*
Dosage: Place bundles of plant in water.
Remarks: None.
References: Hickling (1962); Hoffman & Meyer (1974).

CATENULIN—See Paramomycin.

CAUSTIC LIME—See Lime.

CAUSTIC POTASH—See Potassium hydroxide.

CAUSTIC SODA—See Sodium hydroxide.

CELBENIN—See Methacillin sodium.

CEPHALORIDINE

Composition: Penicillin-related antibiotic originating from the fungus *Cephalosporium*.
Synonyms: Loridine.

Uses or Treatment for: Bacteria (gram-positive and some gram-negative bacteria).
Dosage: Undetermined.
Remarks: Potentially nephrotoxic; shelf life when in solution is 5 days; available as sterile powder in 500 mg and 1 gm quantities; manufactured by Lilly.
References: Kingsford (1975); Sampson et al. (1973).

CESTOCIDE—See Niclosamide.

CHELATED COPPER
Composition: $CuSO_4$ + EDTA (ethylenediamine tetraacetic acid).
Synonyms: None.
Uses or Treatment for: Protozoacide *(Ichthyophthirius)*.
Dosage: 1 ppm applied daily.
Remarks: None.
References: Hoffman & Meyer (1974).

CHESTNUT DECOCTION
Composition: Unknown.
Synonyms: None.
Uses or Treatment for: Vermicide; Turbellaria *(Hydra)*.
Dosage: Flour from one chestnut stirred in 5-15 liters of water, poured into a cheesecloth bag and suspended in the aquarium.
Remarks: None.
References: Reichenbach-Klinke & Landolt (1973).

CHEVREUL'S SALT
Composition: $CuSO_3 \cdot CuSO_3 \cdot 2H_2O$.
Synonyms: None.
Uses or Treatment for: Molluscicide (snails).
Dosage: 2.25 ppm applied one time.
Remarks: 2 ppm = LC_{25} to *Lebistes reticulatus* and 16 ppm toxic to *Lepomis auritus;* however, 16 ppm was not toxic to *Tilapia* or *Micropterus salmoides*.
References: Berrios-Duran et al. (1964); Deschiens et al. (1963); Gamet et al. (1964); Hoffman & Meyer (1974).

CHINACRINE—See Atabrine hydrochloride.

CHINA OIL—See Balsam of Peru oil.

CHLORAMIN—See Chloramine-T.

CHLORAMINE—See Chloramine-T.

CHLORAMINE-B

Composition: Sodium benzenesulfonchloramide.

Synonyms: Halamid.

Uses or Treatment for: Disinfectant; protozoacide [*Chilodonella, Costia, Ichthyophthirius, Trichodina (= Cyclochaeta)*]; monogenetic trematodes *(Gyrodactylus).*

Dosage: (1) 10 ppm for 24 hours; (2) 20 ppm.

Remarks: Do not use in metal tanks.

References: Goncharov (1966); Hoffman & Meyer (1974); Van Duijn (1973).

CHLORAMINE-T

Composition: Sodium *p*-toluenesulfonchloramide.

Synonyms: Chloramin; Chloramine; Chlorazene; Chlorazone; Halamid.

Uses or Treatment for: Antiseptic; fungicide *(Saprolegnia);* protozoacide *(Costia necatrix, Ichthyophthirius);* Turbellaria; monogenetic trematodes *(Gyrodactylus);* ectoparasites.

Dosage: (1) 0.067 gm/l in water, in the form of a bath lasting 2 to 4 hours; (2) 1 gm/15 l of water for 2 to 4 hours; (3) 10 ppm; (4) 66 ppm for 2 to 4 hours; (5) 5-20 ppm twice daily in soft water (pH 6-7); (6) 18-20 ppm in water with pH 7.5-8, change 50 percent of water once each week if water temperature is 10°C or below; at 25°C use 1 treatment for 2 to 3 days.

Remarks: 75 ppm for 1 hour and 166 ppm for 30 minutes not effective against Ich; 67 ppm slightly toxic to young *Cyprinus carpio.*

References: Deufel (1970); Fish (1939); Goncharov (1966); Hoffman & Meyer (1974); Postema (1956); Reichenbach-Klinke (1966); Reichenbach-Klinke & Elkan (1965); Reichenbach-Klinke & Landolt (1973); Schäperclaus (1954); Snieszko (1975).

CHLORAMPHENICOL

Composition: D(—)-threo-2,2-dichloro-*N*-[β-hyroxy-α(hydroxymethyl)-*p*-nitrophenethyl] acetamide.

CH₂OH

CHLORAMPHENICOL

Synonyms: Amphicol; Chloramphenicol palmitate; Chloro-mycetin; Chloronitrin; Leukomycin; Mychel-Vet.

Uses or Treatment for: Antibiotic; bacteria (gram-negative bacteria, *Aeromonas punctata,* bacterial hemorrhagic septice-mia, bacterial fin rot, Furunculosis *(Aeromonas salmonicida), Pseudomonas,* redmouth disease of trout, staphylococci, ulcer disease *(Hemophilus piscium);* fungicide *(Ichthyophonus);* protozoacide *(Ichthyophthirius).*

Dosage: (1) 3 mg/150-400 gm body weight, dilute in water by means of Butylene glycol, 1 cc should contain 3 mg of anti-biotic, administer as intraperitoneal injection of 1 cc of an aqueous solution in 150-400 gm fish, in bigger fish, a little more; (2) dissolve 80 mg/l of water as a long duration bath (24 hours) ; (3) In feed—50-75 mg/kg of body weight per day for 5 to 10 days; (4) dissolve 50 mg/l in water for fish of 10 gm weight as a long duration bath; (5) 2.5-3.5 gm/100 lb of fish per day in food; (6) 0.05-0.1 gm/kg of fish in food over a period of 10 days; (7) as an injection—per 10 gm of fish weight —0.1 mg in 0.1 cc of water in the visceral cavity; (8) as a bath —per 10 gm of fish weight—80 mg/l of water, 8 hours duration; (9) as a food additive—1 mg mixed with 1 gm of corn flour, given once or twice; (10) 10 mg/lb of fish intraperitoneally; (11) 5-10 ppm (12) 0.001 ppm in diet; (13) 50-80 mg/l as a long duration bath; (14) a single intraperitoneal injection of soluble form—10-30 mg/kg of body weight; (15) add to water—10-50 ppm for an indefinite time as needed; (16) 7.5 gm/100 kg per day in feed for 14 days; (17) 1 mg/100 gm in-traperitoneally; (18) 50 mg/gal in salt water.

Remarks: Avoid overdose and use judiciously in food. One of the greatest dangers in the use of antibiotics is the develop-ment of resistant strains of bacteria. Chloramphenicol palmi-tate is insoluble in water; marginally effective in marine aquaria as it is inactivated at a pH of around 8.2-8.4; available as capsule (250 mg and 500 mg) or as a sterile powder; manufactured by Aberdeen, McKesson, PD, Rachelle.

References: Amlacher (1970); Anderson & Battle (1967); Evelyn (1968); Herman (1972); Hoffman & Meyer (1974); Kingsford (1975); Mattheis (1961); Reichenbach-Klinke & Elkan (1965); Schäperclaus (1957, 1958); Smith (1950); Snieszko (1975); Van Duijn (1973).

CHLORAMPHENICOL PALMITATE—See Chloramphenicol.

CHLORAMPHENICOL, Sodium succinate—See Chloramphenicol.

CHLORAZENE—See Chloramine-T.

CHLORBENSIDE—See Mitox.

CHLORIDE OF LIME—See Calcium chloride.

CHLORINATED LIME—See Calcium hypochlorite.

CHLOROZONE—See Chloramine-T.

CHLORINE

Composition: As Cl_2 gas or available element.

Synonyms: None.

Uses or Treatment for: Disinfectant; protozoacide *(Ceratomyxa shasta)*; fungicide *(Ichthyophonus hoferi)*; monogenetic trematodes *(Gyrodactylus)*; Crustacea *(Lernaea)*.

Dosage: (1) 200 ppm; (2) 0.3 ppm; (3) 2.5 ppm as a dip for 10 seconds; (4) 1.0 ppm for 3 days; (5) 50 ppm in seawater for sterilization.

Remarks: Toxic to many fish.

References: Bedell (1971); Connell (1937); Erickson (1965); Hoffman & Meyer (1974); Kingsford (1975); Leith & Moore (1967); Lewis & Ulrich (1967); Putz & Bowen (1964).

CHLORINE BLEACH—See Sodium hypochlorite.

CHLORITE +—See Sodium chlorite.

CHLOROFOS—See Dylox.

CHLOROMYCETIN—See Chloramphenicol.

CHLOROPHENOXETHOL—See Phenoxethol.

CHLOROPHOS—See Dylox.

CHLORONITRIN—See Chloramphenicol.

CHLOROQUINE, Diphosphate—See Chloroquine phosphate.

CHLOROQUINE PHOSPHATE

Composition: 4-aminoquinoline derivative.

Synonyms: Aralen phosphate; Chloroquine diphosphate; Roquine; Truxquine.

Uses or Treatment for: Protozoacide *(Cyptocaryon irritans)*.

Dosage: 40 mg/gal in salt water.

Remarks: Available as 250 mg tablets; manufactured by Arcum, Barre, Bates, Columbia, COT, Medic, Premo, Robinson Lab, Stanley Drug, United, West-Ward, Winthrop.

References: Kingsford (1975).

CHLORTETRACYCLINE—See Aureomycin.

CIODRIN

Composition: Commercial formulation.

Synonyms: None.

Uses or Treatment for: Crustacea *(Lernaea)*; pesticide.

Dosage: Undetermined.

Remarks: Pesticide manufactured by Shell Petroleum Co.; used in Japanese eel culture.

References: Snieszko (1975).

CITRIC ACID

Composition: 2-hydroxy-1,2,3-propanetricarboxylic acid.

Synonyms: None.

Uses or Treatment for: Protozoacide *(Ichthyophthirius, Oodinium)*.

Dosage: (1) $CuSO_4$ + citric acid (1 ppm + 2 ppm) on alternate days; (2) Copper sulfate pentahydrate (3 parts) to citric acid monhydrate (2 parts)—maintain 0.15 ppm copper by water analysis for 10 days.

Remarks: See Copper sulfate.

References: Hoffman & Meyer (1974); Nigrelli & Ruggieri (1966).

CLOROX—See Sodium hypochlorite.

CLOXACILLIN, SODIUM

Composition: Semisynthetic penicillin salt similar to oxacillin sodium.

Synonyms: Tegopen.
Uses or Treatment for: Bacteria (gram-positive and some gram-negative bacteria).
Dosage: Undetermined.
Remarks: Has a shelf life of one day when in solution; available in capsules (250 mg) or powders; manufactured by Bristol Labs.
References: Kingsford (1975).

COGLA (D²n Cogla)—See Bithionol.

COLISTIN SULFATE
Composition: Sodium colistimethate of Colistin sulfate.
Synonyms: Colymycin S; Colymycin M.
Uses or Treatment for: Bacteria (gram-positive and some gram-negative bacteria, *Pseudomonas*).
Dosage: Undetermined.
Remarks: Has a shelf life of one week when mixed in solution; moderately effective in salt water; Colymycin M is sodium colistimethate; Colymycin S is Colistin sulfate; manufactured by WC.
References: Kingsford (1975).

COLLARGOL
Composition: Collodial silver—Silver Oxide (AgO)—78% Ag.
Synonyms: Argentum crede; Aquari-sol.
Uses or Treatment for: Disinfectant; fungicide *(Saprolegnia);* protozoacide *(Chilodonella, Cyclochaeta, Ichthyophthirius).*
Dosage: (1) 1 mg/l of water as a short bath of 20 minutes; (2) 0.1 ppm for 20 minutes; (3) 1-3 ppm for 1 to 3 hours.
Remarks: Not as effective as Malachite green; 10 ppm toxic to *Carassius vulgaris* (5 cm) in 24 hours at 20°C.
References: Amlacher (1961b, 1970); Hoffman & Meyer (1974); Reichenbach-Klinke (1966); Reichenbach-Klinke & Elkan (1965); Reichenbach-Klinke & Landolt (1973); Schäperclaus (1954); Van Duijn (1973).

COLYMYCIN M—See Colistin sulfate.

COLYMYCIN S—See Colistin sulfate.

CONCURAT
Composition: 2,3,5,6-tetrahydro-6-phenylimidazo(2,1,-6)thiazol-hydrochloride.
Synonyms: None.
Uses or Treatment for: Broad spectrum anthelminthic *(Capillaria).*
Dosage: Immerse live chironomid larvae in a solution of 2-4 gm/l until the larvae are beginning to die, then feed.
Remarks: None.
References: Schubert (1974).

COPPER CARBONATE
Composition: $CuCO_3 \cdot Cu(OH)_2 \cdot H_2O$.
Synonyms: Cupric carbonate.
Uses or Treatment for: Molluscicide (snails).
Dosage: (1) If Methyl orange alkalinity is 50 ppm or greater —2 lb of $CuSO_4$ + 1 lb of $CuCO_3 \cdot Cu(OH)_2 \cdot H_2O$ at 3 lb/ 1000 sq ft; (2) 9.76 gm/m^2 (2 lb/1000 sq ft)—if Methyl orange alkalinity is less than 50 ppm.
Remarks: None.
References: Barbosa (1961); Hoffman & Meyer (1974); Mackenthun (1958).

COPPER, micronized
Composition: Micronized copper.
Synonyms: None.
Uses or Treatment for: Unknown.
Dosage: Unknown.
Remarks: None.
References: Harris (1960); Hoffman & Meyer (1974).

COPPER PROTOXIDE—See Cuprous oxide.

COPPER SULFATE
Composition: $CuSO_4 \cdot 5H_2O$ (crystalline); $CuSO_4$ (anhydrous).
Synonyms: Bluestone.
Uses or Treatment for: Algicide (blue-green algae; *Pyrmnesium);* bactericide (bacterial fin rot); fungicide *(Branchiomyces sanguinis, B. demigrans, Saprolegnia);* external protozoacide

(Ambiphyra sp., Chilodonella, Costia, Cryptocaryon irritans, Epistylis, Ichthyophthirius, Ichthyobodo, Myxosoma cerebralis, Oodinium ocellatum, O. pillularis, Trichodina, Trichophyra); monogenetic trematodes *(Gyrodactylus, Dactylogyrus);* Hirudinea (leeches); molluscicide (snails); ectoparasitic worms; Crustacea *(Argulus, Ergasilus, Salmincola, Sinergasilus major). Dosage:* (1) Less than 1 ppm if $CaCO_3$ level in fresh water is less than 50 ppm—use with extreme caution; (2) 1-2 ppm if $CaCO_3$ level is 50-200 ppm; (3) 2 ppm mixed with 3 ppm Citric acid in ponds with $CaCO_3$ levels above 200 ppm; (4) 500 ppm + 500 ppm of Acetic acid as a dip for 1 to 2 minutes; (5) $CuSo_4$ + DMSO (0.1-1.0 ppm + 0.5-5.0 ppm) on alternate days; (6) 0.25-2.0 ppm, add 3 ppm Acetic acid in hard waters on alternate days (to ponds); (7) Dylox (1 ppm) + $CuSO_4$ (2 ppm)—toxic to fish; (8) Ammonia (25 ppm) + $CuSO_4$ (0.5 ppm); (9) 0.5 ppm for 5 to 6 hours (leeches); (10) 1.5 mg/41 of fresh water; (11) 2-3 ppm in fresh water; (12) 1 gm/1 of water as a short duration for 10 to 30 minutes (fresh water); (13) stock solution—1 gm/l, use 1.5-2 cc/l in aquarium as a long duration bath (3 to 10 days), if unsuccessful, repeat (salt water); (14) 8-10 gm/m^3 in a pond; (15) 1:2000 (500 ppm) solution for 1 to 2 minutes, in hard water add 1 ml glacial acetic acid/1; (16) 5 parts $CuSO_4$ mixed with 2 parts $(FeSO_4)_2$ administered to 0.7 ppm level; (17) 5 ppm for one hour as a fungus preventative on fish eggs; (18) 100 ppm for 10 to 30 minutes; (19) 500 ppm for 1 minute; (20) 0.15 ppm (salt water); (21) 9.0 ppm to sterilize a marine aquarium from which all infected life has been removed.

Remarks: Copper sulfate is toxic to most aquatic forms of life. Its effectiveness depends on the concentration being high enough to kill pathogens, yet low enough to not kill desirable life forms; use with extreme caution at all times; 500 ppm not effective against *Myxosoma* in 14 days; 0.30 ppm toxic to marine fish; 0.01 ppm toxic to marine invertebrates (do not use in marine aquaria containing invertebrates); see also Citric acid and Copper carbonate; quantity used depends on hardness of water, hard water requires more; medical purity manufactured by Lilly.

References: Amlacher (1961b, 1970) ; Avdosev et al. (1962); Batte et al. (1951) ; Braker (1961) ; Davis (1953) ; Dempster (1955) ; Dempster & Shipman (1969) ; Fasten (1912) ; Herman (1972) ; Hoffman (1969) ; Hoffman & Hoffman (1972) ; Hoffman & Meyer (1974); Højgaard (1962); Hsu & Jen (1965); Ivasik, Stryzhak, and Turkevich (1968) ; Jen & Hsu (1958) ; Kabata (1970); Kemp (1958); Kingsford (1975); Leitritz (1960); McKee & Wolf (1963); Mackenthun (1958); Mellen (1928); Moore (1923); Moyle (1949); Musselius & Strelkov (1968); Nichols et al. (1946); Nigrelli & Ruggieri (1966); Osborn (1966); Reichelt (1971); Reichenbach-Klinke (1966) ; Reichenbach-Klinke & Elkan (1965); Reichenbach-Klinke & Landolt (1973) ; Sarig (1971); Schäperclaus (1954) ; Scheneberger (1941) ; Shilo et al. (1954); Sneiszko (1975) ; Surber (1948) ; Van Duijn (1973) ; Wellborn (1967, 1969).

COPPER SULFATE plus ACETIC ACID
Composition: $CuSo_4 + CH_3COOH$.
Synonyms: None.
Uses or Treatment for: Algicide; protozoacide (*Ichthyophthirius*).
Dosage: (1) 2 ppm $CuSO_4$ + 3 ppm CH_3COOH is used in ponds with $CaCO_3$ levels above 200 ppm; (2) 500 ppm $CuSO_4$ + 500 ppm Acetic acid as a dip for 1 to 2 minutes.
Remarks: None.
References: Hoffman & Meyer (1974).

CO-RAL—See 7-Co-Ral.

7-CO-RAL
Composition: O,O-diethyl O-(3-chloro-4-methyl-2-oxo-2H-1-benzopyran-7-yl)phosphorothioate.
Synonyms: Co-Ral; Coumaphos; Muscatox; Resitox.
Uses or Treatment for: Protozoacide (*Ichthyophthirius*); Monogenea (*Cleidodiscus*); Crustacea (*Lernaea cyprinacea*); insecticide.
Dosage: (1) 1 ppm; (2) 0.4% of diet daily (proved toxic to fish).
Remarks: 0.1 ppm not effective; 0.18 ppm = LC_{50} in *Lepomis macrochirus*; 18 ppm = LC_{50} in *Pimephales promelas* in 96

hours; 45 ppm $=LC_{16}$ in small *Roccus saxatilis* in 96 hours at 21°C; 1.5 ppm was nontoxic to *Ictalurus punctatus*.
References: R. Allison (1969); Hoffman & Meyer (1974); McKee & Wolf (1963); Wellborn (1971); Willford (1967a).

CORROSIVE SUBLIMATE—See Mercuric chloride.

COTTONSEED OIL
Composition: Gossypium sp.
Synonyms: None.
Uses or Treatment for: Food additive; air-breathing insects.
Dosage: 2.5-5 gal/acre spread on surface of ponds (insects).
Remarks: Acts to suffocate air-breathing insects.
References: Hoffman & Meyer (1974).

COUMAPHOS—See 7-Co-Ral.

CRESOL—See Lysol.

CUPRAVIT
Composition: Unknown.
Synonyms: None.
Uses or Treatment for: Algicide; molluscicide (pond snails).
Dosage: 1-2 kg/hectare.
Remarks: None.
References: Reichenbach-Klinke & Elkan (1965).

CUPRIC ACETATE
Composition: $Cu(CH_3COO)_2$.
Synonyms: Verdigris.
Uses or Treatment for: Protozoacide *(Cryptocaryon irritans)*.
Dosage: Cupric acetate (0.42 ppm) + Formalin (5.26 ppm) +Tris buffer (4.8 ppm).
Remarks: None.
References: Hoffman & Meyer (1974); Nigrelli & Ruggieri (1966).

CUPRIC CARBONATE—See Copper carbonate.

CUPRIC CHLORIDE
Composition: $CuCl_2$.
Synonyms: None.
Uses or Treatment for: Hirudinea *(Piscicola geometra)*.

Dosage: 5 ppm for 5 minutes.

Remarks: None.

References: Bauer (1958) ; Hoffman & Meyer (1974) .

CUPRIC SULFATE, anhydrous—See Copper sulfate.

CUPROUS CHLORIDE

Composition: CuCl.

Synonyms: Nantokite.

Uses or Treatment for: Molluscicide (snails) .

Dosage: (1) 2 ppm; (2) CuCl + KCl (5:6) at 20 ppm; (3) CuCl + KCl at 1.4 ppm.

Remarks: None.

References: Chabaud et al. (1965) ; Deschiens & Floch (1964); Deschiens et al. (1965) ; Floch et al. (1964) ; Hoffman & Meyer (1974) .

CUPROUS OXIDE

Composition: Cu_2O.

Synonyms: Copper protoxide.

Uses or Treatment for: Molluscicide (snails) .

Dosage: 5-50 ppm in water.

Remarks: 50 ppm not toxic to adult fish—toxic to fry.

References: Deschiens & Floch (1964) ; Frick et al. (1964); Hoffman & Meyer (1974) .

CUTRINE

Composition: Copper sulfate + triethanolamine and other additives (commercial formulation) .

Synonyms: None.

Uses or Treatment for: Algicide; aquatic herbicide.

Dosage: According to recommendations on label.

Remarks: Chelated copper compound, less toxic to fish than Copper sulfate.

References: Hoffman & Meyer (1974) ; Snieszko (1975) .

CYANAMIDE—See Calcium cyanamide.

CYANTIN—See Nitrofurantoin sodium.

CYCLOSERINE

Composition: Antibiotic.

Synonyms: Seromycin.

Uses or Treatment for: Gram-positive and gram-negative bacteria.

Dosage: (1) In food—3 mg/100 gm of food; (2) in salt water —50 mg/gal.

Remarks: May be effective as antituberculosis drug; less active than most antibiotics; available in 250 mg capsules; manufactured by Lilly.

References: Kingsford (1975).

CYPREX

Composition: N-dodecylguandine acetate.

Synonyms: Dodine.

Uses or Treatment for: Fungicide *(Saprolegnia)*.

Dosage: 4 ppm is inhibitory.

Remarks: None.

References: Hoffman & Meyer (1974).

CYZINE

Composition: 2-acetylamino-5-nitrothiazole.

Synonyms: Enheptin-A; Trichorad.

Uses or Treatment for: Protozoacide [*Hexamita (= Octomites)*].

Dosage: 20 ppm in dry food for 3 days.

Remarks: None.

References: Herman (1972); Hoffman & Meyer (1974); McElwain & Post (1968); Snieszko (1975).

DALF—See Methyl parathion.

DALIMYCIN—See Oxytetracycline.

DARAMMON—See Ammonium chloride.

DARAPRIM

Composition: 2,4-diamino-5-(p-chlorophenyl)-6-ethylpyrimidine.

Synonyms: Pyrimthamine.

Uses or Treatment for: Protozoacide (anti-malarial, *Cryptocaryon irritans, Ichthyophthirius*).

Dosage: (1) 1 ppm; (2) 4-8 mg/gal.

Remarks: Not particularly effective; different bottles have different strengths; toxic reactions are typified by a marked darkening of the colors and death with open gaping mouth; manufactured by BW.

References: Hoffman & Meyer (1974) ; Kingsford (1975) .

DDFT

Composition: Difluorodiphenyltrichloroethane or difluorodiphenyltrimethylmethane.

Synonyms: DFDT; GIX.

Uses or Treatment for: Insecticide; Crustacea *(Argulus)*.

Dosage: (1) 2 drops/m³ of aquarium content; (2) 1:1000 (1000 ppm) for 15 minutes.

Remarks: Repeated use causes buildup in fish.

References: Hoffman & Meyer (1974) ; Kabata (1970) ; Meinken (1954) ; Stammer (1959) .

DDT

Composition: 1,1,1-trichloro-2,2-bis(parachlorophenyl)ethane or dichlorodiphenyltrichloroethane.

Synonyms: Gesarol.

Uses or Treatment for: Hirudinea (leeches, *Piscola geometra)*; Crustacea *(Argulus, Ergasilus, Lernaea, Tracheliastes)*; insecticide.

Dosage: (1) 1:50-100 million in water for several days *(Lernaea)*; (2) 0.1% emulsion for 24 hours; (3) 20,000 ppm for 30 minutes; (4) 0.01-0.02 ppm; (5) 1000 ppm as a dip for one minute.

Remarks: An accumulative poison—leaves residue in fish flesh; toxic to crayfish; banned in U.S.; 0.025-0.51 ppm toxic to fish fry; prepare concentrated stock solution in alcohol and dilute slowly in water over a period of time.

References: Bauer (1959) ; Cherrington et al. (1969); Clemens & Sneed (1959) ; Hoffman & Meyer (1974) ; Johnson (1968) ; Kabata (1970) ; Marking (1966) ; Reichenbach-Klinke

(1966) ; Reichenbach-Klinke & Landolt (1973) ; Schäperclaus (1949, 1950, 1954) ; Surber (1948) ; Van Duijn (1973; Woyanrovich (1954) ; Yousuf-Ali (1968) .

DDVP

Composition: O,O-dimethyl O-(2,2-dichlorovinyl) phosphate.

Synonyms: Dichlorvos; Shell No-Pest Strip; Vapona.

Uses or Treatment for: Monogenea *(Dactylogyrus);* Digenea; Crustacea (Copepods, *Argulus, Lernaea);* Insecticide.

Dosage: (1) 0.4 ppm; (2) 0.1 ppm; (3) 0.225 ppm weekly for 4 weeks.

Remarks: None.

References: Hoffman & Meyer (1974) ; Kabata (1970) ; Sarig (1966, 1968, 1971) .

DEMETON-S—See Di-Syston.

DETRAPAN

Composition: Unknown.

Synonyms: None.

Uses or Treatment for: Systemic antifungal drug.

Dosage: (1) 0.25 ml/kg intramuscularly used twice every 48 hours.

Remarks: Used in France for fish after spawning.

References: Snieszko (1975) .

DEVERMIN

Composition: Unknown.

Synonyms: None.

Uses or Treatment for: Cestodes.

Dosage: 0.1 gm/kg of fish orally with food.

Remarks: None.

References: Snieszko (1975) .

DFD—See GIX.

DFDT—See DDFT or GIX.

DIAZIL—See Sulfamethazine, sodium.

DIBROM, emulsifiable concentrate—See Bromex-50.

DIBUTYLTIN DILAURATE

Composition: $(C_9H_9)_2Sn(O_2C(CH_2)_{10}CH_3)_2$.

Synonyms: Butynorate; Tinostat.

Uses or Treatment for: Anthelminthic (cestodes).

Dosage: (1) 250-500 mg/kg of fish daily for 3 days; (2) 0.3% of total food for 5 days.

Remarks: None.

References: Hoffman & Meyer (1974) ; Snieszko (1975).

DICHLORODIPHENOLTRICHLOROETHANE—See DDT.

DICHLORVOS—See DDVP.

DICRYL

Composition: Unknown.

Synonyms: None.

Uses or Treatment for: Herbicide (blue-green algae).

Dosage: According to recommendations on label.

Remarks: Experimental algistatic agent.

References: Sarig (1971).

DIESEL FUEL, commercial grade

Composition: Unknown.

Synonyms: None.

Uses or Treatment for: Kills air-breathing insects.

Dosage: 2.5-5 gal/acre, spread on surface of water.

Remarks: Kills by suffocation.

References: Hoffman & Meyer (1974).

DIHYDROSTREPTOMYCIN—See Streptomycin.

DIKAR—See Karathane.

DIMETHYL SULFOXIDE—See DMSO.

DIMETON—See Sulfamonomethoxine.

DIMETRIDAZOLE

Composition: 1,2-dimethyl-5-nitroimidazole.

Synonyms: Emtryl.

Uses or Treatment for: Protozoacide [*Hexamita (= Octomites)*].

Dosage: 0.15% mixed in food daily for 3 days.

Remarks: None.

References: Hoffman & Meyer (1974) ; Snieszko (1975).

DI-N-BUTYL TIN OXIDE

Composition: Di-n-butyl-oxo-stannate.

Synonyms: Biocidal rubber; Butyl tin oxide; Tin oxide.

Uses or Treatment for: All helminths; Acanthocephala; digenetic trematodes; Cestoda *(Alloglossidium, Crepidostomum farionis, Corallobothrium fimbriatum, Eubothrium, Pomphorhynchus);* molluscicide (snails) .

Dosage: (1) 25 gm/100 kg of fish weight = total dose—in feed spread over 3 days; (2) 0.3% of body weight mixed into the food, over 1 to 5 days; (3) 1.0 ppm in water; (4) 3.5 mg/kg of fish daily for 3 days.

Remarks: Toxic to fry but not adult largemouth bass.

References: R. Allison (1957b); Amlacher (1970) ; Herman (1972) ; Hnath (1970) ; Hoffman & Meyer (1974) ; Mitchum & Moore (1966) ; Reichenbach-Klinke & Elkan (1965) ; Snieszko (1975) .

DINOCAP—See Karathane.

DIPTEREX, 5% wettable powder—See Dylox.

DIQUAT

Composition: 1,1'-ethylene-2,2'-dipyridylium dibromide.

Synonyms: Bipyridilium; Reglone.

Uses or Treatment for: Herbicide (blue-green algae) ; bacteria [bacterial gill disease, cold-water disease *(Cytophaga psychrophila),* Columnaris *(Chondroccus columnaris)*].

Dosage: (1) 2-4 ppm of the active agent for 1 hour; (2) 1-2 ppm of medication or 8.4 ppm as purchased, added to water—treat for 30 to 60 minutes.

Remarks: Experimental algicide; activity much reduced in turbid waters; patented herbicide by Ortho; contains 35.3% of active compound.

References: Amlacher (1970) ; Hoffman & Meyer (1974) ; Sarig (1971); Snieszko (1975) ; Surber & Pickering (1962); Wellborn (1969) ; J. Wood (1968) .

DI-SYSTON

Composition: O,O - diethyl S - [2 - (ethylthio)ethyl]phosphorothiotate.

Synonyms: Demeton-S; Isosystox.

Uses or Treatment for: Insecticide.

Dosage: Unknown.

Remarks: None.

References: Hoffman & Meyer (1974).

DIURON

Composition: Unknown.

Synonyms: None.

Uses or Treatment for: Herbicide (blue-green algae).

Dosage: Unknown.

Remarks: Experimental algistatic agent.

References: Sarig (1971).

DIVERCILLIN—See Ampicillin trihydrate.

DMSO

Composition: $(CH_3)_2SO$.

Synonyms: Dimethyl sulfoxide.

Uses or Treatment for: Protozoacide *(Ichthyophthirius)*.

Dosage: (1) $CuSO_4$ + DMSO (0.1-1.0 ppm + 0.5-5.0 ppm) on alternate days; (2) 2500 ppm; (3) Formalin + DMSO (10 ppm + 50 ppm) is not effective, (25 ppm + 125 ppm) is inhibitory, (50 ppm + 250 ppm) is effective but slow to control; (4) Malachite green + DMSO (0.1 ppm + 0.5 ppm) is inhibitory and not toxic to fish, (0.5 ppm + 2.5 ppm) is inhibitory but toxic to fish, (1 ppm + 5 ppm) is toxic to fish.

Remarks: 43,000 ppm = LC_{50} to fish; reportedly not very effective against Ich.

References: Hoffman & Meyer (1974); Willford (1967b).

DOBELL'S SOLUTION—See Sodium borate.

DODINE—See Cyprex.

DOWCO 212

Composition: Experimental compound (Dow Chemical Co.).

Synonyms: None.

Uses or Treatment for: Molluscicide (snails).

Dosage: 0.25 ppm.

Remarks: None.

References: Hoffman & Meyer (1974).

DOWICIDE G—See Pentachlorophenol.

DOXYCLINE HYCLATE

Composition: Tetracycline derivative.

Synonyms: Vibramycin hyclate.
Uses or Treatment for: Gram-positive and some gram-negative bacteria.
Dosage: Undertermined.
Remarks: Has a shelf life of 2 weeks when in solution; only slightly soluble in water; does not appreciably impair renal function, therefore is safe for use in kidney diseases; available as 50 or 100 mg capsules or powder; manufactured by Pfizer Labs.
References: Kingsford (1975).

DURSBAN

Composition: O,O-diethyl-O-3,5,6-trichloro-2-pyridyl phosphorothioate.
Synonyms: None.
Uses or Treatment for: Crustacea *(Lernaea);* insecticide.
Dosage: 0.02-0.05 ppm weekly for five weeks.
Remarks: Caused scoliosis and was toxic to fish; 0.035 ppm = LC_{100} to fish.
References: Hoffman & Meyer (1974); Johnson (1968); F. Meyer (1969).

DVP—See DDVP.

DYLOX

Composition: O,O-dimethyl-2,2,2-trichloro-1-hydroxyethyl phosphonate or O,O-dimethyl-1-hydroxy-2-trichloro methyl phosphonate.
Synonyms: Chlorofos; Chlorophos; D50; Dipterex; Foschlor; Lifebearer; Masoten; Metrifonat; Neguvon; Trichlorofon.
Uses or Treatment for: Ectoparasites; Protozoa *(Ichthyophthirius, Trichodina);* broad spectrum anthelminthic; Monogenea *(Benedenia, Cleidodiscus, Dactylogyrus, Gyrodactylus);* Cestoda; Hirudinea, *(Placobdella parasitica, Illinobdella moorei, Piscicola salmositica, Theromyzon sp.);* Crustacea (parasitic copepods, *Achtheres micropteri, Argulus foliaceus, Argulus sp., Ergasilus sieboldi, Ergasilus sp., Lernaea cyprinacea, Philometra sp., Salmincola, Sinergasilus major);* insecticide; molluscicide (snails).

Dosage: (1) 0.4 ppm; (2) 0.1 ppm; (3) 0.25 ppm (active ingredient) once a week for 4 weeks; (4) 800 ppm for 3 hours; (5) 25 gm/l for 5 minutes as a bath; (6) 0.5 to 1 ppm for leeches; (7) 0.8 ppm is used in Europe for small crustaceans; (8) 100 ppm for 1 to 3 hours; (9) 1 ppm when temperature is above 29°C; (10) 0.0625 ppm when temperature is below 20°C; (11) 10,000 ppm for 1-5 minutes; (12) 2 ppm; (13) Dylox + Copper sulfate (1 ppm + 0.5-1.0 ppm) for Ich; (14) 0.4 ppm for 48 hours; (15) 25,000 ppm as a dip for 5 to 10 minutes (Masoten); (16) 0.2-0.3 mg/l of active substance administered over a period of 3 to 4 days at a temperature of not less than 20°C (68°F) and not above 28°C (82.4°F); (17) 0.25 ppm to water in aquaria and 0.25-1.0 ppm in ponds for an indefinite period.

Remarks: 25.5 ppm = LC_{50} in *Anguilla japonica* in 96 hours at 15-16°C; 50 ppm = LC_{100} in *Carassius auratus* in 2 hours at 19-22°C, 27 ppm = LC_{50} in 96 hours at 16-19°C; 27.5 ppm = LC_{50} in *Cyprinus carpio* in 96 hours at 16-20°C; 1 ppm = LC_{50} in young *Esox sp.;* 79.2 ppm = LC_{50} in *Oryzias latipes* in 96 hours at 16-20°C; 180 ppm = LC_{100} in *Pimephales promelas,* 51 ppm = LC_{50}; 3.2 ppm = LC_{16} in young *Roccus saxatilis* in 96 hours at 21°C; 8.6 ppm = LC_{16} in *Salmo gairdneri* in 48 hours at 12°C; 0.8 ppm = LC_{50} in young *Salmo;* Dylox is easily removed by filtering over charcoal; extremely toxic to sharks, producing severe disorientation and nervous disorder; extremely toxic to waterfowl.

References: R. Allison (1969); Amlacher (1970); Bailosoff (1963); Bauer & Babaev (1964); Funnikova & Krivova (1966); Ghittino & Arcarese (1970); Grabda & Grabda (1968); Herman (1972); Hoffman & Meyer (1974); D. Johnson (1968); Kabata (1970); Kasahara (1962, 1968); Kimura (1967); Lahav & Sarig (1967); Lahav, Sarig, and Shilo (1964); McKee & Wolf (1963); F. Meyer (1966a, 1968, 1969a, 1970); Musselius (1967); Musselius & Laptev (1967); Naumova (1968); Osborn (1966); Plate (1970); Prost & Studnicka (1968); Prowse (1965); Reichenbach-Klinke (1966); Rogers (1966); Sarig (1966, 1968, 1971); Sarig et al. (1965); Schubert (1974);

Snieszko (1975) ; Sukhenko (1963) ; Wellborn (1967, 1969); Willford (1967a.)

EMTRYL—See Dimetridazole.

EMTRYSIDINA

Composition: N'-(3-methoxy-2-purazinyl)sulfanilamide   plus amminosidin.

Synonyms: Amminosidine; Kelfizina; Sulfalene; Sulfalent.

Uses of Treatment for: Antimicrobial; Protozoa *(Hexamita).*

Dosage: 15,000 ppm in dry food daily for 3 days.

Remarks: Available as tablets; manufactured by Lentag.

References: Ghittino (1968) ; Hoffman & Meyer (1974) .

E-MYCIN—See Erythromycin.

ENHEPTIN

Composition: 2-amino-5-nitrothiazol.

Synonyms: None; see also Cyzine.

Uses or Treatment for: Protozoacide *(Hexamita (= Octomites), Ichthyophthirius).*

Dosage: (1) 0.2% (2000 ppm) in food for 3 days; (2) 10 ppm.

Remarks: No longer manufactured in U.S.; banned in U.S.

References: Herman (1972) ; Hoffman & Meyer (1974); Post & Beck (1966) ; Sneiszko (1975) ; Yasutake et al. (1961) .

ENHEPTIN A—See Cyzine.

ENTEX—See Baytex.

ENTOBEX

Composition: 4,7-phenanthroline-5,6-dione.

Synonyms: Phanquone.

Uses or Treatment for: Protozoacide *(Hexamita).*

Dosage: 10,000 ppm in food for 4 days.

Remarks: None.

References: Hoffman & Meyer (1974) ; Van Duijn (1973) .

EOSIN

Composition: 2',4',5',7'-tetrabromofluorescein.

Synonyms: None.

Uses or Treatment for: Aniline dye; protozoacide *(Ichthyophthirius).*

Dosage: 60 ppm for 15 days.

Remarks: Killed free parasites in 16 to 60 minutes; 100 ppm not toxic to *Rutilus sp.* and trout.

References: Hoffman & Meyer (1974); Stiles (In Mellen, 1928).

EPSOM SALTS—See Magnesium sulfate.

ERYPAR—See Erythromycin.

ERYTHROCIN—See Erythromycin.

ERYTHROMYCIN

Composition: Antibiotic derived from *Streptomyces erythreus.*

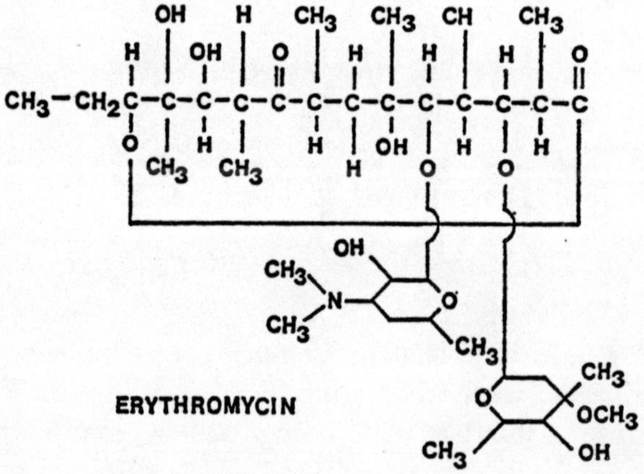

ERYTHROMYCIN

Synonyms: E-Mycin; Erypar; Erythrocin; Ilotycin; Maracyn.

Uses or Treatment for: Bacteria [kidney disease *(Corynebacterium)*, gram-positive and many gram-negative bacteria].

Dosage: (1) 100 mg/kg of fish/day in feed for 21 days; (2) 10 gm/100 kg/day for 21 days.

Remarks: Erythromycin ethylsuccinate, Erythromycin ethylcarbonate ester, Erythromycin stearate, and Erythromycin estolate are insoluble in water; Erythromycin, Erythromycin glucceptate, and Erythromycin lactobionate are slightly soluble in water; not very effective in salt water; available in 100 and 250 mg tablets; manufactured by Abbott, PD, Alliance, Columbia Medic, Lilly, Upjohn, and Zenith.

References: Amlacher (1970); Herman (1972); Kingsford (1975); Piper (1961); Warren (1963).

ETHANEDIOIC ACID—See Oxalic Acid.

ETHER

Composition: Ethyl ether or diethyl ether.

Synonyms: None.

Uses or Treatment for: General anesthesia.

Dosage: (1) 10-15 ml/l of water will anesthetize a fish in 2 to 3 minutes.

Remarks: Works well with recovery also in 2 to 3 minutes when fish is placed in clean water. *CAUTION:* EXPLO-SIVE. Available as a liquid; manufactured by Med Spec and Squibb.

References: "General Anesthesia in Exotics." *Vet Med Small Anim Clin,* Sept. 1974, p. 1185.

ETHIONAMIDE

Composition: Derivative of isonicotinic acid.

Synonyms: Trecator SC.

Uses or Treatment for: Bacteria (fish tuberculosis).

Dosage: Undetermined.

Remarks: More toxic than Isoniazid; unreliable unless used in conjunction with other drugs, e.g. Streptomycin, Rifampin, Cycloserine; available in 250 mg tablets; manufactured by Ives.

References: Kingsford (1975).

ETHYLENE GLYCOL

Composition: 1,2-ethanediol.

Synonyms: None.

Uses or Treatment for: Protozoa *(Ichthyophthirius).*

Dosage: 1000 ppm daily for 5 days.

Remarks: Not effective.

References: Hoffman & Meyer (1974).

ETHYLMERCURIC PHOSPHATE

Composition: Ethylmercuric phosphate.

Synonyms: Lignasan (6.25%); Timsan.

Uses or Treatment for: Algicide *(Pyrmnesium);* bacteria

(bacterial gill disease) .

Dosage: (1) 1-2 ppm (6.25% active) for one hour bath; (2) 0.5 ppm.

Remarks: None.

References: Amlacher (1970) ; Herman (1972) ; Rucker et al. (1956) ; Sarig (1971) .

ETHYL PARATHION

Composition: O,O-dimethyl O-p-nitrophenyl phosphoro-thioate.

Synonyms: Methyl parathion; Niran; Parathion; Phoskil; Thiophos.

Uses or Treatment for: Crustacea *(Argulus sp.);* insecticide.

Dosage: (1) 0.1 ppm for 3 hours; (2) 1.0 ppm for 2 hours; (3) 10 ppm for one hour; (4) 100 ppm for 4 to 5 minutes.

Remarks: 3-3.5 ppm = LC_{50} to young *Cyprinus carpio* and *Esox sp.;* 0.063-0.250 ppm toxic to *Lepomis macrochirus* and *Micropterus salmoides;* 2.7 ppm = LC_{100} to *Pimephales promelas.*

References: Hoffman & Meyer (1974) ; Johnson (1968); Kabata (1970) ; Osborn (1966) ; Reichenbach-Klinke (1966); Stammer (1959) ; Surber (1948) .

EVERGREEN B—See Malachite green.

FENASAL—See Niclosamide.

FENCHLOROPHOS—See Korlan.

FENOVERM—See Phenothiazine.

FENTHION—See Baytex.

FERBAM

Composition: Ferric dimethyldithiocarbamate.

Synonyms: Fermate.

Uses or Treatment for: Fungicide *(Saprolegnia).*

Dosage: 8 ppm.

Remarks: 20 ppm nontoxic to *Ictalurus punctatus.*

References: Clemens & Sneed (1959) ; Hoffman & Meyer (1974) .

FERMATE—See Ferbam.

FERRIC SULFATE
Composition: $Fe_2(SO_4)_3$.
Synonyms: None.
Uses or Treatment for: Crustacea *(Sinergasilus major)*.
Dosage: $CuSO_4$ + $Fe_2(SO_4)_3$ (5:2) used at a 0.7 ppm concentration in water.
Remarks: 500 ppm toxic to fish.
References: Hoffman & Meyer (1974); Hsu & Jen (1955); Musselius & Strelkov (1968); Reichenbach-Klinke (1966).

FINTROL—See Antimycin A.

FLAGYL
Composition: 1-(2-hydroxyethyl)-2-methyl-5-nitroimidazole.

Synonyms: Metronidazole.
Uses or Treatment for: Protozoacide *(Cryptocaryon irritans, Hexamita, Ichthyophthirius, Trichomonas)*.
Dosage: (1) 10,000 ppm in feed for 5 days; (2) 1.5-25 ppm, 4 mg/l for 3 to 4 days in water (inhibitory); (3) one 250 mg tablet/20 gallons.
Remarks: Quickly removed by carbon filtration; anti-trichomonad drug in humans; available in 250 mg tablets; manufactured by Searle.
References: Hoffman & Meyer (1974); Kingsford (1975); Schubert (1974); Willford (1967a).

FORMALDEHYDE—See Formalin.

FORMALIN (37-40%), commercial grade
Composition: HCHO 37-40% by weight of Formaldehyde in water; usually containing 12-15% Methanol.
Synonyms: Formaldehyde.
Uses or Treatment for: External fungicide *(Achyla, Aphanomyces, Branchiomyces demigrans, B. sanguinis, Leptomitus, Pythium, Saprolegnia)*; external protozoacide *(Ambiphyra*

macropoda, A. pyriformis, amoebae, *Chilodonella, Costia, Epistylis, Glossatella, Ichthyophthirius, Oodinium ocellatum, O. pillularis, Trichodina (= Cyclochaeta), Trichophyra, Tripartellia,* ciliates); ectoparasites; Monogena *(Benedenia, Cleidodiscus pricei, C. sp., Dactylogyrus, Gyrodactylus wagneri, G. sp.);* Hirudinea *(Piscicola salmositica);* Crustacea *(Lernaea, Salmincola).*

Dosage: (1) 250 ppm for one hour; (2) 100 ppm for 3 hours; (3) 40 ppm for 24 hours; (4) 20-25 cc of 37-40% Formalin/ 100 l of water for 30 to 40 minutes *(Costia);* (5) 15-20 ppm in ponds or aquarium for indefinite period—long bath; (6) 0.2-0.5 gm/l of water —bath of 30-40 minutes; (7) 2000 ppm for 15 minutes; (8) 250 ppm for 1 hour daily if water temperature equals 10°C or less, 200 ppm for 1 hour daily if water temperature equals 10-15°C, 166 ppm for one hour daily if water temperature is above 15°C; (9) 15-25 ppm on alternate days until control is achieved; (10) 25 ppm on alternate days; (11) 350-500 ppm for 10 to 15 minutes; (12) 0.42 ppm Cupric acetate + 5.26 ppm Formalin + 4.8 ppm Tris buffer; (13) Formalin + DMSO (10 ppm + 50 ppm) is not effective, 25 ppm + 125 ppm is inhibitory, 50 ppm + 250 ppm is effective, but slow to control; (14) Malachite green (0.05-10 ppm) + Formalin (15-50 ppm) for 3 applications on alternate days in aquariums and for indefinite periods in ponds; (15) 200 ppm as a dip for 4 to 8 minutes; (16) 25 ppm of mixture of Malachite green (14 gm) per 1 gal Formalin, use for up to 6 hours daily in tanks or raceways and at 3 to 4 day intervals in ponds; (17) 1:500 for 15 minutes as a dip; (18) 1:4000 to 1:6000 for 1 hour; (19) 2000 ppm bath for 1 hour for egg fungus; (20) 6-7 cc/l of a stock solution [1 cc/99 cc of water (Monogenea) (3.5 minims/U.S. gal) (4 minims/Imp gal)] of 37-40% solution, repeat in 3 days after replacing one half of the water.

Remarks: 124 ppm = LC_{11} in *Salmo trutta* in 48 hours at 12°C, 124 ppm = LC_1 in *Salvelinus fontinalis* in 48 hours at 12°C; oxygen depletion may follow application in hot weather; 250 ppm toxic to *Dorsoma cepadianum;* 167 ppm = LC_{50} in *Ictalurus punctatus* in 48 hours and 126 ppm = LC_{100} in 96

TABLE 5-I

TREATMENT CONVERSION CHART FOR FORMALIN
(37-40% COMMERCIAL FORMALDEHYDE)*

parts per million (ppm)	equivalent in thousands	ml† per liter	ml per gallon	pints per 100 cu ft	quarts per acre ft
1	1:1,000,000	0.001	0.0038	0.0598	1.304‡
2	1:500,000	0.002	0.0076	0.1196	2.608
3	1:333,333	0.003	0.0114	0.1794	3.912
4	1:250,000	0.004	0.0152	0.2392	5.216
5	1:200,000	0.005	0.0190	0.2990	6.520
6	1:166,666	0.006	0.0228	0.3588	7.824
7	1:142,857	0.007	0.0266	0.4186	9.128
8	1:125,000	0.008	0.0304	0.4784	10.432
9	1:111,111	0.009	0.0343	0.5382	11.736
10	1:100,000	0.010	0.0380	0.5980	13.040
15	1:66,666	0.015	0.0570	0.8970	19.560
20	1:50,000	0.020	0.0760	1.1960	26.080
25	1:40,000	0.025	0.0950	1.4950	32.600
100	1:10,000	0.100	0.3800	5.9800	130.400
166	1:6000	0.166	0.6300	9.9300	216.460
200	1:5000	0.200	0.7600	11.9600	260.800
250	1:4000	0.250	0.9500	14.9500	323.000
1000	1:1000	1.000	3.8000	59.8000	1304.000

*From Hoffman, G.L. and Meyer, F.P. *Parasites of Freshwater Fishes.* Neptune, New Jersey, T.F.H. Publications, 1974.
†ml = milliliter (cubic centimeter). Local druggist can probably supply a dropper calibrated to deliver milliliters. For measuring small amounts one can determine the number of drops a dropper will deliver into one milliliter, e.g. many eye droppers will deliver approximately 20 drops of water per milliliter.
‡One gallon of Formalin will yield 3 ppm in 1 acre-foot of water.

hours at 25°C, but 316 ppm = LC_0 in one hour at 25°C, 28.2 ppm = LC_{100} in *Oncorhynchus tschawytscha;* medical purity manufactured by Canfield and by Parker.

References: R. Allison (1957a, 1962, 1963, 1966); Amlacher (1970); Bogdanova (1962); BSFW (1960, 1969); Burrows (1949); Clemens & Sneed (1959); Davis (1953); Earp & Schwab (1954); Fish (1940); Fish & Burrows (1940); Gopalakrishnan (1963); Herman (1972); Hoffman & Meyer (1974); Hora & Pillay (1962); H. Johnson (1956); Kabata (1970); Kingsbury & Embody (1932); Kumar (1958); Leger (1909); Leifson

(1961); Leteux & Meyer (1972); Lewis & Lewis (1963); McKee & Wolf (1963); McNeil (1963); F. Meyer (1966b, 1966c, 1967); Meyer & Collar (1964); Nigrelli & Ruggieri (1966); O'Brien (In Mellan, 1928); Osborn (1966); Peterson et al. (1966); Plehn (1924); Putz & Bowen (1964); Reddecliff (1958); Reichenbach-Klinke & Elkan (1965); Reichenbach-Klinke & Landolt (1973); Roth (1910); Rucker et al. (1963); Sachachte (1974); Sarig (1971); Schäperclaus (1954); Sneiszko (1974, 1975); Steffens (1962); Tripathi (1954); Van Duijn (1973); Watanabe (1940); Wellborn (1967, 1969); Willford (1967a); Zschiesche (1910).

FOSCHLOR—See Dylox.

FOSFOMICINA
Composition: $C_3H_7O_4P$.
Synonyms: None.
Uses or Treatment for: Infections in fishes; bacteria (*Aeromonas*).
Dosage: Unknown.
Remarks: Spanish antibiotic.
References: Snieszko (1975).

FRESCON—See *n*-tritylmorpholine.

FRESH WATER
Composition: H_2O.
Synonyms: None.
Uses or Treatment for: Marine ectoparasites; protozoacide (*Cryptocaryon irritans*).
Dosage: (1) Immerse marine fish in 100% fresh water for 5 to 10 minutes; (2) euryhaline species for 5 hours.
Remarks: Effective, enters the cell of marine microorganisms rapidly, expanding it by osmotic pressure until it ruptures; larger parasites try to escape the irritation caused by immersion in fresh water and release their hold and drop off.
References: Gowanloch (1927); Hoffman & Meyer (1974); Isakov & Shulman (1956); Kingsford (1975).

FUKLASIN—See Zinc dimethyldithiocarbamate.

FULCIN—See Grieseofulvin.

FULVICIN—See Grieseofulvin.

FUMAGILLIN

Composition: 2,4,6,8-decatetraenedioic acid mono [4-(1,2-epoxy-1,5-dimethyl-4-hexenyl)5-methoxy-1-oxaspiro(2,5)oct-6-yl]-ester.

Synonyms: Amebacilin; Fumidil.

Uses or Treatment for: Antimicrobial; protozoacide *(Hexamita);* fungicide *(Branchiomyces, Saprolegnia).*

Dosage: 20,000 ppm in food for 3 days.

Remarks: None.

References: Hoffman & Meyer (1974); Yasutake et al. (1961).

FUMIDIL—See Fumagillin.

FURACIN, 4.59% water mix—See Nitrofurazone.

FURADANTIN—See Nitrofurantoin sodium.

FURAGENT—See Nitrofurantoin sodium.

FURALOID—See Nitrofurantoin sodium.

FURAN—See Nitrofurantoin sodium.

FURANACE

Composition: 6-hydroxymethyl-2-[2-(5-nitro)2-furyl)vinyl]pyridine.

Synonyms: Furpyridinol; Nifurpirinol; P-7138.

Uses or Treatment for: Antimicrobial; bacteria (bacterial gill diseases, bacterial hemorrhagic septicemia, cold-water disease *(Cytophaga psychrophila),* Columnaris *(Chondrococcus columnaris),* fin rot, Furunculosis *(Aeromonas salmonicida),* Pseudomonas, *Vibrio anguillarum);* fungicide *(Saprolegnia);* Protozoa *(Costia, Ichthyophthirius).*

Dosage: (1) 10 ppm; (2) 1 ppm; (3) 1-2 ppm as a dip for 5 to 10 minutes; (4) 0.05-0.2 ppm added to water for an indefinite time; (5) 1 ppm for 1 hour; (6) orally for treatment—2-4 mg/kg of fish per day for 3 to 5 days; (7) orally as a prophylaxis—0.4-0.8 mg/kg of fish per day for as long as needed.

Remarks: 10 ppm toxic to *Oncorhynchus sp.;* intended to be used as a bath but may be added to food; not particularly effective in salt water; see also Furpyridinol.

References: Amend (1969, 1972); Farwell (1972); Hoffman

& Meyer (1974); Holt et al. (1975); Kingsford (1975); Shimizu & Takase (1967); Snieszko (1975); Takase et al. (1971).

FURANTONIN—See Nitrofurantoin sodium.

FURAZOLIDONE—See Furoxone.

FURAZONE GREEN—See Nitrofurazone.

FUROXONE

Composition: N-(5-nitro-2-furfurylidine)-3-amino-2-oxazolidone.

$$O_2N-\overset{O}{\underset{}{\boxed{}}}-CH-N\quad\text{FUROXONE}$$

Synonyms: Furazolidone; Furozone; Nf-180; Nitrofuran.
Uses or Treatment for: Bacteria [Furunculosis *(Aeromonas salmonicida)*]; protozoacide *(Ceratomyxa shasta, Eimeria, Myxosoma cerebralis).*
Dosage: (1) 2.5 gm/100 kg per day in feed for 20 days; (2) 25-75 mg/kg of body weight per day up to 20 days, orally with food on the basis of pure drug activity.
Remarks: Hess & Clark commercial products contain Furazolidone mixed with inert materials; also manufactured by Eaton; available as liquid or tablets; see also Nifurprazine HCl.
References: Amend & Ross (1970); Amlacher (1970); Herman (1972); Hoffman & Meyer (1974); Kulow & Spangenberg (1969); Musselius & Strelkov (1968); Post (1959); Post & Keiss (1962); Reichenbach-Klinke & Elkan (1965); Snieszko (1975).

FUROZONE—See Furoxone.

FURPYRIDINOL
Composition: Product containing 1% Furanace (P-7138).
Synonyms: None.
Uses or Treatment for: Bacteria.
Dosage: Added to water—0.3-10 ppm, for 30 to 60 minutes.

Remarks: See also Furanace.
References: Snieszko (1975).

GAMMEXANE—See Benzene hexachloride.

GANTRISIN—See Sulfisoxazole.

GARAMYCIN—See Gentamycin sulfate.

GARLIC

Composition: Grated seed pods of *Allium sativum.*
Synonyms: None.
Uses or Treatment for: Helminthic.
Dosage: Grind up and mix with fish food.
Remarks: Effective; old Chinese goldfish remedy.
References: Bauer (1958).

GENTAMYCIN SULFATE

Composition: Antibiotic obtained from cultures of *Micromonospora purpurea.*
Synonyms: Garamycin.
Uses or Treatment for: Gram-negative bacteria *(Aeromonas, Pseudomonas).*
Dosage: (1) 5 mg/kg of body weight intramuscularly; (2) 20 mg/gal in salt water.
Remarks: May be nephrotoxic; effective in both fresh water and salt water; probably the most powerful broad spectrum antibiotic currently available; available as ointment or sterile solution; manufactured by Schering.
References: Kingsford (1975).

GENTIAN VIOLET

Composition: Methylrosaniline chloride.
Synonyms: Bismuth violet; Pyoktanin.
Use or Treatment for: Dye, fungicide *(Saprolegnia)* protozoacide *(Costia);* Monogenea *(Cleidodiscus).*
Dosage: 0.3 ppm.
Remarks: May be toxic to weak fish; also toxic to many species of fish; use with extreme caution; not particularly effective; manufactured by Barre, BBC, Rondex, Tablroc, Vitarine, and Webster.
References: Hoffman & Meyer (1974).

GEOPEN—See Carbenicillin disodium.

GERMICIDAL—See Benzalkonium chloride.

GESAROL, proprietary compound of 5% DDT with Kaolin—See DDT

GIX
Composition: 1,1,1-trichloro-2,2-bis(*p*-fluorophenyl)ethane.
Synonyms: DFD; DFDT.
Uses or Treatment for: Crustacea *(Argulus);* insecticide.
Dosage: (1) 1-2 drops/l of water (1:10,000) as a short bath; (2) 2 drops/m³; (3) 100 ppm as a dip for 5 minutes; (4) 1 ppm for 30 minutes.
Remarks: An accumulative poison in fishes and other life forms; see also DDFT.
References: Hoffman & Meyer (1974).

GLOBUCID, sodium
Composition: N^1-(5-ethyl-1,3,4-thiadiazol-2-yl)sulfanilamide.
Synonyms: Albucidnatrium; Sulfaethidole; Sulspantab.
Uses or Treatment for: Antimicrobial (bacterial fin rot); fungicide *(Saprolegnia);* protozoacide [*Chilodonella, Costia Trichodina (= Cyclochaeta)*].
Dosage: (1) 1 gm/10 l of water; (2) 200 ppm for 8 hours (not effective) ; (3) 2000 ppm for 24 hours.
Remarks: 4500 ppm was not toxic to fish after several days; available as 650 mg tablets; manufactured in U.S. by SKF; see also sulfonamides and Albucid.
References: Amlacher (1970) ; Hoffman & Meyer (1974); Schäperclaus (1954).

GRAMOXONE—See Paraquat.

GRIFULVIN of GRIFULVIN V—See Griseofulvin.

GRISACTIN 125, 250, or 500—See Griseofulvin.

GRISEOFULVIN
Composition: 7-chloro-4,6-dimethoxycoumaran-3-one-2-spiro-1'-(2'-methoxy-6'-methylcyclohex-2'-en-4'-one) .

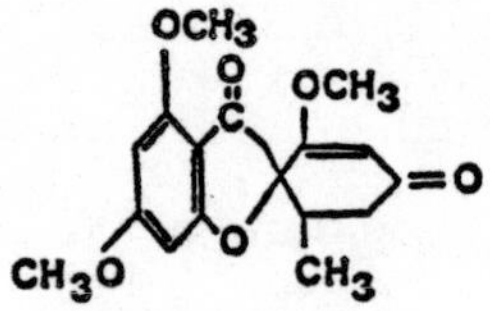

GRISEOFULVIN

Synonyms: Fulcin; Fulvicin; Grifulvin or Grifulvin V; Grisactin 125, 250, or 500; Griseokin; Grisowen.

Uses or Treatment for: Antibiotic; fungicide (Mycosis, *Saprolegnia*).

Dosage: (1) 10 mg/l of water; (2) 10 ppm; (3) 500 mg in water applied daily for 6 days.

Remarks: 50 ppm not toxic; available in 125, 250, and 500 mg tablets or capsules; manufactured by Aberdeen, Ayerst, Balkins, Columbia Medic, McNeil, Owen, Schering, and Westward.

References: BSFW (1960); Hoffman & Meyer (1974); Reichenbach-Klinke (1966); Reichenbach-Klinke & Elkan (1965); Sandler (1966).

GRISEOKIN—See Griseofulvin.

GRISOWIN—See Griseofulvin.

HALAMID—See Chloramine-T.

HARTSHORN—See Ammonium carbonate.

HB-115—See Nifurprazine HCl.

HEXACHLOROCYCLOHEXANE

Composition: Hexachlorocyclohexane.

Synonyms: None.

Uses or Treatment for: Parasitic crustaceans.

Dosage: 2.5 gm/l of water.

Remarks: None.

References: Reichenbach-Klinke & Elkan (1965).

HOTLIME—See Calcium oxide.

HTH—See Calcium hypochlorite.

HUMATIN—See Paramomycin.

HYAMINE
Composition: Quaternary Ammonium germicide.
Synonyms: None.
Uses or Treatment for: Bacterial gill disease.
Dosage: 1.0-2.0 ppm (on basis of 100% product) in water for one hour.
Remarks: Available as crystals or as 50% solution; manufactured by Rohm & Hass; see also Benzalkonium chloride.
References: Hogan (1969); Snieszko (1975); Surber & Pickering (1962).

HYDRATED LIME—See Calcium hydroxide or Lime.

HYDROCHLORIC ACID
Composition: HCl.
Synonyms: Muriatic acid.
Uses or Treatment for: Crustacea *(Salmincola).*
Dosage: 0.08% solution (800 ppm).
Remarks: Torrance manufactures a 1:500 sterile solution if medical quality is desired, but commercial grade is adequate.
References: Edminster & Gray (1948); Fasten (1912); Hoffman & Meyer (1974); Kabata (1970).

HYDROGEN PEROXIDE, 3% solution
Composition: H_2O_2.
Synonyms: None.
Uses or Treatment for: Skin parasites; protozoacide; monogenetic trematodes; antiseptic.
Dosage: (1) 17.5 gm/l of the 3% standard solution as a quick bath for 10 to 15 minutes; (2) 525 ppm as a dip for 10 to 15 minutes; (3) 5000 ppm as a dip for 5 minutes; (4) 30.5 ml of standard 3% solution added to aquarium water.
Remarks: Manufactured by Barre, Bowman Pharm, CLI, CPI, PD, Purepac Pharm, Rexall, Rondex, Shearton.
References: Dempster & Shipman (1970); Hoffman & Meyer (1974); Reichenbach-Klinke (1966); Reichenbach-Klinke & Elkan (1965); Shäperclaus (1954).

HYDROGEN SULFIDE
Composition: H_2S.
Synonyms: "Rotten egg gas."

Uses or Treatment for: Crustacea *(Ergasilus sieboldi).*
Dosage: Unknown.
Remarks: Not thoroughly tested, but probably effective.
References: Gnadeberg (1949) ; Hoffman & Meyer (1974).
β-HYDROXYNAPTHOL—See Betanaphthol.
HYZYD—See Isoniazid.
ILOTYCIN—See Erythromycin.
IODINE—See Alcohol, iodated.
IODOFORM
Composition: Triiodomethane.
Synonyms: None.
Uses or Treatment for: Antiseptic; fungicide *(Saprolegnia);* protozoacide [*Ambiphyra (= Scyphidia), Trichodina (= Cyclochaeta)];* Monogenea *(Cleidodiscus).*
Dosage: 2 ppm (Inhibitory).
Remarks: Not effective.
References: Hoffman & Meyer (1974).
IODOPHORS
Composition: Various iodine solutions.
Synonyms: Alcohol, iodated; Betadine; Bridine; Buffodine; Iodoform; Povadine-Iodine; PVP-I; Wescodyne.
Uses or Treatment for: Disinfection of eggs; bacteria *(Pseudomonas,* bacterial hemorrhagic septicemia disinfection).
Dosage: 50-200 ppm (usually 100 pm) for 10 to 15 minutes (disinfection of eggs).
Remarks: Different commercially available Iodophors contain different concentrations of Iodine, to be used on a basis of pure Iodine present in the product; toxic to newly hatched fish; probably also assists in control of some virus fish diseases; Wescodyne is 1.6% Iodine; Buffodine is a neutral formulation of an Iodophor giving nearly neutral solutions in water; see also Alcohol, iodated, Betadine, Iodoform, Povadine-Iodine, PVP-I.
References: Snieszko (1975).
IRON SULFATE
Composition: Ferric or Ferrous sulfate (not specified).
Synonyms: None.

Uses or Treatment for: Used in combination with Copper sulfate.

Dosage: Unknown.

Remarks: See Copper sulfate.

References: Hoffman & Meyer (1974).

ISODINE—See Povidone-Iodine.

ISOHYDRAZIDE—See Isoniazid.

ISONAPHTHOL—See Betanaphthol.

ISONIAZID

Composition: Iso-nicotinic-acid hydrazide.

Synonyms: Hyzyd,; Isohydrazide; Laniazid; Niconyl; Nicozide; Nydrazid; Teebaconin; Triniad; Uniad.

Uses or Treatment for: Bacteria (saltwater tuberculosis).

Dosage: 40 mg/gal.

Remarks: Available as 50, 100, or 300 mg tablets or as a sterile lypholyzed powder; manufactured by Amer Quinine, APC, Arcum, Barnes-Hind, Barre, Bates, Carchem, Clifford, CMC, Columbia Medic, Corvit, Kasar, Kirkman, Lannett, Lilly, Mallinckrodt, Panray, Pb, Premo, Purepac Pharm, Rondex, Sheraton, Squibb, Stanley Drug, Stayner, Tablroc, Towne, United, Vitarine, West-Ward Xttrium, Zenith.

References: Kingsford (1975).

ISONICOTINIC ACID HYDRAZIDE—See Isoniazid.

ISOSYSTOX—See Di-syston.

KAMALA

Composition: Extract of glands and hairs on fruit of *Mallotus phillippinensis*.

Synonyms: None.

Uses or Treatment for: Anthelminthic; cestodes *(Bothriocephalus, Corallobothrium fimbriatum)*.

Dosage: (1) 75,000 ppm in food; (2) 2% of diet for 7 days, feed to starved fish for 3 days.

Remarks: Not as effective as Di-*n*-butyl tin oxide.

References: R. Allison (1957b); Bauer (1959, 1966); Hoffman & Meyer (1974); McKernan (1940); Nazarova et al. (1969); Snieszko (1975).

KAMYCIN—See Kanamycin.

KANAMYCIN

Composition: Antibiotic derived from *Streptomyces kanamyceticus.*

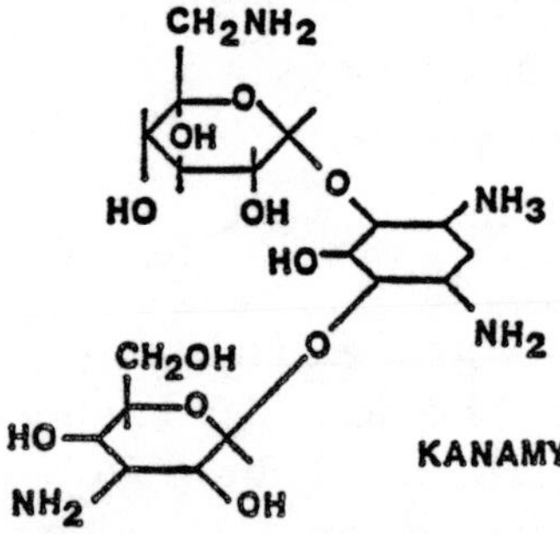

CH₂NH₂ / OH / HO / OH / HO / NH₃ / HO / CH₂OH / O / NH₂ / HO / NH₂ / OH / **KANAMYCIN**

Synonyms: Cantrex, Kamycin; Kantrex; Resistomycin.

Uses or Treatment for: Antibiotic; bacteria [*Aeromonas* (especially *A. punctata*), bacterial fin rot, *Pseudomonas, Mycobacterium, Vibrio,* some gram-positive bacteria]; protozoacide (*Ichthyophthirius*).

Dosage: (1) 20 mg/kg of fish weight as intraperitoneal injecttion or in feed; (2) 0.02-0.05 gm/l of water; (3) 12.5 ppm daily (not effective against Ich); (4) 50 mg/kg of fish or 25-100 mg/kg of food; feed for one week.

Remarks: Shelf life when in solution, over 2 days; moderately effective in salt water; available as capsules or sterile solution; manufactured by Bristol Labs.

References: Amlacher (1970); Conroy (1961a, 1961b, 1962, 1963); Hoffman & Meyer (1974); Kingsford (1975); Reichbach-Klinke & Elkan (1965); Snieszko (1975).

KANTREX—See Kanamycin.

KARATHANE

Composition: 2,4-dinitro-6-(2-octyl)phenyl crotonate.
Synonyms: Dikar; Dinocap; Mildex.
Uses or Treatment for: Fungicide (*Saprolegnia*).
Dosage: 0.1 ppm.
Remarks: Toxic to fish.
References: Hoffman & Meyer (1974).

KELFIZINA—See Emtrysidina.

KEROSENE

Composition: Hydrocarbon derivitive.

Synonyms: None.

Uses or Treatment for: Crustacea *(Argulus);* insecticide.

Dosage: (1) 2.5 to 5 gal/acre poured onto surface of pond; (2) touched to *Argulus* at full strength with a cotton-tipped applicator.

Remarks: Dosage no. 2 not recommended; kills (by suffocation) air-breathing insects that prey on fish.

References: Hoffman & Meyer (1974) ; Van Duijn (1973) .

KORLAN

Composition: O,O-dimethyl O-(2,4,5-trichlorophenyl)-phosphorothioate.

Synonyms: Fenchlorophos; Ronnel, Trolene.

Uses or Treatment for: Crustacea *(Lernaea cyprinacea);* insecticide.

Dosage: (1) 0.25 ppm weekly for 4 weeks; (2) 0.25% in diet daily; (3) 0.8% in diet.

Remarks: Toxic to fish at higher concentrations, toxic to fry, less than 0.74 ppm not appreciably toxic to fish.

References: Hoffman & Meyer (1974) ; Willford (1967a) .

LANIAZID—See Isoniazid.

LEUKOMYCIN—See Chloramphenicol.

LEXONE—See Benzene hexachloride.

LIFEBEARER—See Dylox.

LIGHT GREEN N—See Malachite green.

LIGNASAN—See Ethylmercuric phosphate.

LILAC LEAVES

Composition: Leaves of *Syringya vulgaris.*

Synonyms: None.

Uses or Treatment for: Anti-protozoal agent.

Dosage: Leaves placed in water.

Remarks: None.

References: Bauer (1959) ; Hoffman & Meyer (1974) .

LIME

Composition: Ca(OH)$_2$ · Mg(OH)$_2$ or CaCO$_3$.

Synonyms: Caustic lime; Hydrated lime; Slaked lime.

Uses or Treatment for: Control of *Tubifex* as intermediate host.

Dosage: Apply liberally on drained but wet pond bottoms.

Remarks: Partially effective; see also calcium carbonate.

References: Bauer (1959); Hoffman & Meyer (1974) ; Quebec Game & Fisheries Dept. (1948) .

LINCOCIN—See Lincomycin.

LINCOMYCIN

Composition: Lincomycin hydrochloride.

Synonyms: Lincocin.

Uses or Treatment for: Bacteria (gram-positive bacteria) .

Dosage: Undetermined.

Remarks: Shelf life when in solution is 2 years; available as capsules or as sterile solution; manufactured by Upjohn.

References: Kingsford (1975) .

LINDANE—See Benzene hexachloride.

LINTEX—See Niclosamide.

LORIDINE—See Cephaloridine.

LOROTHIDOL—See Bithionol.

LYE—See Sodium hydroxide.

LYSOL

Composition: Cresol derivative—50% cresol + 50% potash soap; Methyl phenol—CH$_3$ · C$_6$H$_4$OH.

Synonyms: Cresol; Priasol (German trade name) .

Uses or Treatment for: Disinfectant; protozoacide [*Chilodonella, Costia, Trichodina* (= *Cyclochaeta*)]; Monogenea *(Gyrodactylus);* Hirudinea (leeches, *Piscicola geometra);* Crustacea [carplice *(Argulus)*].

Dosage: (1) 2 cc/l of water—dip fish for 5 to 15 seconds; (2) 1 cc/5 l of water as a bath; (3) 0.02% (1 cc/5 l of water) for 5 to 15 seconds; (4) 4 cc /l of water—immersion bath for 5 to 15 seconds; (5) 200 ppm as a dip for 30 seconds; (6) 2000 ppm as a dip for 5 to 15 seconds; (7) 400 ppm as a dip for 5 to 15 seconds (Priasol); (8) 4000 ppm as a dip for 5 to 15 seconds (Priasol).

Remarks: Not as a good as Formalin; 8 ppm toxic to trout; commercial product of Lehn & Fink Division of Sterling Drug Co.

References: Amlacher (1961b, 1970); Bauer (1958); Hoffman & Meyer (1974); Kabata (1970); Reichenbach-Klinke (1966); Reichenbach-Klinke & Elkan (1965); Reichenbach-Klinke & Landolt (1973); Schäperclaus (1954).

MADRIBON—See Sulfadimethoxine sodium.

MAGNESIUM SULFATE
Composition: $MgSO_4 \cdot 7 H_2O$.
Synonyms: Epsom salts.
Uses or Treatment for: Cathartic; protozoacide [*Hexamita (= Octomites)*]; monogenetic trematodes *(Dactylogyrus)*; Crustacea *(Salmincola)*.
Dosage: (1) 1.5% solution; (2) 30,000 ppm in dry food for 3 days; (3) $MgSO_4$ (300,000 ppm) + NaCl (70,000 ppm) as a dip for 5 to 10 minutes; (4) $MgSO_4$ (30,000 ppm) + NaCl (7000 ppm) as a dip for 5 to 10 minutes; (5) 15,000 ppm.
Remarks: Fresh water only; 15,500 ppm toxic to *Gambusia affinis* in 96 hours; 20,000-27,500 ppm toxic to *Perca flavescens* in 72 hours; available as a sterile solution of medical purity from Abbott, Amer Quinine, Atlas Pharceut, Bel-Mar, Elkins-Sinn, Lilly, PD, Robinson Lab, Vitarine.
References: Bauer (1958); BSFW (1968); Fasten (1912); Hoffman & Meyer (1974); Kabata (1970); McKee & Wolf (1963).

MALACHITE GREEN G SULFATE — See Malachite green, zinc free oxalate.

MALACHITE GREEN, zinc free oxalate
Composition: *p,p*-benzylidenebis-*N,N*-dimethyl aniline.
Synonyms: Aniline green; Bright green; Evergreen B; Light green N; Malachite green G sulfate; Malachite oxolate; Nox-Ich; Victoria green B or WB.
Uses or Treatment for: Ectoparasites; bacteria *(Columnaris)*;

fungicide *(Achyla, Aphanomyces, Ichthyophonus hoferi, Sap-rolegnia);* external protozoacide [*Ambiphyra* (= *Scyphidia*), *Chilodonella, Costia, Cryptocaryon irritans, Epistylis, Ichthy-ophthirius, Leptomitus, Oodinium ocellatum, O. pillularis, Pythium, Trichodina* (= *Cyclochaeta*), *Trichophyra*]; mono-genetic trematodes *(Gyrodactylus).*

Dosage: (1) 0.15 ppm—3 times, 3 days apart; (2) 1 gm/10 m^2 of tank surface—2 to 3 times on alternate days, up to a concen-tration of 0.15 mg/l; (3) 1:15,000 solution for 10 to 30 seconds; (4) 5 ppm as a 1 hour flush used daily; (5) 66 ppm for 10 to 30 second dip (trout) ; (6) 0.1-0.15 ppm for 1 hour flush (catfish, bass) ; (7) 1-3 ppm for 1 hour flush (use with caution for trout) ; (8) in flowing water—6 gm to each battery with a flow rate of 50 gpm, at 5 day intervals; (9) in flowing water—90 ml of a 1% solution to head of trough, twice daily; (10) 500 ppm as a flush; (11) 10 ppm for 15 minutes on alternate days; (12) 0.005-0.01 ppm—twice daily; (13) 100,000 ppm applied topi-cally biweekly for 2 weeks (fungus) ; (14) NaCl (30,000 ppm) + Malachite green (66 ppm) ; (15) Basic bright green (Bril-liant green), which is 18 times less expensive than Malachite green—0.12-1.0 ppm; (16) Malachite green (0.005-0.10 ppm) + Formalin (50 ppm) on alternate days for 3 applications; lower doses may not be effective; higher dosage effective, but may be toxic to fish; (17a) Malachite green (0.1 ppm) + DMSO (0.5 ppm) is inhibitory only, but not toxic to fish; (17b) Mal-achite green (0.5 ppm) + DMSO (2.5 ppm) is inhibitory, but toxic to fish; (17c) Malachite green (1 ppm) + DMSO (5 ppm) is toxic to fish; all applications on alternate days; (18) 15 ppm for 6 to 24 hours; (19) standard solution of 1.5 mg/l, add 2 ml/100 ml of water to give 0.03 mg/l concentration; (20) 0.05-2.0 ppm in ponds or aquaria for indefinite time; (21) 0.5 ppm bath for 1 hour (egg fungus) .

Remarks: 1 ppm = LC$_{50}$ in young *Salmo;* 1 ppm toxic to *Salvelinus fontinalis;* 0.5 ppm not toxic to *Tilapia;* 1 ppm = LD$_{100}$ in carp, mullet, *Tilapia,* toxic to many species of fish; 2-5 ppm toxic to *Lebistes reticulatus;* 2 ppm toxic to *Os-phronemus;* 75 ppm not toxic to *Cyprinus carpio,* 0.4 ppm not toxic to *Ictalurus punctatus;* 2 ppm not toxic to *Lepomis macrochirus;* may be toxic to small marine fish.

References: Avdosev (1962); L. Allison (1954); R. Allison (1963, 1966); Amlacher (1961a, 1961b, 1970); Arasaki et al. (1958); Askerov (1968); Astakhova & Martino (1968); Beckert & Allison (1964); Bulkey & Hlavek (1976a 1976b); Burrows (1949); Clemens & Sneed (1958, 1959); Cummins (1954); Deufel (1960); Erickson (1965); Fischthal (1949); Fish (1939); Foster & Woodbury (1936); Glagoleva & Malikova (1968); Gottwald (1961); Havelka & Petrovicky (1967); Herman (1972); Hoffman & Meyer (1974); Hublou (1958); Ivasik & Svirepo (1964); Johnson (1961); Johnson et al. (1955); Kingsford (1975); Knittel (1966); Kocytowski & Antychowicz (1964); Kubu (1962); Lanzing (1965); Leteux & Meyer (1972); McKee & Wolf (1963); Martin (1968); Merriner (1969); O'Donnell (1947); Peterson et al. (1966); Prost & Studnicka (1971); Reichenbach-Klinke & Elkan (1965); Reichenbach-Klinke & Landolt (1973); Robertson (1954); Rucker & Whipple (1951); Sachachte (1974); Sakowicz & Gottwald (1958); Sarig (1968, 1971); Scott & Warren (1964); Snieszko (1974, 1975); Sokolov & Maslyukova (1971); Steffens (1962); Steffens et al. (1961); Tesarick & Havelka (1966); Tesarick & Mares (1966); Van Duijn (1973); Willford (1967a); J. Wood (1968).

MALACHITE OXALATE—See Malachite green, zinc free oxalate.

MALATHION

Composition: O,O-dimethyl S-(1,2 biscarbethoxyl ethyl) phosphorothioate.

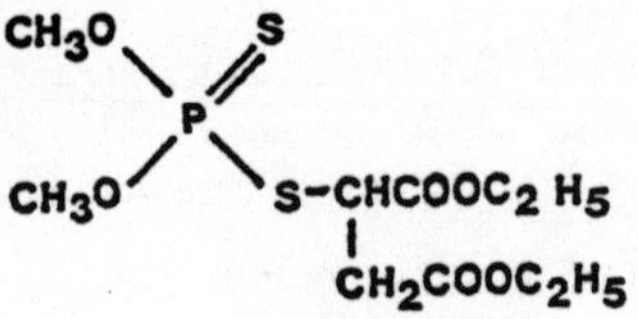

$$CH_3O-\overset{\displaystyle S}{\underset{\displaystyle CH_3O}{P}}-S-CHCOOC_2H_5$$
$$CH_2COOC_2H_5$$

MALATHION

Synonyms: None.

Uses or Treatment for: Crustacea *(Argulus, Ergasilus);* insecticide.

Dosage: (1) 0.20-0.25 ppm; (2) 0.5-1.0 ppm.

Remarks: 29.4 ppm = LC_{50} in young *Cyprinus carpio;* 1 ppm = LC_{50} in young *Esox;* 16-400 ppm not toxic to *Ictalurus punctatus;* 0.13-0.25 ppm toxic to *Lepomis macrochirus;* 0.13-0.5 ppm toxic to *Micropterus salmoides;* 12.5 ppm = LC_{50} in *Pimephales promelas* in 96 hours at 20°C, but 0.2 ppm is nontoxic; 0.13-0.16 ppm = LC_{15} to *Roccus chrysops* and *R. saxitilis.*

References: Clemens & Sneed (1959); Hoffman & Meyer (1974); Johnson (1968); Kabata (1970); Kennedy & Walsh (1970); Lahav & Sarig (1967); Larsen (1964); Mount & Stephan (1967); Peterson et al. (1966); Reichenbach-Klinke (1966); Sarig (1966, 1968, 1971); Wellborn (1971).

MARACYN—See Erythromycin.

MASOTEN—See Dylox.

MEFAROL

Composition: Probably similar to Hyamine.

Synonyms: None.

Uses or Treatment for: Unknown.

Dosage: 1-2 ppm in water for one hour.

Remarks: Toxic in very soft water; less effective in hard water.

References: Snieszko (1975).

MEFENAL—See Sulfamethazine, sodium.

MENAZON

Composition: S-[(4,6-diamino-*s*-triazin-2-yl)methyl] *O,O*-dimethyl phosphorodithioate.

Synonyms: None.

Uses or Treatment for: Crustacea *(Lernaea cyprinacea);* insecticide.

Dosage: 0.4% in diet daily.

Remarks: Not effective; toxic to fry.

References: Hoffman & Meyer (1974).

MEPACRINE—See Atabrine, hydrochloride.

MERBROMEN—See Mercurochrome.

MERCURAM—See Thiram.

MERCURIC CHLORIDE

Composition: $HgCl_2$.

Synonyms: Corrosive sublimate.

Uses or Treatment for: Disinfectant; germicide.

Dosage: 1:1000 solution as a disinfectant.

Remarks: 0.008-0.5 ppm toxic to fish.

References: Hoffman & Meyer (1974); McKee & Wolf (1963); Reichenbach-Klinke (1966).

MERCURIC NITRATE

Composition: $Hg(NO_3)_2 \cdot H_2O$.

Synonyms: Mercuric pernitrate.

Uses or Treatment for: Protozoacide *(Ichthyophthirius multifiliis)*.

Dosage: 0.1-0.3 ppm for 4 days at 10-20°C or higher.

Remarks: None.

References: Hoffman & Meyer (1974); Ivasik & Svirepo (1964).

MERCURIC PERNITRATE—See Mercuric nitrate.

MERCUROCHROME

Composition: Disodium 2,7-dibromo-4-hydroxy-mercurifluorescein.

Synonyms: Merbromin.

Uses or Treatment for: Antiseptic; disinfectant; fungicide *(Saprolegnia)*; protozoacide *(Ichthyophthirius multifiliis);* monogenetic trematodes *(Gyrodactylus)*.

Dosage: (1) Paint on wounds; (2) 10 ppm for 12 hours; (3) 1.34 ppm; (4) 1:10 solution touched to wounds *(Lernaea* produced lesions).

Remarks: Large amounts may be toxic to fish; do not get in gills; available as a bulk powder from HWD; manufactured as a solution by Barre, BBC, HWD, Rondex.

References: Detwiler & McKennon (1929); Hoffman & Meyer (1974); Seale (In Mellen, 1928); Van Duijn (1973).

MERTHIOLATE

Composition: Thimerosal (50% Hg).

Synonyms: None.

Uses or Treatment for: Bacteria (fin rot, ulcers); fungicide *(Saprolegnia).*
Dosage: Swab onto fish's skin.
Remarks: Rinse fish before returning to aquaria; do not get in gills; available as powder, sterile solutions, or tinctures; manufactured by Lilly, Barre, BBC, Rondex.
References: Kingsford (1975); Rucker (1961).

METACIDE—See Methyl parathion.

METASOL L

Composition: *m*-cresol anylol.
Synonyms: None.
Uses or Treatment for: Disinfectant; protozoacide *(Ichthyophthirius multifiliis).*
Dosage: 0.05 ppm.
Remarks: Kills trophs and tomites.
References: Hoffman & Meyer (1974).

METHACILLIN SODIUM

Composition: Sodium methacillin.
Synonyms: Celbenin; Staphcillin.
Uses or Treatment for: Bacteria (gram-positive bacteria).
Dosage: Undetermined.
Remarks: Has a shelf life of 4 days when in solution; available as a sterile powder; manufactured by Beech-Mass Phar and Bristol Labs.
References: Kingsford (1975).

METHYLENE BLUE

Composition: 3,7-bis(dimethylamino)-phenazathionium chloride.

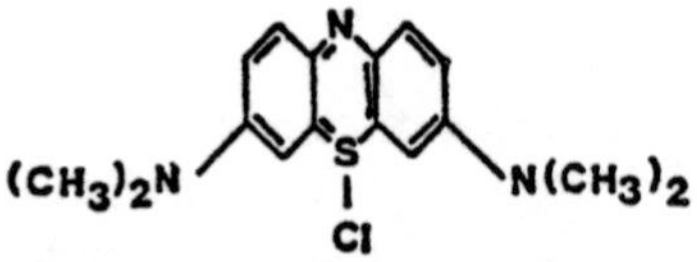

METHYLENE BLUE

Synonyms: Methylene blue-B; Methylthionine chloride; Urolene blue.

Uses or Treatment for: Dye; antifungal agent on fish eggs; fungicide *(Saprolegnia);* external protozoacide [*Ambiphyra* (= *Scyphida*), *Chilodonella, Costia, Cryptocaryon irritans, Epistylis, Ichthyophthirius, Oodinium, Trichodina* (= *Cyclochaeta*), *Trichophyra*]; monogenetic trematodes (*Cleidodiscus, Gyrodactylus*).

Dosage: (1) 2 ppm daily ; (2) 3 cc of a 1% solution in 10 liters of water as a long duration bath (3 to 5 days) ; (3) 10 ppm—not effective; (4) 50 ppm is inhibitory; (5) 3 ppm; (6) 0.15 ppm $CuSO_4$ + Citric acid + 0.2 ppm Methylene blue at 5 day intervals, 3 times, for marine aquarium fishes; (7) 5 ppm; (8) 1.0-3.0 ppm in water for 3 to 5 days; (9) 0.2-0.4 cc/1 (= 3-6 drops/1 = 2-4 cc/Imp gal = 1.7-3.4 cc/U.S. gal) of a stock solution prepared by adding 1 gm to 100 cc (approx. 0.09 qt) of water *(Gyrodactylus)*—good, effective treatment.

Remarks: May be used as a substitute oxygen donor in any case of respiratory distress; absorbed through the skin independently of gill condition; over 4 ppm is toxic to plants; as long as water remains blue, chemical is still active; easily removed by carbon filtration; available in medical purity as solution or tablets (65 mg) ; manufactured by Amer Quinine, Star.

References: R. Allison (1962, 1966) ; Amlacher (1961b, 1970) ; Havelka & Tesarick (1965) ; Herman (1972) ; Hoffman & Meyer (1974) ; Ivasik & Sutyagin (1967) ; Johnson (1968); Kingsford (1975) ; Kumar (1958) ; Nigrelli & Ruggieri (1966); Reichenbach-Klinke (1966) ; Reichenbach-Klinke & Elkan (1965) ; Schäperclaus (1954) ; Snieszko (1975) ; Stiles (In Mellen, 1928) ; Van Duijn (1973) .

METHYLENE BLUE B—See Methylene blue.

METHYL PARATHION

Composition: O,O-dimethyl O-*p*-nitrophenyl phosphorothioate.

Synonyms: Dalf; E605; Metacide; Metron; Nitrox 80.

Uses or Treatment for: Crustacean parasites *(Argulus, Lernaea cyprinacea);* insecticide.

Dosage: 0.125 ppm.

Remarks: Chemically related to Parathion.
References: Bowen & Putz (1966) ; Hoffman & Meyer (1974); Kabata (1970) .

METHYLTHIONINE CHLORIDE—See Methylene blue.

METHYL VIOLOGEN—See Paraquat.

METRIFONAT—See Dylox.

METRON—See Methyl parathion.

METRONIDAZOLE—See Flagyl.

MICROCIDE—See Anthium dioxide.

MICROMYCIN—See Oxytetracycline.

MICROPUR

Composition: German silver compound.
Synonyms: None.
Uses or Treatment for: Drinking water disinfectant; external protozoacide [*Chilodonella, Costia, Trichodina (= Cyclochaeta)*].
Dosage: 10 ppm for 24 hours.
Remarks: May be toxic to weak fish.
References: Hoffman & Meyer (1974) ; Schäperclaus (1954) .

MILBAM—See Zinc dimethyldithiocarbamate.

MILDEX—See Karathane.

MITOX

Composition: *p*-chlorobenzyl *p*-chlorophenyl sulfide.
Synonyms: Chlorbenside.
Uses or Treatment for: Crustacea *(Lernaea cyprinacea);* miticide.
Dosage: 20 ppm weekly for 4 weeks.
Remarks: None.
References: Hoffman & Meyer (1974) .

MONURON

Composition: Unknown.
Synonyms: None.
Uses or Treatment for: Herbicide (blue-green algae) .
Dosage: Undetermined.
Remarks: Experimental algistatic agent.
References: Sarig (1971) .

MS-222

Composition: Tricaine methanesulfonate.

Synonyms: Finquel; Sandoz.

Uses or Treatment for: Fish anesthetic; tranquilizer.

Dosage: 50-100 mg/l depending upon the size and species of fish (increase dosage 5 times to euthanize—kill—fish), will anesthetize a fish in 1 to 3 minutes with an uneventful recovery in 3 to 15 minutes.

Remarks: Application to FDA is necessary to obtain drug for use in food fish; fasting for 24 to 48 hours prior to use is recommended; zinc or copper in tank will react with drug producing toxic effects; inert material (glass, plastic) is recommended; the safest and most effective fish anesthetic available; safe for use with sharks.

References: Allen et al. (1970, 1972); Amlacher (1970); Dawson & Marking (1973); Gilderhus et al. (1973a); Hunn (1970); Luhning (1974a, 1974b); Marking (1967); Meister & Ritzi (1958); Reichenbach-Klinke & Landolt (1973); Schoettger (1967); Schoettger & Julin (1967); Schoettger et al. (1967); Schubert (1974); "General Anesthesia in Exotics." *Vet Med Small Anim Clin*, Sept. 1974, p. 1185; Walker & Schoettger (1967a, 1967b); Willford (1970).

MURIATIC ACID—See Hydrochloric acid.

MUSCATOX—See 7-Co-Ral.

MYCIFRADIN SULFATE—See Neomycin.

NALED—See Bromex-50.

NANTOKITE—See Cuprous chloride.

2-NAPTHOL—See Betanaphthol.

NAPTHOL B

Composition: Unknown.

Synonyms: None.

Uses or Treatment for: Protozoa *(Hexamita).*

Dosage: 5 gm/kg of fish weight in food for 4 to 5 days.

Remarks: None.

References: Reichenbach-Klinke & Elkan (1965).

NEGUVON

Composition: (2,2,2-trichloro-1-hydroxyethyl)-phosphonic acid-dimethylethol.

Synonyms: Dylox.

Uses or Treatment for: Skin parasites; protozoacide *(Ichthyophthirius)*; Monogenea *(Dactylogyrus, Gyrodactylus)*; Hirudinea (leeches) ; Crustacea (copepods, *Argulus, Lernaea)*; insecticide.

Dosage: (1) 0.25-0.50 ppm added to pond water, repeat weekly for 4 weeks; (2) 20,000-35,000 ppm (2-3.5% solution) as a dip for 2 to 3 minutes at a temperature of 15-20°C (kills *Argulus* in 50 to 60 seconds in aquaria, kills *Gyrodactylus* in 15 seconds) ; (3) 5000 ppm as a dip for 5 minutes; (4) 1 ppm for 48 hours; (5) 50,000 ppm as a flush for 30 minutes (ponds); (6) 1:1000 (1 gm/l or 68 gr/Imp gal or 57 gr/U.S. gal) in ponds as an indefinite bath.

Remarks: May be absorbed through the skin; avoid contact with the skin or wear rubber gloves when using; related to Dipterex, manufactured by Messrs. Bayer AG, see also Dylox.

References: Bailosoff (1963) ; Hoffman & Meyer (1974) ; Kabata (1970) ; Prost & Studnicka (1967) ; Reichenbach-Klinke & Elkan (1965) ; Van Duijn (1973) .

NEMAZINE—See Phenothiazine.

NEOBIOTIC—See Neomycin.

NEOMYCIN

Composition: Neomycin sulfate.

Synonyms: Mycifradin sulfate; Neobiotic.

Uses or Treatment for: Bacteria (gram-positive or gram-negative bacteria; *Pseudomonas).*

Dosage: 250 mg/gal in salt water.

Remarks: Shelf life when in solution is 2 years; very effective in salt water; 15 manufacturers produce ointments; available as ointment, tablets, sterile solutions, or powder; manufactured by APC, Barre, Bates, Canfield, Columbia Medic, Lannett, Lilly, Pfizer Labs, Prend, Squibb, Trent, Vitarine, Upjohn.

References: Kingsford (1975) .

NFZ—See Nitrofurazone.

NF-180—See Furoxone.

NICKEL SULFATE
  Composition: $NiSO_4 \cdot 6H_2O$.
  Synonyms: None.
  Uses or Treatment for: Protozoa *(Ichthyophthirius).*
  Dosage: 10 ppm.
  Remarks: Killed trophs and tomites, 24.6-300 ppm = LC_1 in *Ictalurus, Lepomis, Salmo salvelinus.*
  References: Hoffman & Meyer (1974) ; Willford (1967a) .

NICLOSAMIDE
  Composition: 2',5-dichloro-4'-nitrosalicylanilide.

NICLOSAMIDE

  Synonyms: Bayer 2353; Cestocid; Fenasal; Lintex; Phenasal, Yomesan.
  Uses or Treatment for: Anhelminthic; Cestoda *(Bothriocephalus gowkongensis, Proteocephalus ambloplifis).*
  Dosage: (1) 226 mg/lb of fish used as an oral drench; (2) 1 gm/kg of fish daily for 6 days (feed as pellets) ; (3) 10,000 ppm in food daily for 3 days.
  Remarks: Expect reinfection in one month.
  References: Hoffman & Meyer (1974) ; Klenov (1970) ; Larsen (1964) ; Muzykovski (1968, 1971) ; Nazarova et al. (1969).

NICONYL—See Isoniazid.

NICOTINE SULFATE
  Composition: $(C_{10}H_{14}N_2)_2 \cdot H_2SO_4$.
  Synonyms: None.
  Uses or Treatment for: Hirudinea (leeches); insecticide; molluscicide (snails) .

Dosage: 12-15 kg/hectare applied to pond bottom before filling.

Remarks: Effective in aquariums, but not in ponds, for leeches; 3 ppm toxic to fish.

References: Hoffman & Meyer (1974) ; Moore (1923) ; Reichenbach-Klinke (1966) .

NICOZIDE—See Isoniazid.

NI-FURIN—See Nitrofurazone.

NIFURIPIRINOL—See Furanace.

NIFURPRAZINE HCl

Composition: 1-(5-nitro-2-furyl)-2-(6-amino-3-pyridazyl)ethylene hydrochloride.

Synonyms: Aivet; Carofur; HB-115.

Uses or Treatment for: Bacteria [Furunculosis *(Aeromonas salmonicida), Vibrio anguillarum*].

Dosage: (1) As a bath for an indefinite period—0.01-0.1 ppm; (2) in food—10 mg/kg of food, feed for 3 to 6 days at a time.

Remarks: A Nitrofuran, unstable in prolonged exposure to sunlight; Aivet is a soluble powder containing 6.6% active ingredient; Carofur also contains 6.66% active ingredient.

References: Snieszko (1975) .

NIRAN—See Ethyl parathion.

NITREX—See Nitrofurantoin sodium.

NITRIC ACID

Composition: HNO_3.

Synonyms: None.

Uses or Treatment for: Crustacea *(Salmincola).*

Dosage: 0.03% solution (300 ppm) .

Remarks: Killed larvae only.

References: Hoffman & Meyer (1974) ; Kabata (1970) .

NITROFURAN—See Furoxone.

NITROFURANTOIN SODIUM

Composition: Nitrofurantoin sodium.

Synonyms: Cyantin; Furadantin; Furagent; Furaloid; Furan; Furantonin; Nitrex.

Uses or Treatment for: Bacteria (gram-negative and gram-positive bacteria).

Dosage: Undetermined.

Remarks: Has a shelf life of one day when in solution; not effective in salt water; available as tablets (50 or 100 mg) or powder; manufactured by Aberdeen, APC, AUI, Barre, BBC, Beach, Carbide Chemco, Columbia Medic, Dorasol, Eaton, EPC, Lederle, Purepac Phar, Rondex, Sheraton, Star, Steri-Med, Towne, West-Ward, Zenith.

References: Kingsford (1975).

NITROFURAZONE

Composition: 5-nitro-2-furaldehyde semicarbazone.

$$O_2N - \underset{\text{(furan ring)}}{} - CH = N - \underset{H}{N} - \underset{O}{C} - NH_2$$

NITROFURAZONE

Synonyms: Furacin; Furazolidone; Furazone green; Furoxone; NFZ; Nifuran.

Uses or Treatment for: Antiseptic; disinfectant; bacteria *(Vibrio anguillarum)*; Protozoa *(Ichthyophthirius)*.

Dosage: 10 ppm.

Remarks: Not particularly effective in fresh water against Ich (ineffective against trophs and tomites); available as powder, drops, or cream; manufactured by Eaton, Lannett, MCC-M; see also Furoxone.

References: Hoffman & Meyer (1974); Kubota & Hagita (1963); Snieszko (1975).

p-NITROPHENACYL CHLORIDE

Composition: *p*-nitrophenacyl chloride.

Synonyms: None.

Uses or Treatment for: Molluscicide *(Bulinus)*.

Dosage: 2.5 ppm.

Remarks: Did not kill *Tilapia sp.*

References: Hoffman & Meyer (1974); Villiere & Mackenzie (1963).

NITROPHENYL AMIDINEURA

Composition: 1-(*p*-nitrophenyl)-2-amidineura hydrochloride.
Synonyms: T-72.
Uses or Treatment for: Molluscicide *(Radix)*.
Dosage: 0.05 ppm.
Remarks: Fish tolerated up to 70 ppm.
References: Hoffman & Meyer (1974); Venulet & Schultz (1964).

NITROX 80—See Methyl parathion.

NORCILLIN—See Ampicillin trihydrate.

NOVOBIOCIN

Composition: Novobiocin calcium or Novobiocin sodium.
Synonyms: Albamycin.
Uses or Treatment for: Bacteria (gram-positive and many gram-negative bacteria).
Dosage: Undetermined.
Remarks: An antibiotic of questionable merits; has a shelf life of 1 day (do not mix until ready for use); manufactured by Upjohn.
References: Kingsford (1975).

NOX-ICH (0.2% solution, Malachite green)—See Malachite green, zinc free oxalate.

NYDRAZID—See Isoniazid.

OLEANDOMYCIN

Composition: Oleandomycin phosphate.
Synonyms: Matromycin; PA-105; Romicil.
Uses or Treatment for: Bacteria (gram-positive bacteria).
Dosage: Undetermined.
Remarks: Shelf life when in solution is 2 weeks; U.S. regulations require zero tolerance for its residues on or in uncooked tissues or by-products from fish that have received this drug.
References: Kingsford (1975).

OMNIPEN—See Ampicillin trihydrate.

OSAROLUM

Composition: Unknown (Russian origin).
Synonyms: None.

Uses or Treatment for: Protozoa (coccidiostat).
Dosage: Unknown.
Remarks: None.
References: Hoffman & Meyer (1974).

OTETRYN—See Oxytetracycline.

OXALIC ACID
Composition: $(COOH)_2 \cdot nH_2O$.
Synonyms: Ethanedioic acid.
Uses or Treatment for: Crustacea *(Salmincola)*.
Dosage: 30% solution (3000 ppm).
Remarks: None.
References: Fasten (1912); Hoffman & Meyer (1974); Kabata (1970).

OXOLINIC ACID
Composition: 1-ethyl-1,4-dihydro-6,7-methylenedioxy-4-oxo-3-quinolinecarboxylic acid.
Synonyms: None.
Uses or Treatment for: Bacteria *(Aeromonas sp., Columnaris)*.
Dosage: (1) Orally: 3 mg/kg of fish once daily for 5 days; (2) as a bath: 1 ppm for 24 hours.
Remarks: None.
References: Snieszko (1975).

OXY-KESSO TETRA—See Oxytetracycline.

OXY-TETRACHEL—See Oxytetracycline.

OXYTETRACYCLINE
Composition: 4-(dimethylamino)-1,4,4α,5,5α,6,11,12a-octahydro-3,5,6,10,12,12a-hexahydroxy-6-methyl-1,11-dioxo-2-naphthacenecarboxamide; also Calcium Oxytetracyline.

OXYTETRACYCLINE

Synonyms: Achromycin; Agmacycline; Amtet; Bristacycline; Dalimycin; Maytrex; Micromycin; Ostotet; Otetryn; Oxy-Kes-so Tetra; Oxy-tetrachel; Rexamycin; Sumycin; Terramycin; Tetrabid; Tetracaps; Tetrachel; Tetra-co; Tetracycline; Tetracyn; Tetrakin; Tetralar; Tetram; Tetramax; Tetramed; Tetramine; Tetra-mycin; Tetra-queen; Tetraspect; Tetratabs; Tetrex; Uri-tet.*

Uses or Treatment for: Antibiotic; bacteria (gram-positive and most gram-negative bacteria, cold-water disease *(Cytophaga psychrophila)*, bacterial hemorrhagic septicemia, Columnaris *(Chondrococcus columnaris)*, Emphysematous putrefactive disease of channel catfish *(Edwardsiella tarda)*, Furunculosis, *Pseudomonas*, redmouth disease of trout, ulcer disease *(Hemophilus piscium)*, Vibriosis) ; fungicide *(Saprolegnia)*; Protozoa *(Ichthyophthirius)*.

Dosage: (1) 3 mg/100-400 gm of fish body weight as intraperitoneal injection; (2) 50-75 mg/kg of fish weight per day in food for 10 days; (3) 10 ppm in water (not effective against *Saprolegnia)*; (4) 12.5 ppm daily (not effective against Ich); (5) 10-20 mg/l as a long duration bath; (6) 5-8 mg/l as a long duration bath.

Remarks: Probably the most widely used and recommended of all antibiotics used in the treatment for fish diseases; U.S. law requires that its use must be discontinued for at least 21 days before fish are killed for human consumption; 125 ppm = LC_{16} in small *Roccus saxatilis* in 96 hours at 21°C; has a shelf life of 2 days (do not mix with solvent until ready for use); not very effective in salt water; do not inject intramuscularly,

---

In addition to the above listed synonyms which are cross-referenced in the text, the following synonym/manufacturers also produce Oxytetracycline drugs: Cancycline/Canfield; G-Mycin/Coast labs; Brodspec/COT; T-250/Elder; Fed-Mycin/Fed; Forbesycline/Forbes; Kay-cycline/Kay Pharmacal; Bicycline/Knight; Maytrex/Mayrand; Mericycline/Merit Pharceut; Tet-Cy/Metro Med; Metzcycline/Metz; Duratet/Meyer; Romycin/Nortex; Paltet/Palmedico; Cyclopar/PD; Promycin/PMS; Progtet/Progress; Rexamycin/Rexall; Desamycin/RIC; Robitet/Robins; Amer-tet/Robinson Lab; Ro-Cycline/Rowell; Retet/RPL; Scottrex/Scott-Corb; Cycline/Scrip; Amycin/SIG; SK-Tetracycline/SKF; Steclin/Squibb; Sumycin hydrochloride/Squibb; Cyltrecin/Trent; Piracaps/Tutag; Panmycin/Upjohn; Dema/USV; Teline/Winston; Zezycin/Zemmer.

as it will produce sterile abcesses in fish tissues; available as sterile solutions, capsules (250 mg), or tablets; manufacturers of those drugs listed as synonyms and cross-referenced in text include, but may not be limited to, the following: Aberdeen, AGM, Alliance, Amer Quinine, Amid, APC, Arcum, Artaco, AUI, Balkins, Barre, Bates, BBC, Berla, Bluline, Bowman Pharm, Bristol Labs, BT, Carchem, Century, Coastal, Columbia Medic, CPI, Century Lab, Dalin, DE, Dunhall, FTD, Invenex, Jenkins, Lannett, Lardon, Lederle, Linden, Mallard, McKesson, Mayrand, Medspec, Meyer, Orbit, Osto, Pfizer Labs, Premo, PRL, Purepac Pharm, Rachelle, Rexall, Roerig, Rondex, SCA, Schlicksup, Sheraton, Squibb, Stanley drugs, Stayner, Steri-Med, Tablroc, Towne, Trent, Tutag, Ulmer Pharcal, United, WestWard, Zenith.

References: Amend (1969); Amlacher (1970); Bullock & Collis (1969); Choate (1964); Curran & Herman (1969); Friborough et al. (1969a, 1969b, 1969c); Herman (1969a, 1969b, 1972); Herman et al. (1969); Hoffman & Meyer (1974); Irwin (1959); Kingsford (1975); NDCD (1972); Reichenbach-Klinke & Elkan (1965); Robinson et al. (1969); Snieszko (1975); Snieszko & Griffin (1951); Weber & Ridgeway (1967), Wellborn (1969, 1971).

OXYTETRACYCLINE HYDROCHLORIDE—See Oxytetracycline.

OZONE

Composition: Triatomic oxygen (O_3).

Synonyms: None.

Uses or Treatment for: Decontamination of water; external infections; bactericide; fungicide.

Dosage: 26-65 ppm bubbled into water.

Remarks: Is being investigated as a remedy for external infections and decontamination of fresh water; useful in salt water aquaria in conjunction with protein skimmer for the separation and removal of organic wastes.

References: Benoit & Matlin (1966); Hoffman & Meyer (1974).

P-7138—See Furanace.

PAA-2056

Composition: Experimental compound by Parke, Davis & Company.

Synonyms: None.

Uses or Treatment for: Antiprotozoal *(Ichthyophthirius).*

Dosage: 2 ppm (not effective).

Remarks: None.

References: Hoffman & Meyer (1974).

PAMAQUINE NAPHTHOATE—See Plasmoquin.

PARACHLOROMETAXYLENOL

Composition: Parachlorometaxylenol.

Synonyms: None.

Uses or Treatment for: Nematoda (ascarids).

Dosage: Moisten dry flakes with the drug.

Remarks: None.

References: Amlacher (1961b, 1970); Hoffman & Meyer (1974).

PARACHLOROPHENOXETHOL

Composition: Unknown (NIPA).

Synonyms: None.

Uses or Treatment for: Bacteriostat; fungicide *(Ichthyophonous).*

Dosage: 1 ml/l of water—stock solution; gradually during the course of 2 days, add 50 cc/l of water.

Remarks: Extremely expensive drug.

References: Hoffman & Meyer (1974); Reichenbach-Klinke & Elkan (1965); Reichenbach-Klinke & Landolt (1973).

PARAFORMALDEHYDE

Composition: Polymerized formaldehyde.

Synonyms: None.

Uses or Treatment for: Disinfectant; Monogenea *(Gyrodactylus wegeneri).*

Dosage: 10 ppm dissolved in Soda ash.

Remarks: None.

References: Hoffman & Meyer (1974); S. Lewis (1967); Lewis & Parker (1965).

PARAMOMYCIN
Composition: Paramomycin sulfate; derived from *Streptomyces rimosus.*
Synonyms: Catenulin; Humatin.
Uses or Treatment for: Antibiotic; bacteria (gram-negative bacteria, *Pseudomonas*).
Dosage: Undetermined.
Remarks: Available as capsules; manufactured by PD.
References: Hoffman & Meyer (1974) ; Kingsford (1975).

PARAQUAT, dichloride
Composition: 1,1'-dimethyl-4,4'-dipyridinium dichloride.
Synonyms: Bipyridilium; Gramoxone; Methyl viologen.
Uses or Treatment for: Herbicide (blue-green algae) ; molluscicide (snails).
Dosage: (1) 2-10 ppm; (2) 0.5 ppm.
Remarks: Experimental algicide; 1.14 ppm toxic in 1 to 16 days at 20-25°C.
References: Camey et al. (1966) ; Earnest (1971) ; Hoffman & Meyer (1974) ; Paulini (1965) ; Paulini & Camey (1965); Sarig (1971).

PARATHION—See Ethyl parathion.

PCP—See Pentachlorophenol.

PENBRITIN—See Ampicillin trihydrate.

PENICILLIN G—See Penicillin, potassium.

PENICILLIN, Potassium
Composition: γ-chlorocrotylmercaptomethylpenicillin potassium.
Synonyms: Calcium Penicillin G; Penicillin G.
Uses or Treatment for: Antibiotic; dermatitis; bacteria (gill infections) ; Fungi *(Saprolegnia);* Protozoa *(Ichthyophthirius).*
Dosage: (1) 40,000 I.U. to 100 liters of water as a bath of 30 seconds duration; (2) 1 ppm daily.
Remarks: Not effective in salt water; shelf life of 70 days when in solution; can induce resistant strains of bacteria; available as tablets, capsules, powders, ointments, sterile powder and sterile solutions; manufactured by Aberdeen, Al-

liance, Amer Quinine, Barre, Bates, BBC, Bowman Pharm, Canfield, Columbia Medic, Carchem, Corvit, CPI, Day Baldwin, Dow Genrc Pharm, Elder, Fellows, Hartford, Jenkins, Lannett, Lilly, Noyes, PD, Premo, PRL, Purepac Pharm, Rexall, Robinson Lab, Rondex, SCA, Sheraton, Stayner, Stanley Drug, Steri-Med, Tablroc, Towne, Tutag, Ulmer Pharcal, United, Vitarine, West-Ward, Wyeth, Zenith.

References: Hoffman & Meyer (1974) ; Kingsford (1975); Reichenbach-Klinke & Elkan (1965) ; Reichenbach-Klinke & Landolt (1973) ; Van Duijn (1973) .

PENTA—See Pentachlorophenol.

PENTACHLOROPHENOL
Composition: C_6Cl_5OH.
Synonyms: Dowicide G; PCP; Penta; Satobrite; Sodium pentachlorophenate; Weedbeads; Weedone.
Uses or Treatment for: Molluscicide (snails) .
Dosage: 5 ppm.
Remarks: Toxic to *Pimephales promelas* and *Ictalurus punctatus;* biodegrades in 10 days; 8 ppm toxic to trout and *Cyprinus carpio* in 20 to 70 minutes.
References: Clemens & Sneed (1959) ; Crandall & Goodnight (1959) ; Hoffman & Meyer (1974) ; Osborn (1966); Reichenbach-Klinke (1966) ; E. Weber (1965) .

PERCHLORON—See Calcium hypochlorite.

PEROXYDOL—See Sodium perborate.

PERU OIL—See Balsam of Peru oil.

PHANQUONE—See Entobex.

PHEMEROL CHLORIDE—See Benzalkonium chloride.

PHEMEROL CRYSTALS—See Benzalkonium chloride.

PHENASAL—See Niclosamide .

PHENOL
Composition: C_6H_5OH.
Synonyms: None.
Uses or Treatment for: Crustacicide.
Dosage: Unknown.

Remarks: Dangerous to use.
References: Goncharov & Mikryakov (1970); Howland (1969b); Mann (1951).

PHENOTHIAZINE
Composition: Thiodiphenylamine.

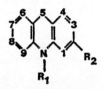

PHENOTHIAZINE

Synonyms: Fenoverm; Nemazine; Phenovis.
Uses or Treatment for: Protozoa *(Hexamita);* Anthelminthic (Cestoda, *Bothriocephalus).*
Dosage: (1) 3 to 4 times, greatly diluted; (2) 75,000 ppm in food; (3) 4-5 gm/kg of fish daily for 3 days.
Remarks: May cause "back peel."
References: Hoffman & Meyer (1974); Kanaev (1967); Kulakovskaya & Musselius (1962); Ivasik & Svirepo (1964); Muzykovski (1968); Nazarova et al. (1969); Reichenbach-Klinke & Elkan (1965); H. Wolf (In Rucker, 1957).

PHENOVIS—See Phenothiazine.

PHENOXETHOL
Composition: 1-hydroxy-2-phenoxyethane.
Synonyms: 2-phenoxyethanol; Chlorophenoxetol.
Uses or Treatment for: Disinfectant; bacteria (bacterial fin rot); fungicide [*Ichthyophonous* (= *Ichthyosporidium) hoferi, Saprolegnia*].
Dosage: (1) Standard solution—1 ml to 99 ml of water; for use, dilute to 10-20 ml/l of water; (2) 100-200 ppm for at least 12 hours.
Remarks: 5000 ppm is toxic to fish; 100 ppm is not toxic to *Lebistes reticulatus* or *Osphronemus.*
References: Amlacher (1970); Hoffman & Meyer (1974); Kingsford (1975); Loader (1963); Rankin (1952); Reichen-

bach-Klinke (1966); Reichenbach-Klinke & Elkan (1965); Reichenbach-Klinke & Landolt (1973); Scott & Warren (1964).

2-PHENOXYETHANOL—See Phenoxethol.

PHENYLMERCURIC ACETATE—See PMA.

PHILIXAN

Composition: Unknown.
Synonyms: None.
Uses or Treatment for: Unknown.
Dosage: Unknown.
Remarks: None.
References: Hoffman & Meyer (1974).

PHOSKIL—See Ethyl parathion.

PICRIC ACID

Composition: 2,4,6-trinitrophenol.
Synonyms: None.
Uses or Treatment for: Monogenetic trematodes; "skin worms."
Dosage: (1) 0.02 gm/l, in the form of a bath for one hour; (2) 20 ppm for one hour.
Remarks: None.
References: Hoffman & Meyer (1974); Reichenbach-Klinke (1966); Reichenbach-Klinke & Elkan (1965); Van Duijn (1973).

PINE NEEDLES

Composition: Leaves of *Pinus sp.*
Synonyms: None.
Uses or Treatment for: Antiprotozoal *(Ichthyophthirius multifiliis).*
Dosage: Nominal amount placed in water.
Remarks: None.
References: Bauer (1959); Hoffman & Meyer (1974).

PLASMOCHIN—See Plasmoquin.

PLASMOCHIN NAPHTHOATE—See Plasmoquin.

PLASMOQUIN

Composition: 6-methóxy-8-(1-methyl-4-diethylamino)   butylaminoquinoline salt of 2,2-dinapthyl-methane 3,3-dicarboxylic acid.

Synonyms: Pamaquine naphthoate; Plasmochin; Plasmochin naphthoate.

Uses or Treatment for: Protozoa (antimalarial, *Ichthyophthirius multifiliis, Cryptocaryon irritans);* skin parasites.

Dosage: (1) 0.01 gm/l of water, in the form of a bath; (2) 0.2 ppm; (3) 20 ppm for 3 to 20 days; (4) 10 ppm.

Remarks: One ppm toxic to *Lebistes reticulatus* in 72 hours at 20°C.

References: Hoffman & Meyer (1974); Reichenbach-Klinke (1966); Reichenbach-Klinke & Elkan (1965); Reichenbach-Klinke & Landolt (1973); Schäperclaus (1954).

PMA

Composition: Pyridyl mercuric acetate.

Synonyms: Nylmerate antiseptic solution concentrate; Phenylmercuric acetate; TAG.

Uses or Treatment for: Algae *(Pyrmnesium);* external parasites; Protozoa [*Ambiphyra* (= *Scyphidia*), *Costia, Colponema, Epistylis, Ichthyophthirius, Trichodina* (= *Cyclochaeta)*]; Monogenea; Hirudinea *(Piscicola salmositica).*

Dosage: (1) 0.2 ppm; (2) 1:500,000; (3) 2-3 ppm for 1 hour.

Remarks: Hazardous to humans, banned by the U.S.D.I. in the United States; LD_{50} = 2 ppm for carp; 5 ppm toxic to *Salmo gairdneri* & trout; 37.6 ppm nontoxic to *Ictalurus punctatus;* 8.4-10 ppm nontoxic to *Lepomis macrochirus* and *Oncorhynchus nerka;* 7.8 ppm nontoxic to *Salvelinus fontinalis;* available as a solution; manufactured by Holland-Rantos.

References: L. Allison (1957); Bryant (1951); Burrows & Palmer (1949); Clemens & Sneed (1958, 1959); Earp & Schwab (1954); Foster & Olson (1951); Hoffman & Meyer (1974); H. Johnson (1956); Reichenbach-Klinke (1966); Reichenbach-Klinke & Landolt (1973); Rogers et al. (1951); Rucker & Whipple (1951); Sarig (1971); Snieszko (1949); Van Horn & Katz (1946); Willford (1967a).

POLYCILLN—See Ampicillin, sodium.

POLYMYXIN B, sulfate
Composition: Antibiotic derived from *Bacillus polymyxa.*
Synonyms: Aerosporin.
Uses or Treatment for: Gram-negative bacteria.
Dosage: Undetermined.
Remarks: Often used in combination with Neomycin and/or Bacitracin; has a shelf life of 2 weeks plus; moderately effective in salt water; produced by BW, Pfizer Labs; available as a powder.
References: Kingsford (1975).

POTASSIUM ANTIMONY TARTRATE
Composition: $C_4H_4KO_7Sb.$
Synonyms: Tartar emetic.
Uses or Treatment for: Monogenea; Nematoda (schistosomiasis).
Dosage: 1.5 ppm.
Remarks: None.
References: Hoffman & Meyer (1974); Reichenbach-Klinke (1966); Van Duijn (1973).

POTASSIUM CHLORATE
Composition: $KClO_3.$
Synonyms: None.
Uses or Treatment for: Crustacea *(Salmincola).*
Dosage: 0.20% (2000 ppm).
Remarks: Used as an explosive; kills larvae only.
References: Fasten (1912); Hoffman & Meyer (1974); Kabata (1970).

POTASSIUM CHLORIDE
Composition: KCl.
Synonyms: None.
Uses or Treatment for: Molluscicide (snails).
Dosage: (1) $CuCl_2$ + KCl (1.4 ppm); (2) $CuCl_2$ (5 pt) + KCl (6 pt) in water at 20 ppm.
Remarks: Nontoxic to *Lebistes reticulatus;* available in medical quality as sterile solutions and tablets; manufactured by Abbott, Amer Quinine, APC, Arcum, Atlas Pharceut, Barre, Bates, Canfield, Columbia Medic, Corvit, CPI, Cutter Labs,

Elkins-Sinn, Fellows, Hartford, Hyrex, Invenex, Kirkman, Lannett, Lentag, Lilly, Lyne, MCC-M, PRL, Progress, Rondex, Stanley Drug, Stayner, Steri-Med, Towne, Travenol, United, Upsher Smith, Vitarine.

References: Floch et al. (1964) ; Hoffman & Meyer (1974) .

POTASSIUM DICHROMATE

Composition: $K_2Cr_2O_7$.

Synonyms: None.

Uses or Treatment for: Wound disinfection; skin parasites; Fungi *(Saprolegnia)*; Protozoa [*Ambiphyra* (= *Scyphidia*), *Trichodina* (= *Cyclochaeta*)]; Monogenea *(Cleidodiscus)*.

Dosage: (1) 10 gm/l of water; (2) 0.005 gm/l as a long duration bath of several days; (3) 20 ppm; (4) 2 ppm daily as needed; (5) 5 ppm for 16 hours; (6) 10 ppm; (7) 1 gm/6 gal of seawater in marine aquaria for fungus.

Remarks: Toxic to many species of fish.

References: Hoffman & Meyer (1974); Kingsford (1975); Meehean (1937) ; Reichenbach-Klinke (1966) ; Reichenbach-Klinke & Elkan (1965) .

POTASSIUM HYDROXIDE

Composition: KOH.

Synonyms: Caustic potash.

Uses or Treatment for: Protozoa *(Myxosoma cerebralis)*.

Dosage: (1) 1000 ppm (not effective in 14 days) ; (2) 10,000 ppm (effective in 2 days) .

Remarks: May have severe effects on fish, not recommended.

References: Hoffman & Hoffman (1972) ; Hoffman & Meyer (1974) .

POTASSIUM IODIDE + IODINE SOLUTION

Composition: KI + I.

Synonyms: None.

Uses or Treatment for: Goiter; benign tumors of the thyroid.

Dosage: (1) Dissolve 0.1 gm of Iodine and ten gm of KI in 100 cc distilled water, add 0.5 cc per liter of water as a long duration bath; (2) mixed into the food—1:2500.

Remarks: Ineffective in cancer of the thyroid; Potassium iodide is available as tablets and solutions; manufactured by

Barre, BBC, Invenex, Jenkins, Lilly, Lyne, PRL, Robinson Labs, Sheraton, Stanley Drug, Vale Chemical, Zemmer.

References: Amlacher (1970); Herman (1972); Schubert (1974) ; Reichenbach-Klinke & Elkan (1965) .

POTASSIUM PENICILLIN G—See Penicillin, potassium.

POTASSIUM PERMANGANATE

Composition: KMnO₄.

Synonyms: None.

Uses or Treatment for: External parasites; external lesions; bacteria (bacteria on skin) ; Fungi *(Saprolegnia,* Achylasis); Protozoa *(Costia, Chilodonella, Cryptocaryon irritans, Epistylis, Ichthyophthirius, Ichthyobodo, Trichodina);* Monogenea *(Benedenia, Cleidodiscus, Dactylogyrus, Gyrodactylus);* Hirudinea (leeches) ; Crustacea *(Argulus, Lernaea).*

Dosage: (1) 20 ppm for one hour; (2) 1 gm/100 l of water— short bath of 90 minutes in a special receptacle; (3) 1 gm/l of water—immersion bath of 30 to 45 seconds; (4) 1 gm/10 l of water—short bath of 5 to 10 seconds; (5) 1 gm/50 l of water as a disinfectant; (6) add 1 gm/100 l of water at 1 cc/l of water as a bath for 30 minutes, 0.01% for 10 minutes, 0.5% for 5 minutes, 0.10% for 2 minutes; (7) 5-10 ppm for 1 to 2 hours; (8) 3-5 ppm in ponds and aquariums for an indefinite period; (9) 5000 ppm; (10) 1000 ppm (1:1000) as a dip for 10 to 45 seconds; (11) 1000 ppm as a flush for 5 to 10 minutes; (12) NaCl (7000 ppm) + KMnO₄ (4-45 ppm) ; (13) 10,000 ppm (not effective as a disinfectant against *Myxosoma cerebralis);* (14) 500 ppm as a dip for 5 minutes; (15) 1000 ppm as a dip for 2 minutes; (16) 50,000 ppm as a dip; (17) 4-5 mg/l (0.25- 0.3 gr/Imp gal or 0.2-0.25 gr/U.S. gal.) added to water, repeat in 10 days if necessary (for *Argulus).*

Remarks: 1-2 ppm may be used to detoxify Antimycin A and Rotenone; effectiveness may be altered by water chemistry or high organic content; alkaline or slightly acid water may cause manganese to precipitate onto a fish's gills; aerate well when using; antiseptic and/or disinfectant; acts by liberating free oxygen; 10 ppm toxic to *Stizostedion sp.;* 11.8 ppm toxic to young *Anguilla* in 8 hours; 6-10 ppm = LC₁₀₀ in *Carassius auratus* in 18 hours; 12 ppm toxic to *Gambusia affinis;* 20 ppm toxic to *Lebistes reticulatus;* 3 ppm = LC_{100} in *Lepomis macrochirus;* 4 ppm = LC_{100} in *Micropterus salmoides;* 20 ppm toxic to *Osphronemus;* 5 ppm = LC_{100} to *Pimephales promelas;* 1.7 ppm = LC_{16} in young *Roccus saxatilis* in 96 hours at 21°C; 6.25 ppm toxic to trout in 24 hours; 9.1 ppm nontoxic to *Ictalurus punctatus* in 1 hour at 25°C, and 3.2 ppm was nontoxic in 24 hours at 25°C; 3 ppm nontoxic to *Dorosoma cepedianum;* available as tablets or crystals; manufactured by Barre, Bowman Pharm, Lilly.

References: R. Allison (1957a); Amlacher (1961b, 1970); Brunner (1943); Chen (1933); Clemens & Sneed (1959); Fish (1933); Fletcher (1961); Gopalakrishnan (1963); Herman (1972); Hess (1930); Hofer (In Mellen, 1928); Hoffman & Hoffman (1972); Hoffman & Meyer (1974); Kabata (1970); Khan (1944); Kingsbury & Embody (1932); Kingsford (1975); Kislev & Ivleva (1950); Kumar (1958); Lahav, Sarig, and Shilo (1964); Lawrence (1956); McKee & Wolf (1963); Meehean (1937); Peterson et al. (1966); Prevost (1934); Reichenbach-Klinke (1966); Reichenbach-Klinke & Elkan (1965); Reichenbach-Klinke & Landolt (1973); Sarig (1966, 1971); Schäperclaus (1954); Schubert (1974); Scott & Warren (1964); Shilo et al. (1960); Snieszko (1975); Van Duijn (1973); Wellborn (1969); L. Wolf (1935a, 1935b); Yin Weng Yin et al. (1963); Yui-fan et al. (1967).

POTENTIATED SULFONAMIDE—See Sulfadimethoxine sodium.

POVIDONE-IODINE

Composition: A water soluble complex of polyvinylpyrrolidone and Iodine.

Synonyms: Betadine; Isodine; PVP-1.

Uses or Treatment for: Disinfection of skin; disinfection of fish eggs.

Dosage: (1) 100 ml/l—painted on skin; (2) 100 ml/l—as a bath for 10 minutes.

Remarks: See also Betadine; manufactured by Blair, Purdue; available as a solution.

References: Reichenbach-Klinke & Elkan (1965) .

PR-3714

Composition: Experimental compound by Abbott Laboratories.

Synonyms: None.

Uses or Treatment for: Protozoa [*Hexamita (= Octomites)*].

Dosage: 2000 ppm in dry food for 3 days.

Remarks: None.

References: Hoffman & Meyer (1974) ; Yasutake et al. (1961).

PRIASOL—See Lysol.

PRIMAQUINE PHOSPHATE

Composition: Primaquine phosphate.

Synonyms: None.

Uses or Treatment for: Protozoa *(Cryptocaryon irritans).*

Dosage: 15 mg/gal in salt water.

Remarks: Prolonged treatment may result in dark pigmentation of the fish, but this resolves itself upon discontinuance of treatment; available as tablets (26.3 mg) ; manufactured by Winthrop.

References: Kingsford (1975) .

PRODOXUR—See Baygon.

PROPOQUIN—See Ampyroquin.

PROPOXATE

Composition: Unknown.

Synonyms: R7464.

Uses or Treatment for: General fish anesthesia.

Dosage: 4-8 ppm in water will anesthetize a fish for 10 to 15 minutes with recovery in approximately 20 minutes at a water temperature of 17°C.

Remarks: Not recommended, as it is not available in the U.S. and is an experimental drug; produced by Janssen Pharmaceuticals, England.

References: "General Anesthesia in Exotics." *Vet Med Small Anim Clin,* Sept. 1974, p. 1185; Thienpoint & Niemegeers (1965) .

PVP-1—See Betadine or Povidone-Iodine.

PYOKTANIA—See Gentian violet.

PYRETHRUM

Composition: Extract of *Chrysanthemum sp.*

Synonyms: Pyrethrins.

Uses or Treatment for: Crustacea *(Argulus);* insecticide.

Dosage: (1) 0.01 ppm fatal to *Argulus*—10 ppm fatal to fish—20-100 ppm for 10 to 20 minute bath; (2) 0.01 ppm for 50 minutes; (3) 0.1 ppm for 20 minutes; (4) 10 ppm for 3 minutes; (5) 20 ppm for 1 minute.

Remarks: 1% powder not a suitable formulation.

References: Bauer (1966) ; Dogiel et al. (1958) ; Hoffman & Meyer (1974) ; Kabata (1970) ; Kemper (1933) ; Stammer (1959) .

PYRETHRINS—See Pyrethrum.

PYRIMETHAMINE—See Daraprim.

QUATERNARY AMMONIUM COMPOUNDS

Composition: Various cationic surface-acting anti-infective detergents or soaps.

Synonyms: Benzalkonium chloride; Hyamine; Roccal.

Uses or Treatment for: Bacteria [Bacterial gill disease, cold-water disease *(Cytophaga psychrophila),* Columnaris *(Chondrococcus columnaris)*].

Dosage: 2-4 ppm (active ingredient) —1 hour bath.

Remarks: See also Benzalkonium chloride, Hyamine.

References: Amlacher (1970) ; Rucker et al. (1949) ; Snieszko (1975) .

QUICKLIME—See Calcium oxide.

QUINACRINE—See Atabrine hydrochloride.

QUINACRINE HYDROCHLORIDE—See Atabrine hydrochloride.

QUINALDINE

Composition: Quinaldine sulfate.

Synonyms: None.

Uses or Treatment for: Anesthetic; fish tranquilizer.

Dosage: Dilute 20:1 with Ethyl alcohol or Acetone (stock solution) , spray into water or gills of fish.

Remarks: CAUTION: Acetone will burn fish's gills, use only in absence of other suitable solvent; vodka or other alcoholic beverage may be substituted for Ethyl alcohol; manufactured by Kodak.

References: Allen & Sills (1973); Amlacher (1970); Dawson & Marking (1973); Dempster (1973); Gilderhus et al. (1973a); Goldstein (1973); Lobel (1974); Locke (1969); Marking (1969a); Marking & Dawson (1973); Reichenbach-Klinke & Landolt (1973); Schoettger & Julin (1969); Sills et al. (1973a); Zeiller (1972).

QUININE HYDROCHLORIDE

Composition: Extract of *Cinchona sp.* bark.

Synonyms: None.

Uses or Treatment for: Skin parasites; Protozoa [*Chilodonella, Costia, Cryptocaryon irritans, Ichthyophthirius, Trichodina (= Cyclochaeta)*]; Monogenea (*Gyrodactylus elegans*).

Dosage: (1) 1 gm to 50-100 l of water (Monogenea); (2) 10 ppm for 7 hours (not effective); (3) 20 ppm for 24 hours; (4) 13-20 ppm as needed at 4 day intervals, change water after each second treatment (salt water); (5) 20 ppm for 3 to 10 days daily; (6) 10-15 ppm in water for indefinite time; (7) 8-12 mg/gal in salt water.

Remarks: Substitute for Quinine sulfate; toxic reaction in fish is evidenced by loss of equilibrium, lying on bottom, rapid breathing, and loss of appetite; Antidote: change water; toxic to carp fry; 100 ppm = LC_1 in 48 hours at 17°C to *Ictalurus punctatus, Lepomis macrochirus, Salmo gairdneri, S. trutta, Salvelinus fontinalis,* and *S. namaycush.*

References: De Graaf (1962); Gopalakrishnan (1963, 1964); Loader (1963); Reichenbach-Klinke (1966); Reichenbach-Klinke & Elkan (1965); Reichenbach-Klinke & Landolt (1973); Schäperclaus (1954); Snieszko (1975); Willford (1967a); Van Duijn (1973).

QUININE SULFATE

Composition: Extract of *Cinchona sp.* bark.

Synonyms: None.

Uses or Treatment for: Protozoa *(Cryptocaryon irritans, Ich-thyophthirius).*

Dosage: (1) 1 gm to 75-100 l of water; (2) 10 ppm—killed trophs in 7 hours at 20°C; (3) 6.4 ppm applied daily for 2 days; (4) 10-15 ppm in water for indefinite time.

Remarks: Substitute for Quinine hydrochloride; 100 ppm was not toxic to *Ictalurus punctatus* in one hour at 23°C; available as capsules, tablets, or powder (bulk) ; manufactured by Aberdeen, Amer Quinine, APC, Arcum, Barre, Barrows, Bates, Canfield, Carchem, Columbia Medic, Cord, Corvit, FTP, Invenex, Kirkman, Lannett, Lilly, Linden, MCD, PD, Premo, Purepac Pharm, Rexall, Robinson Lab, Rondex, Rowell, SCA, Scruggs, Stanley Drug, Stayner, Tablroc, Towne, United, Vitarine, West-Ward, Xttrium, Zenith.

References: Clemens & Sneed (1959) ; Kingsford (1975); Loader (1963) ; Peterson et al. (1966) ; Reichenbach-Klinke (1966) ; Reichenbach-Klinke & Elkan (1965) ; Reichenbach-Klinke & Landolt (1973) ; Schäperclaus (1954) ; Snieszko (1975) .

RANCILLIN—See Ampicillin trihydrate.

REGLONE—See Diquat.

RESISTOMYCIN—See Kanamycin.

RESISTOX—See 7-Co-Ral.

RIFAMPIN

Composition: A semisynthetic antibiotic derived from *Streptomyces mediterranei.*

Synonyms: Rifadin; Rimactane.

Uses or Treatment for: Bacteria (fish tuberculosis) .

Dosage: In food—6 mg/100 gm of food.

Remarks: Works well in conjunction with Isoniazid; insoluble in water; available as capsules (300 mg) ; manufactured by CIBA.

References: Kingsford (1975) .

RIMACTANE—See Rifampin.

RIVANOL

Composition: 6,9-diamino-2-ethoxyacridine lactate · (monohydrate) .

Synonyms: None.

Uses or Treatment for: Disinfectant; skin parasites; fungus; Protozoa *(Ichthyophthirius);* Monogenea.

Dosage: (1) gm/500 l of water; (2) 2.5 mg/l of water in the form of a bath; (3) 10 ppm; (4) 2-5 ppm; (5) 100 mg dissolved in 100 ml of hot water, after cooling, swab onto affected areas, repeat in 48 hours if necessary; do not allow solution to get into gill cavity.

Remarks: 5.6 ppm nontoxic to *Ictalurus punctatus;* 10 ppm nontoxic to *Lebistes.*

References: Amlacher (1961b, 1970) ; Clemens & Sneed (1959) ; Hoffman & Meyer (1974); Reichenbach-Klinke (1966); Reichenbach-Klinke & Elkan (1965) ; Reichenbach-Klinke & Landolt (1973) ; Schäperclaus (1954) ; Schubert (1974) .

RO-AMPEN—See Ampicillin trihydrate.

ROCCAL—See Benzalkonium chloride

ROCK SALT—See Sodium chloride.

RONNEL—See Korlan.

ROQUINE—See Chloroquine phosphate.

ROTENONE

Composition: Most commonly derived from derris roots but may be found in other weeds from the eastern United States.

Synonyms: Cube; Derris; Timbo powder; Rotenoil.

Uses or Treatment for: Fish toxicant.

Dosage: Add to water in sufficient quantity to kill fish.

Remarks: Even distribution over water surface is required for reliable fish kills; 1-2 ppm of Potassium permanganate will detoxify Rotenone.

References: Herman (1972) ; Howland (1969a) ; Menn (1976) .

RUELENE

Composition: 4-*tert*-butyl-2-chlorophenyl *N*-methyl *O*-methylphosphoramidate.

Synonyms: None.

Uses or Treatment for: Protozoa (Ichthyophthirius); Monogenea *(Cleidodiscus);* Crustacea *(Lernaea cyprinacea);* insecticide. •

Dosage: (1) 1 ppm (not effective against Ich) ; (2) 0.53 ppm; (3) 0.1% in diet; (4) 0.25 ppm weekly for 4 weeks (not effective against *Lernaea*).

Remarks: Concentrations up to 28.4 ppm did not exceed LC_1 in *Ictalurus punctatus, Lepomis macrochirus, Salmo gairdneri, S. trutta, Salvelinus fontinalis,* and *S. namaycush.*

References: R. Allison (1969) ; Hoffman & Meyer (1974); Willford (1967a) .

SALICYLIC ACID

Composition: Orthohydroxybenzoic acid.

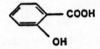

SALICYLIC ACID

Synonyms: None.

Uses or Treatment for: Monogenea *(Gyrodactylus).*

Dosage: 11 ppm for 30 minutes.

Remarks: Available as powder (microcrystals) .

References: Hofer (In Mellen, 1928) ; Hoffman & Meyer (1974) .

SALT—See Sodium chloride.

SALUFER—See Sodium fluosilicate.

SANTONIN

Composition: Extract of dried *Artemisia maritina* (Levant wormwood) .

Synonyms: Artemisin.

Uses or Treatment for: Anthelminthic; Nematoda (roundworms); Cestoda *(Contracaecum bidentatum).*

Dosage: 0.04 gm/fish, combined with sugar and animal fat.

Remarks: Has been used on sturgeon; a very ancient folk remedy.

References: Agapova (1957); Hoffman & Meyer (1974); Snieszko (1975) .

SAPONIN

Composition: Saprogenin glycosides.

Synonyms: None.

Uses or Treatment for:　Fish toxicant; molluscicide (snails).
Dosage:　15-18 kg/hectare, apply to pond bottom before filling.
Remarks:　Toxic to fish.
References:　Hoffman & Meyer (1974).

SATOBRITE—See Pentachlorophenol.

SEAWATER

Composition:　Normal ocean water or synthetic sea salts.
Synonyms:　None.
Uses or Treatment for:　Hirudinea *(Piscicola salmositica).*
Dosage:　Immerse freshwater fish in 100% seawater for one hour (if able to tolerate that length of time).
Remarks:　Effective on *Oncorhynchus gorbuscha.*
References:　Earp & Schwab (1954) ; Hoffman & Meyer (1974).

SEROMYCIN—See Cycloserine.

SHELL NO-PEST STRIP—See DDVP.

SILVER NITRATE

Composition:　$AgNO_3$.
Synonyms:　None.
Uses or Treatment for:　Wounds; mycoses *(Saprolegnia).*
Dosage:　(1) 10 gm/l stock solution; (2) 10,000 ppm applied topically.
Remarks:　0.004 ppm toxic to *Gasterosteus aculeatus;* available in solution form from Day-Baldwin, Lilly, PD.
References:　Hoffman & Meyer (1974) ; Reichenbach-Klinke (1966) ; Reichenbach-Klinke & Elkan (1965).

SILVER PROTEIN—See Silvol.

SILVOL

Composition:　Commercial formulation.
Synonyms:　Argyrol; Silver protein (mild).
Uses or Treatment. for:　Disinfectant; Trematoda *(Microcotyle).*
Dosage:　20,000 ppm as a dip for 3 minutes.
Remarks:　Available as crystals or solution (20%) ; manufactured by Cooper.
References:　Hoffman & Meyer (1974) ; Mellen (1928).

666—See Benzene hexachloride.

SLAKED LIME—See Calcium hydroxide or Lime.

SODIUM BORATE

Composition: $Na_2B_4O_7$.

Synonyms: Dobell's solution; Sodium pyroborate; Sodium tetraborate.

Uses or Treatment for: Protozoa *(Myxosoma cerebralis)*.

Dosage: 1000 ppm (not effective against *Myxosoma* in 14 days).

Remarks: Available as solutions; manufactured by Barre, BBC, Purepac Pharm.

References: Hoffman & Hoffman (1972); Hoffman & Meyer (1974).

SODIUM CHLORATE

Composition: $NaClO_3$.

Synonyms: None.

Uses or Treatment for: Protozoa *(Chilodonella)*; Mongenea *(Dactylogyrus)*.

Dosage: (1) 50,000 ppm; (2) 3000 ppm.

Remarks: May be toxic to fry.

References: Hoffman & Meyer (1974); Popov & Jankov (1968).

SODIUM CHLORIDE

Composition: NaCl.

Synonyms: Rock salt; Table salt.

Uses or Treatment for: Fungus *(Saprolegnia)*; external freshwater protozoa [*Ambiphyra pyriformis, Bodomonas, Chilodonella, Costia, Epistylis, Ichthyobodo, Ichthyophthirius, Trichodina (= Cyclochaeta)*]; ectoparasitic worms; Monogenea *(Dactylogyrus, Gyrodactylus)*; Hirudinea (leeches, *Piscicola geometra, P. salmositica)*; Crustacea *(Argulus, Lernaea cyprinacea, Salmincola)*.

Dosage: (1) 10-15 gm/l of water as a short bath of 20 minutes; (2) 25 gm/l of water as a short bath of 10-15 minutes; (3) first day—26.6 gm/gal (0.7% solution), second day—replace one-half of water with 41.8 gm/gal (1.1% solution), third day—

replace one-half of water with 49.4 gm/gal (1.3% solution), provided water temperature is not below 14°C (57°F) (for *Lernaea*), may be continued for 2 to 3 weeks; (4) 20 ppm; (5) 30,000 ppm as a dip (until fish shows signs of distress) or 5 to 10 minutes to one hour; (6) 2000 ppm; (7) 4000 ppm; (8) 10,000 pm daily as a dip for 2 to 10 minutes to 1 hour as needed; (9) 15,000 ppm daily for 20 minutes as needed; (10) 17,500 ppm as a dip for 3 minutes daily as needed; (11) 25,000 ppm as a dip for 2 to 30 seconds or as a flush for 10 to 15 minutes daily as needed; (12) 175,500 ppm as a dip for 3 minutes per day as needed; (13) 10,000 ppm as a dip for 15 to 30 minutes; (14) 30,000 ppm NaCl + 66 ppm Malachite green as a dip; (15) 20,000 ppm for 15 minutes to 1 hour daily as needed; (16) 7000 ppm built up to 15,000 ppm; (17) 50,000 ppm for from 90 seconds to 2 to 10 minutes daily as needed; (18) 1000 ppm; (19) 6500 ppm; (20) NaCl (7000 ppm) + KMnO$_4$ (4-4.5 ppm); (21) MgSO$_4$ (300,000 ppm) + NaCl (70,000 ppm) as a dip for 5 to 10 minutes; (22) 3000 ppm; (23) MgSO$_4$ (30,000 ppm) + NaCl (7000 ppm) as a flush for 5 to 10 minutes; (24) 100% seawater for one hour; (25) build up to 130,000 ppm in 3 days; (26) 13,000 ppm daily for 4 days; (27) 1-3% in water for from 30 minutes to 2 hours, for freshwater fish only (leeches, skin flukes).

Remarks: Fresh water only remedy; never use a galvanized (zinc) container; 30,000 ppm toxic to *Salmo gairdneri* fry; available as tablets (USP) of medical quality from United and Robinson Labs; Available as crystals of medical purity from Abbott, Atlas Pharceut, Barre, Canfield, CPI, Cutter labs, Elkins-Sinn, Fellows, Invenex, Lilly, PD, Stanley drug, Stayner, USV, Winston, Wyeth.

References: K. Allen & Avault (1970); L. Allison (1950); Amlacher (1961b, 1970); Bauer (1958, 1959, 1966); Bauer & Strelkov (1959); Butcher (1947); Chen (1933); Davis (1953); Dempster (1970a); Edminister & Gray (1948); Fasten (1912); Fischthal (1949); Gopalakrishnan (1963, 1964, 1966); Guberlet et al. (1927); Herbert & Mann (1958); Herman (1972); Hoffman & Meyer (1974); Hora & Pillay (1962);

Ivasik & Svirepo (1964); Kabata (1970); Khan (1944); Leitritz (1960); Lotan (1960); McKee & Wolf (1963); F. Meyer
(1969a); Nakai & Kokai (1931); Reichenbach-Klinke & Elkan
(1965); Reichenbach-Klinke & Landolt (1973); Rucker &
Whipple (1951); Schäperclaus (1954); Shilo et al. (1960);
Sneiszko (1975); Tebo & McCoy (1964); Tripathi (1954);
Van Duijn (1973); Yousuf-Ali (1968).

SODIUM CHLORITE
Composition: NaClO$_2$.
Synonyms: Chlorite +.
Uses or Treatment for: Bacteriostatic agent; Protozoa *(Cryp-
tocaryon irritans, Ichthyophthirius).*
Dosage: 2-5 ppm in fresh water.
Remarks: 12 ppm nontoxic to freshwater fish; may be toxic to
marine invertebrates under certain conditions.
References: Dempster (1970b); Garibaldi (1971); Hoffman
& Meyer (1974); Kingsford (1975).

SODIUM CYANIDE
Composition: NaCN.
Synonyms: None.
Uses or Treatment for: Fish toxicant.
Dosage: (1) 50 ppm fatal (acute toxicity); (2) 1-2 ppm
(chronic toxicity).
Remarks: Used extensively in foreign countries (especially
the Phillipines) in the collection of marine fish; however, it
is lethal, and the practice is deplorable.
References: Herwig (1976).

SODIUM FLUOSILICATE
Composition: Sodium hexafluorosilicate (Na$_2$SiF$_6$).
Synonyms: Salufer.
Uses or Treatment for: Cestoda *(Bothriocephalus);* rodenti-
cide.
Dosage: 10,000 ppm in food for 3 days.
Remarks: Not effective.
References: Hoffman & Meyer (1974); Klenov (1970).

SODIUM HYDROXIDE

Composition: NaOH.

Synonyms: Caustic soda; Lye.

Uses or Treatment for: Protozoa *(Ichthyophthirius)*.

Dosage: 10 ppm.

Remarks: Not effective against Ich.

References: Hoffman & Meyer (1974) .

SODIUM HYPOCHLORITE

Composition: NaOCl.

Synonyms: Chlorine bleach; Clorox; Household bleach; Zonite.

Uses or Treatment for: Disinfection of tanks and equipment; viracidal agent; Protozoa *(Discocotyle)*.

Dosage: (1) 200 ppm for one hour; (2) 10 ppm for 24 hours; (3) 265 ppm as a dip for two minutes; (4) 1 tsp/gal to sterilize raw seawater.

Remarks: May be neutralized with Sodium thiosulfate.

References: Amlacher (1970) ; Hoffman & Meyer (1974); Kingsford (1975) ; Laird & Embody (1931) .

SODIUM METHACILLIN—See Methacillin sodium.

SODIUM PENTACHLOROPHENATE—See Pentachlorophenol.

SODIUM PENTACHLOROPHENOL—See Pentachlorophenol.

SODIUM PERBORATE PEROXYDOL

Composition: $NaBO_3 \cdot 4H_2O$.

Synonyms: None.

Uses or Treatment for: Industrial bleach; Monogenea *(Benedenia seriolae)*.

Dosage: (1) 500 ppm as a dip for 8.5 minutes; (2) 1000 ppm for 30 minutes (as a flush) ; (3) 1000 ppm as a dip for 2 to 3 minutes; (4) 10,000 ppm as a dip for 1 minute.

Remarks: None.

References: Hoffman & Meyer (1974) ; Hoshina (1966); Kasahara (1967, 1968) .

SODIUM PEROXIDE PYROPHOSPHATE

Composition: Sodium peroxide pyrophosphate.

Synonyms: None.
Uses or Treatment for: Disinfectant; Monogenea.
Dosage: (1) 1000 ppm; (2) 10,000 ppm as a dip for 15 to 30 seconds.
Remarks: Interchangeable with Sodium pyrophosphate peroxyhydrate.
References: Hoffman & Meyer (1974); Hoshina (1966); Kasahara (1967).

SODIUM PYROBORATE—See Sodium borate.

SODIUM PYROPHOSPHATE PEROXYHYDRATE
Composition: Sodium pyrophosphate peroxyhydrate.
Synonyms: None.
Uses or Treatment for: Disinfectant; Monogenea.
Dosage: (1) 1000 ppm; (2) 10,000 ppm as a dip for 15 to 30 seconds.
Remarks: Interchangeable with Sodium peroxide pyrophosphate.
References: Hoffman & Meyer (1974).

SODIUM SULFADIAZINE—See Sulfadiazine.

SODIUM TETRABORATE—See Sodium borate.

SODIUM THIOSULFATE
Composition: Sodium thiosulfate.
Synonyms: Hypo; Tioclean.
Uses or Treatment for: Dechlorination of water and neutralization of chlorine bleach.
Dosage: (1) 1 gm/10 l of water; (2) 1 drop/gal (various commercial formulations).
Remarks: Available as sterile solutions of medical purity from Atlas Pharceut, Bel-Mar, Dorasol, Lilly.
References: Amlacher (1970); Reichenbach-Klinke & Elkan (1965); Reichenbach-Klinke & Landolt (1973).

SODIZOLE—See Sulfisoxazole.

STAPHCILLIN—See Methacillin sodium.

STOVARSOLAN—See Acetarsone.

STOVARSOL—See Acetarsone.

STREPTOMYCIN

Composition: Dihydrostreptomycin.

STREPTOMYCIN

Synonyms: Streptomycin sulfate; Strycin.

Uses or Treatment for: Bacteria (gram-positive and gram-negative bacteria, bacterial hemorrhagic septicemia, *Aeromonas punctata*, fish tuberculosis, *Pseudomonas*).

Dosage: (1) 5-10 mg/150-400 gm of fish body weight as intraperitoneal injection; (2) as per Chloramphenicol, with dosage a little higher, as its effect is slightly weaker; (3) 3-4 mg/100 gm intraperitoneally; (4) 40 mg/gal in salt water.

Remarks: One-third of activity of Chloramphenicol; not effective in salt water; greatest efficiency when used in conjunction with other drugs; available as sterile powder or sterile solution; manufactured by Amer Quinine, Lannett, Lilly, Pfizer Labs, Premo, Upjohn, Wyeth.

References: Amlacher (1970); Herman (1972); Kingsford (1975); Reichenbach-Klinke & Elkan (1965); Reichenbach-Klinke & Landolt (1973).

STREPTOMYCIN SULFATE—See Streptomycin.

STRYCIN—See Streptomycin.

SULFACETAMIDE—See Albucid.

SULFACETAMIDE SODIUM—See Albucid.

SULFACYL—See Albucid.

SULFADIAZINE

Composition: Sulfapyrimidine compound.

$$H_2N - \langle \rangle - SO_2NH - \langle \rangle$$

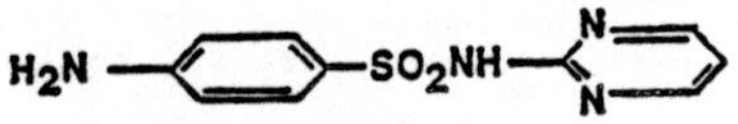

SULFADIAZINE

Synonyms: Sulfadiazine sodium.

Uses or Treatment for: Bacteria (bacterial diseases, gram-negative and some gram-positive bacteria).

Dosage: 100-250 mg/l of water as a long duration bath.

Remarks: Will precipitate in water with pH below 9; shelf life of 1 day when in solution; available as tablets; manufactured by Abbott, Amer Quinine, Arcum, Barre, Canfield, Carchem, Cord, Corvit, Day Baldwin, Kaser, Lederle, Lilly, MA, PD, Premo, Scruggs, Stanley Drug, United, Upjohn, Vale Chemical, Vitarine, West-Ward, Zemmer.

References: Amlacher (1970); Kingsford (1975); Reichenbach-Klinke & Elkan (1965); Reichenbach-Klinke & Landolt (1973); Rucker et al. (1951).

SULFADIAZINE SODIUM—See Sulfadiazine.

SULFADIMETHOXINE SODIUM

Composition: Sulfapyrimidine compound.

Synonyms: Madribon; Potentiated sulfonamide.

Uses or Treatment for: Bacteria (Furunculosis, systemic infections).

Dosage: (1) 100-200 mg (calculated as pure drug)/kg of food; (2) Potentiated sulfonamide—used with feed at 50 mg/kg of fish per day.

Remarks: Available in Japan as a 10% powder; Potentiated sulfonamide is Sulfadimethoxine potentiated with Ormetroprim; available as 500 mg tablets; manufactured in U.S. by Roche.

References: Snieszko (1975).

SULFAETHIDOLE—See Globucid.

SULFAGUANIDINE

Composition: Sulfonamide preparation.

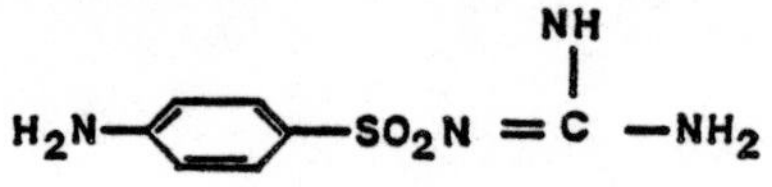

$$H_2N--SO_2N = \overset{\overset{\displaystyle NH}{|}}{C} -NH_2$$

SULFAGUANIDINE

Synonyms: None.

Uses or Treatment for: Bacteria (bacterial diseases).

Dosage: As per sulfamerazine.

Remarks: Available as tablets; manufactured by Robinson Lab.

References: Reichenbach-Klinke & Elkan (1965); Reichenbach-Klinke & Landolt (1973).

SULFALENE—See Emtrysidina.

SULFALENE +—See Emtrysidina.

SULFAMERAZINE

Composition: Sulfonamide compound.

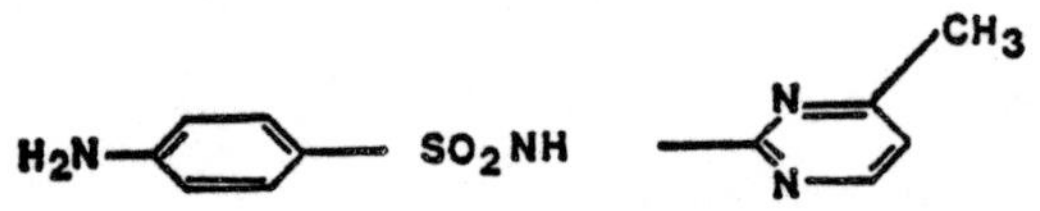

$$H_2N-- SO_2NH -^{CH_3}$$

SULFAMERAZINE

Synonyms: None.

Uses or Treatment for: Bacteria [bacterial diseases, Columnaris disease, kidney disease *(Cornybacterium)*, cold-water disease, Furunculosis *(Aeromonas salmonicida)*, nephritis, redmouth disease of trout, ulcers].

Dosage: (1) 22-24 gm/100 kg/day in feed for 14 days; (1) 100-200 mg/kg of fish mixed into the food every first to third day; (3) 200 mg/kg of body weight per day with food for 14 days.

Remarks: Effective substitutes are Sulfamethazine, Sulfisoxazole; law requires that treatments must be stopped for 21 days before fishes are killed for human consumption; see also Sulfisoxazole; available as tablet (with Sodium bicarbonate) ; manufactured by Jenkins.

References: Amlacher (1970) ; Gutsell & Snieszko (1949a, 1949b) ; Herman (1972) ; Herman & Degurse (1967) ; Johnson & Bruce (1953); Reichenbach-Klinke & Elkan (1965); Reichenbach-Klinke & Landolt (1973) ; Snieszko (1975) ; Snieszko & Friddle (1949, 1952) ; L. Wolf (1947) .

SULFAMETHAZINE—See Sulfamethazine, sodium.

SULFAMETHAZINE, Sodium

Composition: N^1-(4,6-dimethyl-2-pyrimidinyl)sulfanilamide.

Synonyms: Diazil; Mefenal; Sulfamezathine; Sulfamidine.

Uses or Treatment for: Antimicrobial; bacteria [cold-water disease *(Cytophaga psychophila),* Columnaris disease *(Chondrococcus columnaris),* Furunculosis, kidney disease *(Corynbacterium),* peduncle disease, *Vibrio anguillarum];* Protozoa *(Ichthyophthirius).*

Dosage: (1) 22-24 gm/100 kg of fish weight per day in feed for 14 days; (2) 100-200 mg/kg of fish weight per day for 10 to 20 days; (3) 10 ppm once a week for 2 to 3 weeks; (4) for prophylaxis—2 gm/kg per day depending on the type of food with which it is used.

Remarks: Substitutes are Sulfamerazine, Sulfisoxazole; 100 ppm did not exceed LC_1 in *Ictalurus punctatus, Lepomis macrochirus, Salmo gairdneri, S. trutta, Salvelinus fontinalis, S. namaycush.*

References: Amend & Fryer (1968) ; Amend et al. (1965, 1967) ; Amlacher (1970) ; Herman (1972) ; Hoffman & Meyer (1974) ; Postema (1956) ; Snieszko (1975) ; Willford (1967a); E. Wood et al. (1957) .

SULFAMIDINE—See Sulfamethazine, sodium.

SULFAMONOMETHOXINE

Composition: Sulfonamide compound.

Synonyms: Dimeton.

Uses or Treatment for: Bacteria.

Dosage: With feed as is, at a rate of 100-200 mg/kg of feed.

Remarks: Use as needed as treatment; water-soluble.
References: Snieszko (1975).

SULFANILAMIDE

Composition: Sulfonamide compound.

$$H_2N \longrightarrow \langle\ \rangle \longrightarrow SO_2NH_2$$

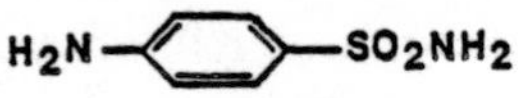

SULFANILAMIDE

Synonyms: None.
Uses or Treatment for: Bacteria; fungal disease.
Dosage: 100-250 mg/l of water as a long duration bath.
Remarks: None.
References: Amlacher (1970); Reichenbach-Klinke & Landolt (1973).

SULFAQUININE

Composition: Sulfonamide compound.
Synonyms: None.
Uses or Treatment for: Protozoa *(Cryptocaryon irritans).*
Dosage: Undetermined.
Remarks: None.
References: Kingsford (1975).

SULFAQUINOXALINE—See Sulguin (Sulquin).

SULFATHIAZOLE

Composition: Sulfonamide compound.

$$H_2N \longrightarrow \langle\ \rangle \longrightarrow SO_2NH$$

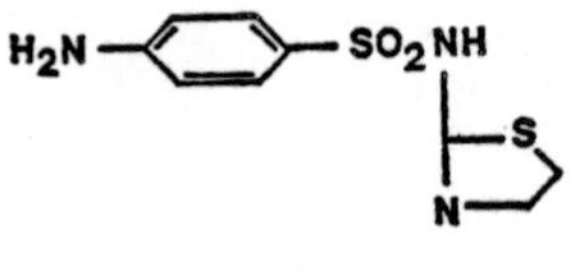

SULFATHIAZOLE

Synonyms: Sulfathiazole sodium.
Uses or Treatment for: Bacteria (gram-positive bacteria); Protozoa *(Cryptocaryon irritans).*
Dosage: 250 mg/10 gal of water.
Remarks: Sulfathiazole sodium works slightly better and is more soluble; available in medical quality as creams, oint-

ments, and tablets; manufactured by Barre, Cord, United; available in pet trade as powder (microcrystals).

References: Allen (1972) ; Kingsford (1975).

SULFATHIAZOLE SODIUM—See Sulfathiazole.

SULFISOXAZOLE

Composition: Acetyl sulfisoxazole or sulfisoxazole diolamine.

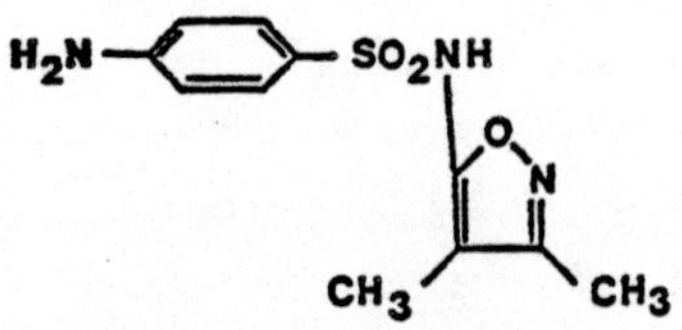

SULFISOXAZOLE

Synonyms: Gantrisin; Sodizole; Sulfazin.

Uses or Treatment for: Bacteria [cold-water disease *(Cytophaga psychrophila)*, Columnaris disease *(Chondrococcus columnaris)*, Furunculosis *(Aeromonas salmonicida)*, kidney disease *(Cornybacterium)*, peduncle disease].

Dosage: (1) 22-24 gm/100 kg of fish weight per day in feed for 14 days; (2) 100-200 mg/kg per day for 10 to 20 days.

Remarks: Substitutes include Sulfamerazine, Sulfamethazine; moderately effective in salt water; available as tablets or solutions; manufactured by Aberdeen, Alliance, Amer Quinine, APC, Arcum, Barre, Canfield, Carchem, Columbia Medic, Corvit, CPI, Fellows, FTP, Invenex, Kasar, Lannett, Premo, PRL, Purepac Pharm, Roche, Scruggs, Sheraton, Stanley Drug, Stayner, Steri-Med, Towne, Trent, Tutag, Ulmer Pharcal, United, Vale Chemical, Vitarine, West-Ward, Zenith.

References: Amlacher (1970); Herman (1972); Snieszko (1975).

SULFISOXAZOLE, DIOLAMINE—See Sulfisoxazole.

SULFONAMIDES—See Sulfamerazine, Sulfadiazine, Sulfaguanidine, Sulfamethazine, or Sulfisoxazole; all are interchangeabe at dosages of 10 gm/100 lb of fish per day or 100 mg/l for 3 to 4 days; also see Albucid or Globucid.

SULFURIC ACID
　　Composition: H_2SO_4.
　　Synonyms: None.
　　Uses or Treatment for: Crustacea *(Salmincola)*.
　　Dosage: 0.015% solution (150 ppm).
　　Remarks: Killed larvae only.
　　References: Edminister & Gray (1948) ; Fasten (1912) ; Hoffman & Meyer (1974) ; Kabata (1970).

SULGUIN (SULQUIN)
　　Composition: 2-sulfanilamidoquinoxaline.
　　Synonyms: Sulfaquinoxaline.
　　Uses or Treatment for: Protozoa (coccidiostat, *Ichthyophthirius*).
　　Dosage: (1) 50 ppm daily; (2) 10,000 ppm in diet daily.
　　Remarks: None.
　　References: Hoffman & Meyer (1974).

SULSPANTABS—See Globucid.

T-72—See Nitrophenyl amidineura.

TABLE SALT—See Sodium chloride.

TAG—See PMA.

TARTAR EMETIC—See Potassium antimony tartrate.

TARTARIC ACID
　　Composition: $C_6H_6O_6$ (isomer unknown).
　　Synonyms: None.
　　Uses or Treatment for: Crustacea *(Salmincola)*.
　　Dosage: 0.45% solution (4500 ppm).
　　Remarks: Killed larvae only.
　　References: Fasten (1912) ; Hoffman & Meyer (1974) ; Kabata (1970).

TBP—See Bithionol.

TEASEED CAKE—See Teaseed meal.

TEASEED MEAL
　　Composition: Unknown.
　　Synonyms: Teaseed cake.
　　Uses or Treatment for: Crustacea *(Argulus)*.

Dosage: 40 pounds, finely fragmented and mixed with mud, treats 1 acre of pond, 2.5 feet deep.

Remarks: Concentrations sufficient to kill *Argulus* are also lethal to fish; old Chinese remedy, probably of no real value.

References: Chen (1933) ; Hoffman & Meyer (1974) ; Kabata (1970) .

TEEBACONIN—See Isoniazid.

TEGOPEN—See Cloxacillin sodium.

TERRAMYCIN—See Oxytetracycline.

TETRACAPS—See Oxytetracycline.

TETRACHEL—See Oxytetracycline.

TETRACYCLINE—See Oxytetracycline.

TETRACYCLINE HYDROCHLORIDE—See Oxytetracycline.

TETRACYN—See Oxytetracycline.

TETRAFINOL

Composition: Unknown.
Synonyms: None.
Uses or Treatment for: Intestinal helminths.
Dosage: Used with food.
Remarks: For control only.
References: Snieszo (1975) .

TETRAKIN—See Oxytetracycline.

TETRALER—See Oxytetracycline.

TETRAM—See Oxytetracycline.

TETRAMAX—See Oxytetracycline.

TETRAMED—See Oxytetracycline.

TETRAMINE—See Oxytetracycline.

TETRASPECT—See Oxytetracycline.

TFM—See Trifluoromethyl nitrophenol.

THIOPHOS—See Ethyl parathion.

THIRAM

Composition: Bis(dimethylthiocarbamyl) disulfide.
Synonyms: Arasan; Mercuram; Thylate.
Uses or Treatment for: Fungicide *(Saprolegnia)*.

Dosage: 1.0 ppm.

Remarks: Not particularly effective; 0.63-1.0 ppm nontoxic to *Ictalurus punctatus.*

References: Clemens & Sneed (1959); Hoffman & Meyer (1974).

THYLATE—See Thiram.

TIGUVON—See Baytex.

TIMSAN—See Ethylmercuric phosphate.

TIN OXIDE—See Di-*n*-butyl tin oxide.

TINCTURE OF IODINE—See Alcohol, Iodated.

TINOSTAT—See Dibutyltin dilaurate.

TIOCLEAN—See Sodium thiosulfate.

TOTACILLIN—See Ampicillin trihydrate.

TRECATOR-SC—See Ethionamide.

TRI-6—See Benzene hexachloride.

TRICAINE METHANESULFONATE—See MS-222.

TRICHLOROFON—See Dylox .

TRICHORAD—See Cyzine.

TRIFLUOROMETHYL NITROPHENOL

Composition: 3-trifluoromethyl-4-nitrophenol.

Synonyms: TFM.

Uses or Treatment for: Molluscicide (snails, *Australorbis glabratus*); lampricide.

Dosage: (1) 9 ppm; (2) 12 ppm.

Remarks: Toxic to *Pimephales promelas, Ictalurus punctatus* and many other fish; only partially effective; 10 ppm was not toxic to *Carassius auratus*; 14 ppm = LC_{100} to tadpoles (*Rana catesbeiana*); 18 ppm = LC_{100} in *Carassius auratus* in 96 hours at 28°C; 5 ppm = LC_{25} in *Catostomus commersoni* in 24 hours at 13°C; 5.75 ppm = LC_{25} in *Ictalurus natalis* in 24 hours at 13°C; 10 ppm was nontoxc, but 18 ppm = LC_{100} in *Ictalurus punctatus* in 96 hours at 28°C; 21.5 ppm = LC_{25} in *Lepomis macrochirus* in 24 hours at 13°C; 22.0-34.5 ppm = LC_{25} in *Micropterus dolomieu* and *D. salmoides* in 24 hours at 13°C; 14.75 ppm = LC_{25} in *Notemigonus crysoleucas* in 24 hours at

13°C; 13.25 ppm = LC$_{25}$ in *Notropis heterolepis* in 24 hours at 13°C; 7.25 ppm = LC$_{25}$ in *Perca flavescens* in 24 hours at 13°C; 16 ppm = LC$_{25}$ in *Pimephales promelas* in 24 hours at 13°C; 12 ppm = LC$_{25}$ in *Salmo gairdneri* in 24 hours at 13°C; 5.75 ppm = LC$_{25}$ in *Stizostedion vitreum* in 24 hours at 13°C.

References: Applegate et al. (1961); Applegate & King (1962); Chandler & Marking (1975); Daniels et al. (1965); Dawson et al. (1975); Fremling (1975); Gilderhus et al. (1975); Hoffman & Meyer (1974); Howell et al. (1964); Jobin & Unrau (1967); Kanayama (1963); Kawatski et al. (1975); Makai et al. (1975); Makai & Johnson (1976); Marking, Bills, and Chandler (1975); Marking & Olson (1975); Piavis & Howell (1975); Sanders & Walsh (1975); Schnick (1972); Sills & Allen (1975); Sills et al. (1973a, 1973b).

TRINIAD—See Isoniazid.

TRINITROPHENOL—See Picric acid.

TRIPLE SULFA

Composition: Mixture of Sulfadiazine, Sulfamethazine, and Sulfamerazine.

Synonyms: None.

Uses or Treatment for: Bacteria (fin and tail rot, gram-positive bacteria); fungus *(Saprolegnia).*

Dosage: (1) As per sulfonamide dosage; (2) as per label of trade preparations.

Remarks: None.

References: None.

TRIS BUFFER

Composition: Commercial formulation containing tris(hydroxymethyl) aminomethane.

Synonyms: None.

Uses or Treatment for: Physiological buffering agent; Protozoa *(Cryptocaryon irritans).*

Dosage: 0.42 ppm Cupric acetate + 5.26 ppm Formalin + 4.8 ppm Tris buffer.

Remarks: For salt water use.

References: Hoffman & Meyer (1974); Nigrelli & Ruggieri (1966).

n-TRITYLMORPHOLINE

Composition: *n*-tritylmorpholine.

Synonyms: Frescon; W1-8008.

Uses or Treatment for: Molluscicide (snails, *Australorbis glabratus*).

Dosage: (1) 0.01-0.50 ppm for one hour (higher concentrations toxic to fish) ; (2) 0.01-0.05 ppm for 24 hours.

Remarks: Is being used in Africa and Great Britain; 0.1 ppm = LC_{100} to *Barbus sp.* and *Tilapia sp.*

References: Boyce et al. (1967) ; Crossland (1967) ; Crossland et al. (1971) ; Hoffman & Meyer (1974) .

TROLENE—See Korlan.

TRUXQUINE—See Chloroquine phosphate.

TRYPAFLAVINE—See Acriflavine.

TURPENTINE

Composition: Unknown.

Synonyms: None.

Uses or Treatment for: Crustacea *(Argulus)*.

Dosage: Dip a cotton swab in turpentine and apply topically to parasite.

Remarks: Not recommended.

References: Van Duijn (1973) .

TV-1096

Composition: Experimental compound by Parke, Davis & Company.

Synonyms: None.

Uses or Treatment for: Antiprotozoal *(Ichthyophthirius)*.

Dosage: 0.2 ppm.

Remarks: Not effective for 6.7-18.2 ppm; did not exceed LC_1 in 48 hours at 12-17°C in *Ictalurus punctatus, Lepomis macrochirus, Salmo gairdneri, S. trutta, Salvelinus fontinalis, S. namaycush.*

References: Hoffman & Meyer (1974) ; Willford (1967a) .

UDEN—See Baygon.

UNIAD—See Isoniazid.

UNSLAKED LIME—See Calcium oxide.

URETHANE, 2-5%
Composition: Unknown.
Synonyms: None.
Uses or Treatment for: Fish anesthetic.
Dosage: As per label.
Remarks: Continued use or overdose may produce bone marrow depression; used in Great Britian, unavailable in U.S.
References: "General Anesthesia in Exotics." *Vet Med Small Anim Clin,* Sept. 1974, p. 1185.

URI-TET—See Oxytetracycline.

VANCOCIN—See Vancomycin hydrochloride.

VANCOMYCIN HYDROCHLORIDE
Composition: A glycopeptide antibiotic of unknown chemical structure.
Synonyms: Vancocin.
Uses or Treatment for: Bacteria (gram-positive cocci).
Dosage: Undetermined.
Remarks: Has a shelf life of two weeks when in solution; available as sterile powder; manufactured by Lilly.
References: Kingsford (1975).

VAPONA—See DDVP.

VERDIGRIS—See Cupric acetate.

VIBROMYCIN—See Doxycycline hyclate.

VICTORIA GREEN B or WB—See Malachite green, zinc free oxalate.

VINEGAR—See Acetic acid, commercial grade.

VIOLET K
Composition: Unknown.
Synonyms: None.
Uses or Treatment for: Protozoa *(Ichthyophthirius).*
Dosage: 0.25-0.5 ppm.
Remarks: Russian dye; less expensive than Malachite green.
References: Hoffman & Meyer (1974); Musselius & Flippova (1968).

VOLAN A ADHESIVE OINTMENT
Composition: Unknown.
Synonyms: None.
Uses or Treatment for: Virus (Lymphocystosis) ; packing or covering wounds.
Dosage: Cortisone or antibiotics mixed into it and applied to epidermis.
Remarks: Inhibits spread of lymphocystis; European product.
References: Schubert (1974) .

WATER—See Fresh Water or Seawater.

WEED BEADS—See Pentachlorophenol.

WEEDONE—See Pentachlorophenol.

WESCODYNE—See Iodophores.

WL-8008—See *n*-tritylmorpholine.

YOMESAN—See Niclosamide.

ZALKONIUM CHLORIDE—See Benzalkonium chloride.

ZECTRAN
Composition: Methyl-4-dimethylamino-2,5-xylyl carbamate.
Synonyms: None.
Uses or Treatment for: Crustacea *(Lernaea cyprinacea);* insecticide; molluscicide (snails) .
Dosage: (1) 1 ppm/week for 4 weeks; (2) 7 ppm.
Remarks: Toxic to fry; fish tolerance is 6-12 ppm; 10 ppm = LC_{100} to *Notemigonus crysoleucas.*
References: Hoffman & Meyer (1974) .

ZEPHIRAN—See Benzalkonium chloride.

ZEPHIRAN CHLORIDE—See Benzalkonium chloride.

ZEPHIROL—See Benzalkonium chloride.

ZERLATE—See Zinc dimethyldithiocarbamate.

ZINC CHLORIDE
Composition: $ZnCl_2$.
Synonyms: Butter of Zinc.
Uses or Treatment for: Disinfectant; Hirudinea (leeches) .
Dosage: Undetermined.
Remarks: Not effective.

References: Hoffman & Meyer (1974); Moore (1923); Skidmore (1964).

ZINC DIMETHYLDITHIOCARBAMATE

Composition: Zinc dimethyldithiocarbamate.

Synonyms: Fuklasin; Milbam; Zerlate; Ziram.

Uses or Treatment for: Fungicide *(Saprolegnia)*; Cestoda; Crustacea *(Cyclops)*.

Dosage: (1) 2 ppm (inhibitory but not curative); (2) 4 ppm (inhibitory and toxic to fish); (3) 1 ppm (effective in destroying intermediate hosts of Cestoda, i.e. *Cyclops*).

Remarks: 2 ppm nontoxic to *Ictalurus punctatus;* used to destroy *Cyclops* which serves as intermediate host of Cestoda.

References: Clemens & Sneed (1959); Grétillat (1965); Hoffman & Meyer (1974); Skidmore (1964).

ZIRAM—See Zinc dimethyldithiocarbamate.

ZONIUM CHLORIDE—See Benzalkonium chloride.

ZONITE, Stabalized sodium hypochlorite—See Sodium hypochlorite.

APPENDICES

APPENDIX I-A

VIRICIDES

Betadine

Sodium hypochlorite

Volan A adhesive ointment

APPENDIX I-B

BACTERICIDES

Acriflavine, hydrochloride
Acriflavine, neutral
Albucid, sodium
Alcohol, Iodated
Ampicillin, sodium
Ampicillin trihydrate
Aquarol
Arycil
Aureomycin
Bacitracin
Betadine
Bithionol
Carbenicillin disodium
Cephaloridine
Chloramphenicol
Cloxacillin, sodium
Colistin sulfate
Copper sulfate
Diquat
Doxycycline hyclate
Emtrysidina
Erythromycin
Ethionamide
Ethylmercuric phosphate
Fosfomicina
Fumagillin
Furanace
Furoxone
Furpyridinol
Gentamycin sulfate

Globucid, sodium
Griseofulvin
Hyamine
Iodophors
Isoniazid
Kanamycin
Lincomycin
Malachite green, zinc free oxalate
Merthiolate
Methacillin sodium
Neomycin
Nifurprazine HCl
Nitrofurantoin sodium
Nitrofurazone
Novobiocin
Oleandomycin
Oxolinic acid
Oxytetracycline
Ozone
Parachlorophenoxethol
Paramomycin
Penicillin, potassium
Phenoxethol
Polymyxin B, sulfate
Potassium permanganate
Quaternary ammonium
  compounds
Rifampin
Roccal
Streptomycin

Sulfadiazine
Sulfadimethoxine sodium
Sulfaguanidine
Sulfamerazine
Sulfamethazine, sodium

Sulfamonomethoxine
Sulfanilamide
Sulfisoxazole
Vancomycin hydrochloride

APPENDIX I-C

ALGICIDES

Acrolein
Ammonium sulfate
Aqua-ammonia
Copper sulfate
Copper sulfate + Acetic acid
Cupravit
Cutrine

Dicryl
Diquat
Diuron
Ethylmercuric phosphate
Paraquat, dichloride
PMA

APPENDIX I-D

FUNGICIDES

Acriflavine, hydrochloride
Acriflavine, neutral
Aquarol
Aureomycin
Bacitracin
Basic bright green, oxalate
Calcium cyanamide
Calomel
Chloramine-T
Chlorine
Collargol
Copper sulfate
Detrapan
Ferbam
Formalin (37–40%)
Furanace
Gentian violet
Globucid, sodium
Griseofulvin
Iodoform
Karathane
Malachite green, zinc free oxalate
Mercurochrome
Merthiolate
Methylene blue
Oxytetracycline
Ozone
Parachlorophenoxethol
Phenoxethol
Potassium dichromate
Potassium permanganate
Rivanol
Silver nitrate
Sulfanilamide
Thiram
Zinc dimethyldithiocarbamate

PROTOZOACIDES

Acetarsone
Acetic acid, commercial grade
Acnitrazole
Acriflavine, hydrochloride
Acriflavine, neutral
Albucid, sodium
Aluminum sulfate
Ammonium carbonate
Ammonium chloride,
  commercial grade
Amprolium
Ampyroquin
Antimycin A
Aqua-aid
Aquarol
Atabrine, hydrochloride
Aureomycin
Basic bright green, oxalate
Basic violet
Baytex
Betanaphthol
Bithionol
Bromex-50
Calcium carbonate, commercial
  grade
Calcium chloride
Calcium cyanamide
Calcium hydroxide, commercial
  grade
Calcium oxide

Calomel
Carbarsone
Carbarsone oxide
Chelated copper
Chloramine-B
Chloramine-T
Chloramphenicol
Chlorine
Chloroquine
Citric acid
Collargol
Copper sulfate
Copper sulfate + Acetic acid
7-Co-Ral
Cupric acetate
Cyzine
Daraprim
Dimetridazole
DMSO
Dylox
Emtrysidina
Enheptin
Entobex
Eosin
Ethylene glycol
Flagyl
Formalin (37–40%)
Fresh water
Fumagillin
Furanace

Furoxone
Gentian violet
Globucid, sodium
Hydrogen peroxide, 3%
Iodoform
Kanamycin
Lilac leaves
Lysol
Magnesium sulfate
Malachite green, zinc free
  oxalate
Mercuric nitrate
Mercurochrome
Metasol L
Methylene blue
Micropur
Napthol B
Neguvon
Nickel sulfate
Nitrofurazone
Oxalic acid
Oxytetracycline
PAA-2056
Penicillin, potassium
Phenothiazine

Pine needles
Plasmoquin
PMA
Potassium dichromate
Potassium hydroxide
Potassium permanganate
PR-3714
Primaquine phosphate
Quinine hydrochloride
Quinine sulfate
Rivanol
Ruelene
Sodium borate
Sodium chlorate
Sodium chloride
Sodium chlorite
Sodium hydroxide
Sodium hypochlorite
Sulfamethazine, sodium
Sulfaquinine
Sulfathiazole
Sulquin (Sulguin)
Tris buffer
TV-1096
Violet K

APPENDIX I-F

ANTHELMINTHICS

Turbellaria

Acetic acid, commercial grade
Ammonium nitrate
Chestnut decoction
Chloramine-T
Dylox

Monogenea

Acetic acid, commercial grade
Ammonia, 28% in water
Ammonium chloride
Ammonium hydroxide
Antimony potassium tartrate
Bis-oxide
Bromex-50
Calcium oxide
Chloramine-B
Chloramine-T
Chlorine
Copper sulfate
DDVP
Dylox
Formalin (37–40%)
Fresh water
Hydrogen peroxide, 3%
Magnesium sulfate
Malachite green, zinc free
   oxalate
Mercurochrome
Methylene blue
Neguvon
Paraformaldehyde
Picric acid
PMA
Potassium antimony tartrate
Potassium permanganate
Quinine hydrochloride
Rivanol
Roccal
Salicylic acid
Silvol
Sodium chlorate
Sodium chloride
Sodium perborate peroxydol
Sodium peroxide pyrophosphate
Sodium pyrophosphate
   peroxyhydrate

Digenea

Di-n-butyl tin oxide
Potassium antimony tartrate
Tetrafinol

Cestoda

Bithionol
Calcium chloride
Concurat
Devermin
Dibutyltin dilaurate
Di-*n*-butyl tin oxide
Dylox

Garlic
Kamala
Niclosamide
Phenothiazine
Sodium fluosilicate
Tetrafinol
Zinc dimethyldithiocarbamate

Nematoda

Antimony potassium tartrate
Concurat
Garlic

Parachlorometaxylenol
Santonin
Tetrafinol

Acanthocephala

Bithionol
Di-*n*-butyl tin oxide

Garlic
Tetrafinol

Hirudinea

Acetic acid, commercial grade
Baygon, 50% wettable powder
Baytex
Benzene hexachloride
Calcium oxide
Copper sulfate
Cupric chloride
DDT
Dylox

Formalin (37–40%)
Lysol
Neguvon
PMA
Potassium permanganate
Seawater
Sodium chloride
Zinc chloride

APPENDIX I-G

CRUTACICIDES

Acetic acid, commercial grade
Ammonium chloride,
  commercial grade
Anthium dioxide
Antimycin A
Balsam of Peru oil
Baygon, 50% wettable powder
Baytex
Benzene hexachloride
Bromex-50
Calcium chloride
Calcium hypochlorite
Calcium oxide
Castor bean plant
Chlorine
Ciodrin
Copper sulfate
7-Co-Ral
DDFT
DDT
DDVP
Dursban
Dylox
Ethyl parathion
Ferric sulfate
Formalin (37–40%)

Fresh water
Gix
Hexachlorocyclohexane
Hydrochloric acid
Hydrogen sulfide
Korlan
Lysol
Magnesium sulfate
Malathion
Menazon
Methyl parathion
Mitox
Neguvon
Nicotine sulfate
Nitric acid
Potassium chlorate
Potassium permanganate
Pyrethrum
Ruelene
Sodium chloride
Sulfuric acid
Tartaric acid
Teaseed meal
Zectran
Zinc dimethyldithiocarbamate

APPENDIX I-H

INSECTICIDES

Balsam of Peru oil
Bayer 9015
Baytex
Benzene hexachloride
Bromex-50
7-Co-Ral
Cottonseed oil
DDFT
DDT
DDVP
Diesel fuel, commercial grade
Di-syston
Dursban

Dylox
Ethyl parathion
GIX
Kerosene
Korlan
Malathion
Menazon
Methyl parathion
Neguvon
Nicotine sulfate
Pyrethrum
Ruelene
Zectran

APPENDIX I-I

MOLLUSCICIDES

Acrolein

Barium carbonate

Barium chloride

Bayluscide

Cadmium sulfate

Calcium carbonate, commercial grade

Calcium hydroxide, commercial grade

Calcium oxide

Chevreul's salt

Copper carbonate

Copper sulfate

Cupravit

Cuprous chloride

Cuprous oxide

Di-*n*-butyl tin oxide

Dowco 212

Nicotine sulfate

p-Nitrophenacyl chloride

Nitrophenyl amidineura

Paraquat, dichloride

Pentachlorophenol

Potassium chloride

Saponin

Trifluoromethyl nitrophenol

n-Tritylmorpholine

Zectran

APPENDIX I-J

FISH TOXICANTS

Antimycin A
Rotenone
Saponin

Sodium cyanide
Trifluoromethyl nitrophenol

APPENDIX I-K

DISINFECTANTS

Betadine
Boric acid
Calcium chloride
Calcium cyanamide
Calcium hypochlorite
Calcium nitrate
Calcium oxide
Chloramine-B
Chlorine
Collargol
Iodophors
Lime
Lysol

Metasol L
Micropur
Paraformaldehyde
Phenoxethol
Potassium dichromate
Povidone-Iodine
Rivanol
Roccal
Silvol
Sodium hypochlorite
Sodium pyrophosphate peroxy-
hydrate
Zinc chloride

APPENDIX I-L

MISCELLANEOUS

Fish Anesthetics and Tranquilizers

Alcohol, ethyl
Aspirin
Ether
MS-222

Propoxate
Quinaldine
Urethane, 2-5%

Antiseptics

Betanapthol
Chloramine-T
Iodoform

Mercurochrome
Nitrofurazone

Coelenteraticides (Cnideria)

Ammonium nitrate, commercial
   grade

Aquarol
Chestnut decoction

Dyes

Gentian violet

Methylene blue

Dechlorinators

Sodium thiosulfate

Miticides

Mitox

Cathartics

Magnesium sulfate

Tumors-Goiters

Potassium Iodide-Iodine solution

Rodenticides

Sodium fluosilicate

Bleaches

Sodium perborate peroxydol

Others

Copper, micronized
Cycloserine

Philixan

225

PARTIAL LISTING OF MANUFACTURERS AND/OR DISTRIBUTORS OF DRUGS AND CHEMICALS LISTED IN TEXT*

Abbott
Abbott Laboratories
14th & Sheridan Road
North Chicago, Illinois 60064

Aberdeen
Aberdeen Pharmacals Corporation
140 Le Grande Avenue
Northvale, New Jersey 07647

Adams Chemical Corp.

AGM
AGM Drug Company
124 Covington Street
Montgomery, Alabama 36104

Alliance
Alliance Laboratories, Inc.
330 Oak Street
Columbus, Ohio 43216

Amer Quinine
American Quinine Company, Inc.
10 Fairchild Court
Plainview, New York 11803

Amid
Amid Laboratories, Inc.
611 Moore Street
Marion, Alabama 36756

APC
American Pharmaceutical Company
120 Bruckner Boulevard
Bronx, New York 10454

Aquatrol Co.
237-H N. Euclid
Anaheim, California 92801

Arcum
Arcum Pharmaceutical Corp.
P.O. Box 267
Vienna, Virginia 22180

Artaco
The Archer-Taylor Drug Co.
P.O. Box 636
335 West Lewis
Wichita, Kansas 67201

*NDCD code name, if any, followed by company address. The majority of these manufacturers are drug companies supplying human drugs and may not be available as sources for fish medications, but nonetheless should be able to provide informtion on the various drugs they manufacture or distribute.

Ascher
B.F. Ascher & Company, Inc.
5100 E. Street
Kansas City, Missouri 64130

Atlas Pharceut
Atlas Pharmaceutical Laboratories,
Inc.
13211 Conant Avenue
Detroit, Michigan 48212

AUI
American Urologicals, Inc.
432 N.E. 191st Street
Miami, Florida 33162

Ayerst
Ayerst Laboratories
Div. of American Home Products
Corp.
685 Third Avenue
New York, New York 10017

Balkins
Balkins Laboratories, Inc.
P.O. Box 307
Columbus, Kansas 66725

Barnes-Hind
Barnes-Hind Laboratories, Inc.
Div. of Barnes-Hind Pharmaceuti-
cals, Inc.
895 Kifer Road
Sunnyvale, California 94086

Barre
Barre Drug Co., Inc.
4128 Hayward Avenue
Baltimore, Maryland 21215

Barrows
Barrows Biochemical Products
Corp.
300-303 Prospect Street
Inwood, L.I., New York 11696

Bates
Bates Laboratories Division
LTC Pharmaceutical Corp.
2312 West Main Street
Evanston, Illinois 60202

———

Messers. Bayer AG
Leverkusen, Germany

Baylor
Baylor Laboratories, Inc.
P.O. Box 552
Hurst, Texas 76053

BBC
BBC Laboratories
700 N. Sepulveda Boulevard
El Segundo, California 90245

BCR
BCR Pharmacal Co., Inc.
P.O. Box 213
Florala, Alabama 36442

Beach
Beach Products, Inc.
5220 S. Manhatten Ave.
Tampa, Florida 33611

Beech-Mass Phar
Beecham-Massengill Pharmaceuti-
cals
Div. of Beecham, Inc.
Bristol, Tennessee 37620

Bel-Mar
Bel-Mar Labs
6-10 Nassau Ave.
Inwood, L.I., New York 11696

Berla
Berkeley Laboratories
356 Warren Avenue
Stirling, New Jersey 07890

———

Bioquatic Laboratories
Victoria Mill, Blakewell
Derbyshire, England, DE4 1DA

Blair

Blair Laboratories, Inc.
99-101 Saw Mill River Rd.
Yonkers, New York 10701

Bluline

The Blueline Chemical Co.
302 South Broadway
St. Louis, Missouri 63102

Bowman Pharm

Bowman-Braun Pharmaceuticals,
Inc.
119 Schroyer Ave., S.W.
Canton, Ohio 44702

Bristol Labs

Bristol Laboratories, Inc.
Div. of Bristol-Myers Co.
Thompson Road
P.O. Box 657
Syracuse, New York 13201

Brunswick

Brunswick Laboratories, Inc.
5836 W. 117th Place
Worth, Illinois 60482

BT

Bruner-Tillman Company
1009 N. Third Street
Phoenix, Arizona 85004

BW

Burroughs Wellcome & Co.
3030 Cornwallis Road
Research Triangle Park
North Carolina 27709

Calgon

Calgon Corporation
Subsidiary of Merck & Co., Inc.
Calgon Center, Box 1346
Pittsburgh, Pennsylvania 15230

Canfield

C.R. Canfield & Co.
2744-46 Lyndale Ave. S.
Minneapolis, Minnesota 55408

Carchem

Carroll Chemical Co.
2301 Hollins St.
Baltimore, Maryland 21223

Caribe Chemco

Caribe Chemical Co., Inc.
Kingshell P.O.
St. Croix, U.S. Virgin Islands
00850

Century Lab

Century Laboratories, Inc.
P.O. Box 1038
3 Birches Hall
Turnersville, New Jersey 08012

Chemagro Corp.

P.O.Box 4913—Hawthorn Road
Kansas City, Missouri 64120

Ciba

Ciba Pharmaceutical Co.
Div. of Ciba-Geigy Corp.
556 Morris Ave.
Summit, New Jersey 07901

CLI

Certified Laboratories, Inc.
400 Valley Road
Warrington, Pennsylvania 18976

Clifford

Clifford Chemical Corp.
852 Clinton Ave.
Newark, New Jersey 07108

CMC

Consolidated Midland Corp.
Div. of CMC Research
15 Parkway
Katonah, New York 10536

Coast Labs
Coast Laboratories, Inc.
521 West 17th Street
Long Beach, California 90813

Coastal
Coastal Pharmaceutical Co., Inc.
1229 W. Olney Road
Norfolk, Virginia 23507

Columbia Medic
Columbia Medical Co.
38 East 19th Street
New York, New York 10003

Cooper
Cooper Laboratories, Inc.
2900 N. 17th St.
Philadelphia, Pennsylvania 19132

Cord
Cord Laboratories, Inc.
19191 Filer Ave.
Detroit, Michigan 48234

Corvit
Corvit Pharmaceuticals
P.O. Box 165
Orinca, California 94563

COT
C.O. Truxton, Inc.
1458-60 Haddon Ave.
Camden, New Jersey 08103

CPI
Century Pharmaceuticals, Inc.
6383 Monitor Dr.
Indianapolis, Indiana 46220

Cutter Labs
Cutter Laboratories
820 Parker Street
Berkeley, California 94710

Dalin
Dalin Pharmaceuticals, Inc.
30 Van Siclen Avenue
Floral Park, New York 11001

Day Baldwin
Day-Baldwin, Inc.
1460 Chestnut Ave.
Hillside, New Jersey 07205

DE
Davis-Edwards Pharmacal Corp.
Davis-Edwards Road
Danbury, Connecticut 06810

———
Dixie Chemical Co.
P.O. Box 13410
Houston, Texas 77019

DHL
Don Hall Laboratories
1935 N. Argyle
Portland, Oregon 97217

Dorasol
Dorasol Laboratories
G.P.O. Box 3906
San Juan, Puerto Rico 00936

Dow Genrc Pharm
Dow Chemical Company
P.O. Box 1656
Indianapolis, Indiana 46206

———
Dow Chemical Co.
P.O. Box 512
Midland, Michigan 48640

Dunhall
Dunhall, Inc.
P.O. Box 100
Gravette, Arkansas 72736

DuPont

E.I. DuPont de Nemours & Co.,
Inc.
Pharmaceutical Division
1007 Market Street
Wilmington, Delaware 19898

———

Dyna-Pet, Inc.
Campbell, California 95008

Eaton

Eaton Laboratories
Div. Norwich Pharmacal Co.
17 Eaton Ave.
Norwich, New York 13815

Elder

Paul B. Elder Co.
705 E. Mulberry St.
P.O. Box 31
Bryan, Ohio 43506

Elkins-Sinn

Elkins-Sinn, Inc.
22 Cherry Hill Industrial Center
Cherry Hill, New Jersey 08034

EPC

Edwards Pharmacal Co.
1474 South Trezevant
Memphis, Tennessee 38114

Fed

Federal Pharmacal Corp.
1260 N.E. 35th St.
Fort Lauderdale, Florida 33308

Fellows

Fellows-Testagar
Div. Fellows Medical Mfg. Co.,
Inc.
12741 Capital Avenue
Oak Park, Michigan 48237

Flar

Flar Medicine Co.
P.O. Box 256
Coamo, Puerto Rico 00640

Forbes

Forbes Pharmacal, Inc.
1825 N.E. 164th St.
N. Miami Beach, Florida 33162

FTP

First Texas Pharmaceuticals, Inc.
1810-16 N. Lamar St.
P.O. Box 5026
Dallas, Texas 75222

———

General Aniline Dye Co.
Chattanooga, Tennessee 37401

Hartford

Hartford Laboratories, Inc.
40 W. Brook St.
Manchester, New Hampshire 03105

———

Hess & Clark
Div. of Vick Chemical Co.
Ashland, Ohio 44805

Holland-Rantos

Holland-Rantos Co., Inc.
P.O. Box 5
865 Centennial Ave.
Piscataway, New Jersey 08854

Humco

Humco Laboratories, Inc.
1008 Whitaker St.
Texarkana, Texas 75501

HWD

Hynson, Wescott & Dunning, Inc.
Charles and Chase Streets
Baltimore, Maryland 21201

Hyrex
Hyrex Co.
832 S. Cooper Street
Memphis, Tennessee 38114

Invenex
Invenex Pharmaceuticals
377 Genesee St.
Buffalo, New York 14204

Ives
Ives Laboratories, Inc.
685 Third Ave.
New York, New York 10017

Jenkins
Jenkins Laboratories, Inc.
Auburn, New York 13021

Jungle Laboratories Corp.
P.O. Box 2018
Sanford, Florida 32771

Kasar
Kasar Laboratories
7313 N. Harlem Ave.
Niles, Illinois 60648

Kay Pharmacal
Kay Pharmacal Co.
1312 N. Utica
Tulsa, Oklahoma 74150

Kirkman
Kirkman Laboratories, Inc.
934 N.E. 25th Ave.
Portland, Oregon 97208

Knight
Knight Pharmacal Co.
705 W. Kirk
San Antonio, Texas 78226

Lannett
Lannet Co., Inc.
9000 State Road
Philadelphia, Pennsylvania 19136

Lardon
Lardon Laboratories
522 Glen Echo Road
Philadelphia, Pennsylvania 19119

Lederle
Lederle Laboratories
Div. American Cyanamid Co.
W. Middleton Road
Pearl River, New York 10965

Lentag
Len-tag Co. Pharmaceuticals
1501 E. Davison Ave.
Detroit, Michigan 48212

Lilly
Eli Lilly & Co.
740 S. Alabama St.
Indianapolis, Indiana 46206

Linden
Linden Laboratories, Inc.
8454 Steller Dr.
Culver City, California 90230

Lyne
Lyne Laboratories
750 Main Street
Winchester, Massachusetts 01890

McCrary's Farm Suply
114 Park St.
Lonoke, Arkansas 72086

MA
Medical Arts Supply Co.
706-08-10 Fourth Avenue
Huntington, West Virginia 25715

Mac Eslin
Mac Eslin & Co.
251 S. George St., Box 92
York, Pennsylvania 17403

Mallard

Mallard, Inc.
3021 Wabash Avenue
Detroit, Michigan 48216

Mallinckrodt

Mallinckrodt Chemical Works
3600 N. Second St.
St. Louis, Missouri 63160

―――

Moreco
Costa Mesa, California 95626

―――

Mardel Laboratories, Inc.
Carol Stream, Illinois 60187

―――

Marineland Aquarium Products,
Inc.
800 N. Cole Ave.
Los Angeles, California 90038

―――

Mathieson, Coleman & Bell
2909 Highland Ave.
Norwood, Ohio 45212

Mayrand

Mayrand, Inc.
P.O. Box 20246
1026 E. Lindsay St.
Greensboro, North Carolina 27420

MCC-M

Medical Chemical Corp.
2137 N. 15th Avenue
Melrose Park, Illinois 60160

MCD

Merck Chemical Division
Merck & Co., Inc.
Rahway, New Jersey 07065

McKesson

McKesson Laboratories
Div. of Foremost-McKesson, Inc.
P.O. Box 548
Bridgeport, Connecticut 06602

McNeil

McNeil Laboratories, Inc.
Div. Johnson & Johnson
Camp Hill Road
Fort Washington, Pennsylvania
19034

Med Spec

Medical Specialties Corp.
6900 Second Ave. South
Birmingham, Alabama 35212

Merit Pharceut

Merit Pharmaceutical Co., Inc.
P.O. Box 12625
Houston, Texas 77017

―――

Metal And Thermit Co.
P.O. Box 471
Rahway, New Jersey 07065

―――

Mesco
P.O. Box 7944
Louisville, Kentucky 40207

Metro Med

Metro Med, Inc.
P.O. Box 6532
2510 South Blvd.
Houston, Texas 77005

Metz

Metz Pharmacal Co., Inc.
644 Mt. Prospect Ave.
Newark, New Jersey 07104

Meyer

Meyer Laboratories, Inc.
1900 W. Commercial Blvd.
Fort Lauderdale, Florida 33309

MSD

Merck Sharp & Dohme
Div. Merck & Co., Inc.
West Point, Pensylvania 19486

―――

National Aniline Division
Allied Chemical Corp.
40 Rector St.
New York, New York 10006

National Drug
National Drug Co.
Div. Richardson-Merrell, Inc.
4663 Stenton Ave.
Philadelphia, Pennsylvania 19144

Nortex
Nortex Laboratories, Inc.
P.O. Box 506
McKinney, Texas 75069

Noyes
P.J. Noyes Co.
101 Main St.
Lancaster, New Hampshire 03584

———

Nyanza Color and Chemical Corp.
49 Blanchard St.
Lawrence, Massachusetts 01843

Orbit
Orbit Pharmaceutical Co., Inc.
P.O. Box 1241
Kansas City, Kansas 66117

Ortho
Ortho Pharmaceutical Corp.
Div. Johnson & Johnson
Rt. 202
Raritan, New Jersey 08869

Osto
Osto Pharmaceutical Co.
200 Elmora Ave.
Elizabeth, New Jersey 07207

Owen Labs
Owen Laboratories, Inc.
8911 Directors Row
Dallas, Texas 75247

Palmedico
Palmedico, Inc.
Ethical Pharmaceuticals
P.O. Drawer 3397
Columbia, South Carolina 29203

Panray
Panray Div. Ormont Drug &
    Chemical Co., Inc.
520 S. Dean Street
Englewood, New Jersey 07631

Parker
Parker Laboratories, Inc.
P.O. Box 184
Irvington, New Jersey 07111

PD
Parke, Davis & Company
Jos Campau Ave., at the River
Detroit, Michigan 48232

———

S.B. Pennick Co.
50 Church St.
New York, New York 10003

———

Pflatz & Bauer, Inc.
31-20 College Point Causeway
Flushing, New York 11354

Pfizer Labs
Pfizer Laboratories
Div. Chas. Pfizer & Co., Inc.
235 E. 42nd St.
New York, New York 10017

———

Pfizer Laboratories
1151 Chattahooche Ave., N.W.
Atlanta, Georgia 30318

Pharmaderm
Pharmaderm, Inc.
Cantigue Road
Hicksville, L.I., New York 11802

PMS

Parkdale Medical Services, Inc.
7526 Louis Pasteur Dr., Suite 107
San Antonio, Texas 78229

Premo

Premo Pharmaceutical Laboratories, Inc.
111 Leuning St.
South Hackensack, New Jersey
07606

PRL

Philips Roxane Labs
Div. Philips Roxane, Inc.
330 Oak St.
Columbus, Ohio 43216

Prof Pharcal

Professional Pharmacal Co., Inc.
300 W. Josephine St.
San Antonio, Texas 78206

Progress

Progress Laboratories, Inc.
4156 S. Main St.
Los Angeles, California 90037

Purdue

Purdue Fredrick Co.
99-101 Saw Mill River Road
Yonkers, New York 10701

Purepac Pharm

Purepac Pharmaceutical Co.
Div. Elizabeth Laboratories
200 Elmora Ave.
Elizabeth, New Jersey 07207

Rachelle

Rachelle Laboratories, Inc.
700 Henry Ford Ave.
Long Beach, California 90810

Rand Lab

Rand Laboratories, Inc.
P.O. Box 7312
Metairie, Louisiana 70002

Rexall

Rexall Drug Co.
3901 N. Kingshighway
St. Louis, Missouri 63115

RIC

Research Industries Corp.
30 W. 2950 South
Salt Lake City, Utah 84115

Robins

A.H. Robins Co., Inc.
1407 Cummings Dr.
Richmond, Virginia 23220

Robinson Lab

Robinson Laboratory, Inc.
355 Brannan St.
San Francisco, California 94107

Roche

Roche Laboratories
Div. Hoffman-LaRoche, Inc.
Roche Park
Nutley, New Jersey 07110

Roerig

J.B. Roerig & Co.
Div. Chas. Pfizer & Co., Inc.
235 E. 42nd St.
New York, New York 10017

———

Rohm & Hass Co.

Rondex

Rondex Laboratories, Inc.
68 Sixty-ninth St.
Guttenberg, New Jersey 07093

Rowell

Rowell Laboratories, Inc.
Baudette, Minnesota 56623

RPL

Reid-Provident Laboratories, Inc.
25 Fifth Street, N.W.
Atlanta, Georgia 30308

S-K Research
S-K Research Laboratories, Inc.
P.O. Box 230
Phoenix, Arizona 85001

Sandoz
Sandoz Pharmaceuticals
Div. of Sandoz-Wander, Inc.
Route 10
Hanover, New Jersey 07936

SCA
Strong Cobb Arner, Inc.
11700 Shaker Boulevard
Cleveland, Ohio 44120

Schering
Schering Corp.
60 Orange St.
Bloomfield, New Jersey 07003 ´

Schlicksup
Schlicksup Drug Co., Inc.
420 S.W. Washington St.
Peoria, Illinois 61602

Scott-Cord
Scott-Cord Laboratories, Inc.
23 Englewood Ave.
Englewood, New Jersey 07666

Scrip
Scrip, Inc.
1900 N. Missouri Ave.
Peoria, Illinois 61603

Scruggs
Scruggs Pharmacal Co.
611 Moore St.
Marion, Alabama 36756

Searle
G.D. Searle & Co.
San Juan, Puerto Rico 00936

Sheraton
Sheraton Laboratories, Inc.
1400 Coleman Ave., D-12
Santa Clara, California 95050

SIG
SIG, Inc.
P.O. Box 35556
Houston, Texas 77035

SKF
Smith Kline & French Laboratories
1500 Spring Garden Street
Philadelphia, Pennsylvania 19101

Squibb
E.R. Squibb & Sons, Inc.
P.O.Box 4000
Princeton, New Jersey 08540

Stanley Drug
Stanley Drug Products, Inc.
Div. Sperti Drug Corp.
P.O. Box 3108
Portland, Oregon 97208

Star
Star Pharmaceuticals
206 Chanin Building
North Miami Beach, Florida 33162

Stauffer Chemical Co.
P.O. Box 7222
Houston, Texas 77008

Stayner
Stayner Corp.
2531 Ninth St.
Berkeley, California 94710

Steri-Med
Sterimed Division
Ketchum Laboratories, Inc.
26 Edison St.
Amityville, New York 11701

Sutliff & Case
Sutliff & Case Co., Inc.
Pharmaceutical Manufacturers
P.O. Box 838
Peroria, Illinois 61601

Tablroc
Table Rock Laboratories, Inc.
812 Hampton Ave., P.O. Box 1968
Greenville, South Carolina 29602

Thompson-Hayward Chemical Co.
1701 Oliver
P.O. Box 3185
Houston, Texas 77007

Torrance
The Torrance Co.
830 W. Centre Avenue, Box 242
Portage, Michigan 49081

Towne
Towne Paulsen & Co., Inc.
140 E. Duarte Road
Monrovia, California 91016

Travenol
Travenol Laboratories, Inc.
6301 Lincoln Ave.
Morton Grove, Illinois 60053

Trent
Trent Pharmaceuticals, Inc.
233 Broadway
New York, New York 10007

Tutag
S.J. Tutag & Co.
19180 Mt. Elliott Ave.
Detroit, Michigan 48234

Ulmer-Pharcal
Ulmer Pharmacal Co.
1400 Harman Place
Minneapolis, Minnesota 55403

United
United Pharmaceuticals, Inc.
1064 Forty-Fourth
Oakland, California 94601

Upjohn
The Upjohn Co.
7171 Portage Rd.
Kalamazoo, Michigan 49002

Upsher Smith
Upsher Smith Laboratories
529 S. Seventh St.
Minneapolis, Minnesota 55415

USV
USV Pharmaceutical Corp.
1 Scarsdale Road
Tuckahoe, New York 10707

Vale Chemical
Vale Chemical Co., Inc.
1201 Liberty St.
Allentown, Pennsylvania 18102

Vitarine
The Vitarine Co.
227-15 N. Conduit Ave.
Springfield Gardens, New York
   11413

WC
Warner-Chilcott Laboratories
Div. Warner-Lambert Pharma-
   ceutical Co.
201 Tabor Road
Morris Plains, New Jersey 07950

Webster
William A. Webster Co.
P.O. Box 18358
3580 Air Park St.
Memphis, Tennessee 38118

Wendt-Bristol
Wendt-Bristol Co.
1159 Dublin Road
Columbus, Ohio 43215

West-Ward

  West-Ward, Inc.
  745 Eagle Ave.
  Bronx, New York 10456

Winston

  Winston Pharmaceuticals, Inc.
  P.O. Box 5275
  Winston-Salem, North Carolina
    27103

Winthrop

  Winthrop Laboratories
  90 Park Avenue
  New York, New York 10016

  Winthrop Laboratories
  Div. of Sterling Drug Co.
  Sterwin Chemical, Inc.
  6627 Maple Ave.
  Dallas, Texas 75235

Wyeth

  Wyeth Laboratories, Inc.
  Div. American Home Products
    Corp.
  P.O. Box 8299
  Philadelphia, Pennsylvania 19101

Xttrium

  Xttrium Laboratories
  415 W. Pershing Road
  Chicago, Illinois 60609

Zemmer

  The Zemmer Co.
  231 Hulton Road
  Oakmont, Pennsylvania 15139

Zenith

  Zenith Laboratories, Inc.
  140 Le Grand Ave.
  Northvale, New Jersey 07647

BIBLIOGRAPHY

Adamson, R.H. "Drug Metabolism in Marine Vertebrates." *Federal Proceedings; Federation American Societies Experimental Biology,* 26:1047-1055, 1967.

Adlung, K.G.: "Zur Fischtoxizität Einiger Insektizider Wirkstoffe." *Aquaristik, 3*:124-127, 1957a.

Adlung, K.G. "Zur Toxizität Insektizider und Akarizider Wirkstoffe Für Fische." *Naturwissenschaften, 44*:471-472, 1957b.

Adlung, K.G., Bodenstein, G., and Müller-Bastgen, G. "Über Die Toxizität Einiger Pflanzenschutzmittel Für Fische." *Aquaristik, 3*:44-51, 1957.

Adlung, K.G. and Knauth, H. "Insektizide Zur Krabbenbekämpfung." *Anzeiger Fuer Schädlingsk* (now *Anzeiger Fishädlingsk*), 29:75, 1956.

Adlung, K.G. and Müller-Bastgen, G. "Weitere Ergebnisse Über Die Toxizität von Pflanzenschutzmitteln auf Fische." *Aquaristik, 3*:88-92, 1957.

Agapova, A.I. "Results of the Study of Fish Parasites in Waters of Kazakhstan." *Trudi Institute of Zoology. Akademiya Nauk Kazakhskoi SSR,* 7:121-130, 1957.

Agapova, A.I. *"Fish Diseases and Measures for Combating Them."* Alma-Ata, Akademiya Nauk Kazakhstan SSR, 1966.

Alexander, J.W., Fisher, M.W., Macmillan, B.G., and Altemier, W.A. "Prevention of Invasive *Pseudomonas* Infection in Burns With a New Vaccine." *Archives Surgery,* 99:249-256, 1969.

Allen, D.B. "The Use of Sulfathiazole Sodium for Treatment Against a Protozoan Ectoparasite of Marine Fish, and the Effect of the Drug on the Biological Filter of a Closed Recirculating System." *Abstract Proceedings AAZPA Conference,* Oct. 1972, p. 157.

Allen, J.L., Luhning, C.W., and Harman, P.D. *Identification of MS-222 Residues in Selected Fish Tissues by Thin Layer Chromatography.* Investigations in Fish Control, Bureau of Sport Fisheries and Wildlife, Fish and Wildlife Services, U.S. Dept. Interior, Washington, D.C., No. 41, 1970, pp. 1-7.

Allen, J.L., Luhning, C.W., and Harman, P.D. *Residues of MS-222 in Northern Pike, Muskellunge and Walleye.* Investigations in Fish Control, BSFW, FWS, U.S. Dept. Interior, Washington, D.C., No. 45, 1972, pp. 1-8.

Allen, J.L. and Sills, J.B. *Preparation and Properties of Quinaldine Sulfate, an Improved Fish Anesthetic.* Investigations In Fish Control, BSFW,

FWS, U.S. Dept. Interior, Washington, D.C., No. 47, 1973, pp. 1–7.

Allen, K.O. and Avault, J.W. Jr. "Effects of Brackish Water on *Ichthyophthirius*." *Progressive Fish-Culturist*, Supt. of Documents, Washington, D.C., U.S. Govt. Printing Office, *32(4)*:227–230, 1970.

Allison, L.N. "Common Diseases of Fish in Michigan." Michigan Dept. Conservation Miscellaneous Pub. No. 5, 1950, pp. 1–27.

——. "Advancements in Prevention and Treatment of Parasitic Diseases of Fish." *Transactions American Fisheries Society*, *83*:221–228, 1954.

——. "Variation in Strength of Pyridylmercuric Acetate Technical and its Effect on Rainbow Trout." *Prog Fish-Cult*, *19*:108–118, 1957.

——. "Multiple Sulfa Therapy of Kidney Disease Among Brook Trout." *Prog Fish-Cult, 20(2)*:66–68, 1958.

Allison, R. "Some New Results in the Treatment of Ponds to Control Some External Parasites of Fish." *Prog Fish-Cult, 19*:58–63, 1957a.

——. "A Preliminary Note on the Use of Di-*n*-Butyl Tin Oxide to Remove Tapeworms From Fish." *Prog Fish-Cult, 19*:128–130 and 192, 1957b.

——. "The Effects of Formalin and Other Parasiticides Upon Oxygen Concentration in Ponds." *Proceedings 16th Annual Conference Southeastern Association Game and Fish Commissioners*, 1962, pp. 446–449.

——. "Parasite Epidemics Affecting Channel Catfish." *Proc 17th Ann Conf SE Assoc Game & Fish Comm*, pp. 346–347.

——. "New Control Methods for *Ichthyophthirius* in Ponds." *FAO World Symposium on Warmwater Pond Fish Culture*, FR:IX/E-9, 1966.

——. "Parasiticidal Activity of Organophosphate Compounds." Final Report on Project A1-00593, Department of Zoology-Entomology (Fisheries), Auburn University, Auburn, Alabama, 1969.

Amend, D.F. *Oxytetracycline Efficacy as a Treatment for Furunculosis in Coho Salmon*. BSFW, FWS, U.S. Dept. Interior, Washington, D.C., Technical Papers No. 36, 1969a, pp. 1–6.

——. *Progress in Sport Fishery Research*. BSFW, Washington, D.C., U.S. Dept. Interior, Resources Pub. No. 88, 1969b.

——. "Control of Infectious Hematopoietic Necrosis Virus Disease by Elevating the Water Temperature." *Journal Fisheries Research Board Canada*, *27*:265–270, 1970a.

——. *Myxobacterial Infections of Salmonids: Prevention and Treatment.* American Fisheries Society, Special Pub. No. 5, 1970b, pp. 258–265.

——. *Efficacy, Toxicity, and Residues of Nifurpirinol in Salmonids.* BSFW, FWS, U.S. Dept. Interior, Washington, D.C., Technical Papers No. 62, 1972, pp. 1–13.

Amend, D.F. and Fryer, J.L. "The Administration of Sulfonamide Drugs to Adult Salmon." *Prog Fish-Cult, 30*:168–172, 1968.

Amend, D.F., Fryer, J.L., and Pilcher, S.K. "A Comparison of Oregon Pellet and Fish Meal Diets for Administration of Sulfamethazine to Chinook Salmon," *Research Briefs, Fish Commission Oregon*, *13*:20–24, 1967.

Amend, D.F., Fryer, J.L., and Pilcher, S.K. "Production Trials Utilizing Sulfonamide Drugs for the Control of 'Coldwater Disease' in Juvenile Coho Salmon." *Res Briefs*, Fish Comm Oregon, *11(1)*:14–17, 1965.

Amend, D.F. and Ross, A.J. "Experimental Control of Columnaris Disease with a New Nitrofuran Drug, P-7138." *Prog Fish-Cult*, *32*:19–25, 1970.

Amlacher, E. "Die Wirkung des Malachitgruns auf Fische, Fischparasiten *(Ichthyophthirius, Trichodina)* Kleinkrebse und Wasserpflanzen." *Deutsche Fischerei Zeitung*, *8(1)*:12–15, 1961a.

——. "Das Verhalten der Inneren Organe und der Muskulatur Dreisömmeriger Karpfen aus dem Teich des Dresdner Zwingers bei Extremer Kohlehydratfüttereung, 2 teil." *Zeitschrift Fischerei*, Vol 9 (New Series), 1961b.

——. *Taschenbuch der Fischkrankheiten*. Jena, G. Fischer Verlag, 1961; Translated by D.A. Conroy and R.L. Herman. *Textbook of Fish Diseases*. Neptune, New Jersey, T.F.H. Publications, Inc., 1970.

Anderson, P.O. and Battle, H.I. "Effects of Chloramphenicol on the Development of the Zebrafish, *Brachydanio rerio*." *Canadian Journal Zoology*, *45*:191–204, 1967.

Applegate, V.C., Howell, J.H., Moffett, J.W., and Smith, M.A. *Uses of 3-Trifluormethyl-4-Nitrophenol as a Selective Sea Lamprey Larvicide*. Ann Arbor, Michigan, Great Lakes Fishery Commission, Technical Report No. 1, 1961, pp. 1–35.

Applegate, V.C., Johnson, B.G.H., and Smith, M.A. *The Relation Between Molecular Structure and Biological Activity Among Mononitrophenols Containing Halogens*. Ann Arbor, Michigan, Great Lakes Fishery Commission, Technical Report No. 11, 1966, pp. 1–29.

Applegate, V.C. and King, E.L. "Comparative Toxicity of 3-Trifluoramethyl-4-Nitrophenol (TFM) to Larval Lampreys and Eleven Species of Fishes." *Trans Am Fish Soc*, *91(4)*:342–345, 1962.

Arasaki, S.K., Nozawa, K., and Mizaki, M. "On the Pathogenicity of Water Mold. II." *Bulletin Japanese Society Scientific Fisheries*, *23(9)*:593-598, 1958.

Aronson, A.L. and Kirk, R.W. "Antibiotic Therapy." In Kirk, R.W. (Ed.). *Current Veterinary Therapy V*. Philadelphia, W.B. Saunders Co., 1974.

Ashley, L.M. and Halver, J.E. "Dimethylnitrosamine-Induced Hepatic Cell Carcinoma in Rainbow Trout." *Journal National Cancer Institute*, *41*: 531–552, 1968.

Askerov, T.A. "A Method for Control of Saprolegnial Fungus." *Rybnoe Khozyaistvo*, Oct. 10, 1968, pp. 23–24 (English translation by BSFW, U.S. Dept. Interior, Washington, D.C.).

Astakhova, T.V. and Martino, K.V. "Measures for the Control of Fungus Diseases of the Eggs of Sturgeons in Fish Hatcheries." *Voprosy Ikhtiologiii*, *8(2)*:261–268, 1968 *(Problems of Ichthyology* translated into English by American Fisheries Society).

Avdosev, B.S. "New Methods of Malachite Green Used to Control Carp *Ichthyophthirius.*" *Ryb Khoz, 38(7):*27–29, 1962 (In Russian).

Avdosev, B.A. et al. "Lechenic I Nery Profilaktiki Porazheniya Shchuk Pilyavkame" [The treatment and prophylaxis of pike infested by leeches]. *Veterinariia, 60.* Also *Biological Abstracts, 42,* Abs. 8768, 1962.

Babaev, B. and Shcherbakova, A. "The Control of *Bothriocephalus gowkongensis* from *Ctenopharyngodon idella.*" Izvestiia Akademii Nauk SSSR–Seria Biologicheskaia, *4:*86–87, 1963 (In Russian).

Bailosoff, D. "Neguvon, ein Wirksames Mittel Zur Bekampfung der Karpfenlaus und Sonstiger Parasitärer Fischkrankheiten." *Dtsch Fisch Ztg, 10:*181-182, 1963.

Bandt, H.J. "Chemische Pflanzenbekämpfungsmittel (Herbizide) und Fische." *Dtsch Fisch Ztg, 6:*241–244, 1959.

Barbosa, F.S. "Insoluble or Slightly Soluble Chemicals as Molluscicides." *Bulletin World Health Organization, 25:*710–711, 1961.

Batte, E.G., Murphy, J.B., and Swanson, L.E. "New Molluscicides for the Control of Freshwater Snails." *American Journal Veterinary Research, 12:*158–160, 1951.

Bauer, O.N. *Ichthyophthirius in Fish Ponds and Measures Against It.* Leningrad, Institute Freshwater Fisheries, Bull. No. 36, 1955.

———. "Parasitic Diseases of Cultured Fishes and Methods of Their Prevention and Treatment." In Dogiel, V.A., Petrushevski, G.K., and Polyanski, Y.I. (Eds.). *Parasitology of Fishes.* London, Oliver & Boyd, 1961; Translated by Z. Kabata. Neptune, New Jersey, T.F.H. Publications, 1970; Original Russian publication by Leningrad University Press, 1958.

———. *Parasites of Freshwater Fish and the Biological Basis for Their Control.* State Science Research Institute Lake and River Fish, Bull No. 49, 1959 (English translation by U.S. Dept. Commerce, Washington, D.C., OTS-61-31056).

———. "Control of Carp Diseases in the U.S.S.R." *FAO World Symp Warmwater Pond Fish Cult,* FR:IX/E:344–352, 1966.

Bauer, O.N. and Babaev, B. "*Sinergasilus major* (Markewitsch, 1940): Its Biology and its Pathological Importance." *Izvestiia Akademiia Nauk Turmensk SSSR, 3:*63–67, 1964.

Bauer, O.N., Musselius, J., and Strelkov, A. *Bolezny Prudovyh Ryb [Diseases of Pond Fishes].* Moscow, Kolos, 1969 (English translation by U.S. Dept. Commerce, Washington, D.C., TT 72 50070).

Bauer, O.N. and Nikolskaya, N.P. "New Therapeutic Substance Against Dactylogyrosis of the Carp Fry." *Fisheries Industries* (Moscow), Vol. 7, 1951.

Bauer, O.N. and Strelkov, Y.A. "Diseases of Artificially Reared *Salmo salar* Fry." *Proceedings 9th Conference Fish Diseases,* Academy Science, U.S. S.R., 1959, pp. 89–93 (English translation by U.S. Dept. Commerce, Washington, D.C., OTS-61-31058).

Bauer, O.N. and Upenskaya, A.V. "New Curative Methods in the Control of Fish Diseases." *Proc 9th Conf Fish Diseases*, Academy Sciences, U.S. S.R., Ichthyological Committee, 1959, pp. 19–25 (English translation by Israel Program Scientific Translations of Jerusalem For National Science Foundation).

Beckert, H. and Allison, R. "Some Host Responses of White Catfish to *Ichthyophthirius multifiliis* Fouquet." *Proc 18th Ann Conf SE Assoc Game & Fish Comm*, 1964.

Bedell, G.W. "Eradicating *Ceratomyxa shasta* From Infected Water by Chlorination and Ultraviolet Irradiation." *Prog Fish-Cult, 33(1):51–54,* 1971.

Bell, G.R. *A Guide to the Properties, Characteristics and Uses of Some General Anesthetics for Fish.* Fisheries Research Board Canada, Bull. No. 148, 1967 (rev. 1969).

Benoit, R.F. and Matlin, N.A. "Control of *Saprolegnia* on Eggs of Rainbow Trout *(Salmo gairdneri)* With Ozone." *"Trans Am Fish Soc, 95(4):* 430–432, 1966.

Bent, K.J. "Fungicides in Perspective." *Endeavour (London), 28(105):129–134,* 1969.

Beresky, A. and Sarig, S. "Use of Aqua-Ammonia in Fish Ponds." *Agricultural Ammonia News*, May–June, 1965, pp. 55–57.

Berg, G.L. *Farm Chemicals Handbook.* Willoughby, Ohio, Meister Publishing Co., 1970.

Berg, O. and Gorbman, A. "Iodine Utilization by Tumorous Thyroid Tissues of the Swordtail, *Xiphophorus montezumae." Cancer Research, 14:232–236,* 1954.

Berg, O. and Gordon, M. "Thyroid Drugs That Control Growth of Goiters in Xiphophorin Fishes." *Proceedings American Association Cancer Research*, Vol. 1, Abstract 5, 1953.

Berger, B.L., Lennon, R.F., and Hogan, J.W. *Laboratory Studies on Antimycin A as a Fish Toxicant.* Investigations in Fish Control, BSFW, FWS, U.S. Dept. Interior, Washington, D.C., No. 26, 1969, pp. 1–21.

Berrios-Duran, L.A., Ritchie, L.S., Frick, L.P., and Fox, I. *Comparative Piscicidal Activity of "Stabilized Chevreul Salt" (SCS), A Candidate Molluscicide and Bayluscide,* 1964.

Bevan, Billie M. and Zeiller, W. *Ultraviolet Irradiation of Marine Aquaria.* (Published privately), 1967.

Bills, T.D. and Marking, L.L. *Toxicity of 3-Trifluormethyl-4'-nitrosalicylanilide (Bayer 73), and a 98:2 Mixture of Fingerlings of Seven Fish Species and to Eggs and Fry of Coho Salmon.* Investigations in Fish Control, BSFW, FWS, U.S. Dept. Interior, Washington, D.C., No. 69, 1976, pp. 1–9.

Blume, Dorthy M. *Dosages and Solutions.* Philadelphia, Davis Co., 1969.

Bogdanova, E.A. "Malachite Green and Formalin: Effective Agents for the

Control of Trichodiniasis." *Ryb Khoz, 38:(8):*30–31, 1962. Also in *Biological Abstracts, 41,* Abs. 17281 (English translation by FWS, Washington, D.C.).

Borshosh, A.V. and Illesh, V.V. "Elimination of *Ichthyophthirius* From Fish Ponds." *Veterinariia, 39(11),* 1962 (SLA Translation TT-66011296).

Bowen, J.T. and Putz, R.E. *Parasites of Freshwater Fish, IV. Miscellaneous. 3. Parasitic Copepod Argulus.* FWS, U.S. Dept. Interior, Washington, D.C., Fishery Leaflet FDL 3, 1966, pp. 1–4.

Boyce, C., Jones, W.T., and van Tongeren, W.A. "The Molluscicidal Activity of *n-Tritylmorpholine.*" *Bull WHO, 37:*1–11, 1967.

Braker, W.P. "Controlling Saltwater Parasites." *The Aquarium, 30(1):*12–15, 1961.

Brunner, G. "Zur Bekämpfung der Karpfenlaus *(Argulus foliaceus).*" *Allgemeine Fischerei Zeitung, 46:*174–175, 1943.

Bryant, M. Jr. "The Use of PMA in Treating Columnaris." *Prog Fish-Cult, 13:*103-104, 1951.

Bulkley, R.V. and Hlavek, R.R. *Effects of Malachite Green on Fish Blood Composition.* Iowa Cooperative Fishery Research Unit, First Quarter, 1976a.

Bulkley, R.V. and Hlavek, R.R. *Effects of Malachite Green on Fish Blood Composition.* Iowa Cooperative Fishery Research Unit, Second Quarter, 1976b.

Bullock, G.L. and Collis, D. *Oxytetracycline Sensitivity of Selected Fish Pathogens.* BSFW, U.S. Dept. Interior, Washington, D.C., Technical Papers No. 32, 1969.

Bureau of Sport Fisheries and Wildlife, Division of Fish Hatcheries. *Hatchery Biologists Quarterly Report,* Region I, U.S. Dept. Interior, Washington, D.C., 1960.

——. Fourth Quarter, U.S. Dept. Interior, Washington, D.C., 1968.

——. First Quarter, U.S. Dept. Interior, Washington, D.C., 1969.

Burkholder, P.R. "Antibiotic Plankton Diet for Penguins." *International Zoo Year Book, 2:*105, 1960.

Burress, R.M. *Development and Evaluation of On-site Toxicity Test Procedures for Fishery Investigations.* Investigations in Fish Control, BSFW, FWS, U.S. Dept. Interior, Washington, D.C., No. 68, 1975, pp 1–8.

Burress, R.M. and Luhning, C.W. *Field Trials of Antimycin A as a Selective Toxicant in Channel Catfish Ponds.* Investigations in Fish Control, BSFW, FWS, U.S. Dept. Interior, No. 25, 1969a, pp. 3–11.

Burress, R.M. and Luhning, C.W. *Use of Antimycin A for Selective Thinning of Sunfish Populations in Ponds.* Investigations in Fish Control, BSFW, FWS, U.S. Dept. Interior, Washington, D.C., No. 28, 1969b, pp. 1–10.

Burrows, R.E. "Prophylactic Treatment for Control of Fungus *(Saprolegnia parasitica)* on *Salmo* eggs." *Prog Fish-Cult, 11(2):*97–103, 1949.

Burrows, R.E. and Palmer, D.D. "Pyridylmercuric Acetate: Its Toxicity to Fish, Efficacy in Disease Control and Applicability to a Simplified Treatment Technique." *Prog Fish-Cult, 11(3)*:147–151, 1949.

Butcher, A.D. "*Ichthyophthirius* in Australian Trout Hatchery." *Prog Fish-Cult, 9(1)*:21–26, 1947.

Calabrese, A. *Effects of Acids and Alkalies on Survival of Bluegills and Largemouth Bass.* BSFW, U.S. Dept. Interior, Washington, D.C., Technical Papers No. 42, 1969, pp. 1–10.

Calhoun, A. (Ed.). *Inland Fisheries Management.* The Resources Agency, Department of Fish & Game, State of California, 1966.

Camey, T., Paulini, E., and de Souza, C.P. "Aaco moluscicida de Gramoxone (*N,N'*-dimetil-*p,p'*-dipiridila) sobre *B. glabrata* em suas diversas fases de evolucaco." *Revista Brasileira de Malariologia Doencas Tropicans, 18(2)*:235–245, 1966.

Chabaud, A., Deschiens, R., Le Corroller, Y. "Demonstration à Marrakch d'un Traitment Molluscicide des Eaux Douces par le Chlorure Cuivreux Dans le Cadre de la Prophylaxie des Bilharzioses." *Bulletin de Societe de Pathologie Exotique et des Ses Filiales, 58(5)*:885–890, 1965.

Chandler, J.H. and Marking, L.L. *Toxicity of the Lampricide 3-Trifluoromethyl-4-Nitrophenol (TFM) to Selected Aquatic Invertebrates and Frog Larvae.* Investigations in Fish Control, BSFW, FWS, U.S. Dept. Interior, Washington, D.C., No. 62, 1975, pp. 1–7.

Chang, S. *Bulletin Institute of Chemistry, Academia Sinica,* No. 3, 1960, pp. 44–50.

Chechina, A.S. "Sanguinicolsis and Measures for its Control in the Pond Fisheries of the Belo-Russian SSR." *Proc 9th Conf Fish Diseases,* Academy of Science, U.S.S.R. 1959, pp. 56–59 (English translation by U.S. Dept. Commerce, Washington, D.C., OTS-61-31058).

Chen Tung-Pai. "A Study of the Methods of Prevention and Treatment of Fish Lice in Pond Culture." *Lignan Science Journal, 12*:241–244, 1933.

Cherrington, A.D., Paim, U., and Pate, O.T. "In Vitro Degredation of DDT by Intestinal Contents of Atlantic Salmon (*Salmo salar*)." *J Fish Res Bd Can, 26*:47–54, 1969.

Choate, J. "Use of Tetracycline Drugs to Mark Advanced Fry and Fingerling Brook Trout (*Salvelinus fontinalis*)." *Trans Am Fish Soc, 93(3)*: 309–311, 1964.

Clemens, H.P. and Sneed, K.E. "The Chemical Control of some Diseases and Parasites of Channel Catfish." *Prog Fish-Cult, 20(1)*:8–15, 1958.

Clemens, H.P. and Sneed, K.E. *Lethal Doses of Several Commercial Chemicals for Fingerling Channel Catfish.* FWS, U.S. Dept. Interior, Washington, D.C., Special Science Report No. 316, 1959.

Collins, M.T., Gratzek, J.B., Dawe, D.L., and Nemetz, T.G. "Effects of Parasiticides on Nitrification." *J Fish Res Bd Can, 32*:2033–2037, 1975.

Connell, F. "Chlorine Treatment for Bacterial Fin Rot of Trout." *Prog*

Fish-Cult, 34:6–9, 1937.

Conroy, D.A. "Estudio in Vitro de la Accion de la Kanamicina Sobre Bacterias Patogenas Para los Peces." *Microbiologia Espanola, 14*:147–155, 1961a.

Conroy, D.A. "Las Causas de un Brote de Putrefaccion de la Aleta Caudal en los Peces y su Tratamiento con Kanamicinia." *Microbiol Esp, 14*:239–246, 1961b.

Conroy, D.A. "El Tratamiento de "Tail Rot" en Peces con la Kanamicina." *Ciencia e Investigation, 18*:133, 1962.

Conroy, D.A. "Studies of the Application of Kanamycin to the Control and Treatment of Some Bacterial Diseases of Fish." *Journal Applied Bacteriology, 26*:182–192, 1963.

Crandall, C. and Goodnight, C.J. "The Effect of Various Factors on the Toxicity of Sodium Pentachlorophenate to Fish." *Limnology & Oceanography, 4(1)*:53–56, 1959.

Crossland, N.O. "Field Trials to Evaluate the Effectiveness of the Molluscicide N-Tritylmorpholine in Irrigation Systems." *Bull WHO, 37*:23–42, 1967.

Crossland, N.O., Pearson, A.J., and Bennett, M.S. "A Field Trial With the Molluscicide Frescon for Control of *Lymnaea peregra* Miller, Snail Host of *Diplostomum spathaceum* (Rudolphii)." *Journal Fish Biology, 3(3)*: 297–302, 1971.

Cummins, R. Jr. "Malachite Green Oxalate Used to Control Fungus on Yellow Pikeperch Eggs in Jar Hatchery Operations." *Prog Fish-Cult, 16(2)*:79–82, 1954.

Curran, D. and Herman, R.L. *Oxytetracycline Efficacy as a Pretreatment Against Columnaris and Furunculosis in Coho Salmon.* BSFW, FWS, U.S. Dept. Interior, Washington, D.C., Technical Papers No. 34, 1969, pp. 1–6.

Cutting, W.C. *Actions and Uses of Drugs.* Stanford, California, Stanford U Press, 1946.

Daniels, S.L., Kempe, L.L., Billy, T.J., and Beeton, A.M. *Detection and Measurement of Organic Lamricide Residues.* Ann Arbor, Michigan, Great Lakes Fishery Commission, Technical Report No. 9, 1965, pp. 1–9.

Davis, H.S. *Culture and Diseases of Fishes.* Berkeley, U of Cal Pr. 1953.

Dawson, V.K., Cumming, K.B., and Gilderhus, P.A. *Laboratory Efficacy of 3-Trifluoromethyl-4-Nitrophenol (TFM) as a Lampricide.* Investigations in Fish Control, FWS, U.S. Dept. Interior, Washington, D.C., No. 63, 1975, pp. 1–13.

Dawson, V.K. and Marking, L.L. *Toxicity of Mixtures of Quinaldine Sulfate and MS-222 to Fish.* Investigations in Fish Control, BSFW, FWS, U.S. Dept. Interior, Washington, D.C., No. 53, 1973, pp. 1–11.

De Graaf, F. "On the Use of Lindane in Fresh and Seawater." *Bulletin, Aquatic Biology, 1(6)*:41–43, 1959.

De Graaf, F. "A New Parasite Causing Epidemic Infection in Captive Coral Fishes." *Bulletin de L'Institut Oceanographique,* Numero Special 1A, Premier Congrès International d'Aquaraiologie, *A*:93–96, 1962.

DeManche, J.M., Donaghay, P.L., Breese, W.P., and Small, L.F. "Residual Toxicity of Ozonized Seawater to Oyster Larvae." Oregon State University, Corvallis, Oregon, Sea Grant Pub. No. ORESU-T-75-003, 1975, pp. 1–7.

Dempster, R.P. "The Use of Copper Sulfate as a Cure for Fish Diseases Caused by Parasitic Dinoflagellates of the Genus *Oodinium.*" *Zoologica, 40(12)*:133–139, 1955.

———. "Brackish Water as a Cure for *Ichthyophthirius* in Trout." *Drum & Croaker, 70(1)*:17, 1970a.

———. "Sodium Chlorite for Water Clarity in the Marine Dolphin System." *Drum & Croaker, 16(3)*:5–6, 1970b.

———. "Quinaldine." *The Marine Aquarist, 4(2)*:60–61, 1973.

Dempster, R.P. and Shipman, W.H. "The Use of Copper Sulfate as a Medicament for Aquarium Fishes and as an Algaecide in Marine Mammal Water Systems." *Occasional Papers California Academy Sciences,* No. 71, 1969.

Dempster, R.P. and Shipman, W.H. "The Use of Hydrogen Peroxide in the Control of Fish Disease." *Drum & Croaker, 70(1)*:27–29, 1970.

Deschiens, R. "Nots aux Prospecteurs sur les Applications Molluscicides Chimiques en Prophylaxis de la Bilharziose sur le Terrain." *Bull Soc Pathol Exot, 54(2)*:365–375, 1961.

Deschiens, R. and Floch, H. "Controle de l'action des Molluscicides Selectifs sur la Microfaune et sur la Microflore des eaux Douces." *Bull Soc Pathol Exot,* 57:292–299, 1964. Also in *Helminthological Abstracts, 34,* Abs. 1006, 1964.

Deschiens, R., Floch, H., and Le Corroller, Y. "Actions Molluscicide et Piscicide de sel Cuprosulfitique de Chevreul en Prophylaxie des Bilharzioses." *Bull Soc Pathol Exot, 56(3)*:438–442, 1963.

Deschiens, R., Gamet, A., Brottes, H., and Mvogo, L. "Application Molluscicide sur le Terrain, au Camerain, de l'oxyde Cuivereux dans le Cadre de la Prophylaxie des Bilharzioses." *Bull Soc Pathol Exot, 58(3)*:445–455, 1965.

Deschiens, R. and Tahiri, M. "Action Molluscicide Selective du Sulfate de Cadmium." *Bull Soc Pathol Exot, 54(5)*:944–946, 1961.

Detwiler, S.R. and McKennon, G.E. "Mercurochrome (Di-bromoxy-mercuri-Fluorescein) as Fungicidal Agent in Growth of Amphibian Embryos." *Anatomical Record, 41(2)*:205–211, 1929.

Deufel, J. "Malachitgrün zur Bekämpfung von *Ichthyophthirius* bei Forellen." *Fischwirt,* Vol. 1, 1960.

Deufel, J. "Direkte und Indirekte Bekämpfung von *Diplostomum volvens* in Kleinen Gewassern Mit Bayluscid." *Fischwirt, 12*:1–3; also *14*:341–343, 1964.

Deufel, J. "Vorbeugende Behandlung der Furunkulose in der Forellen-zucht Mit Zinkbacitracin." *Allg Fisch Ztg*, 92 Jahrgang, N.R., Vol. 4, 1967.

Deufel, J. "Untersuchungen Mit dem Desinfectionsmittel Halamid." *Fischwirt, 20(5)*:114–117, 1970.

Dogiel, V.A. and Bauer, O.N. *Parasitic Diseases in Pond Fisheries and Measures Against Them*. An S.S.S.R. (Akademii Nauk U.S.S.R.), Popular Science Series, 1955.

Dogiel, V.A., Petrushevski, G.K., and Polyanski, Y.I. (Eds.). *Parasitology of Fishes*. London, Oliver & Boyd, 1961. Translated by Z. Kabata. Neptune, New Jersey, T.F.H. Publications, 1970; Original Russian publication by Leningrad University Press, 1958.

Dulin, ·Mark P. *Diseases of Marine Aquarium Fishes*. Neptune, New Jersey, T.F.H. Publications, 1976.

Earnest, R.D. "The Effect of Paraquat on Fish in a Colorado Farm Pond." *Prog Fish-Cult, 33(1)*:27–31, 1971.

Earp, B.J. and Schwab, R.L. "An Infestation of Leeches on Salmon Fry and Eggs." *Prog Fish-Cult, 16(3)*:122–124, 1954.

Edminister, J.O. and Gray, J.W. "Toxicity Thresholds From Three Chlorides and Three Acids to the Fry of the White Fish (*Coregonus clupeaformis*) and Yellow Pickeral (*Stizotedion v. vitreum*). *Prog Fish-Cult, 10(2)*:105–106, 1948.

Embody, G.C. "Notes on the Control of Gyrodactylus on Trout." *Trans Am Fish Soc, 54*:48–50, 1924.

Ergens, R. "Direct Control Measures for Some Ectoparasites of Fish." *Prog Fish-Cult, 24(3)*:133–134, 1962.

Erickson, J.D. "Report on the Problem of *Ichthyosporidium* in Rainbow Trout." *Prog Fish-Cult, 27*:179–183, 1965.

Evelyn, T.P.T. "Tissue Levels of Chloramphenicol Attained in Sockeye (*Oncorhynchus nerka*) and Coho (*O. kisutch*) Salmon by Feeding." *Bulletin de l'Office International des Epizooties, 69*:1453–1463, 1968.

Falk, H.L. *Potential Hepatocarcinogens for Fish*. BSFW, FWS, Research Report No. 70, 1967, pp. 175–177, 182–192.

Farwell, C.J. "Nitrofuran Compound 'Furanace' for Bacterial Fish Disease Treatment." *Proc AAZPA Conf*, Oct. 1972, p. 176.

Fasten, N. "The Brook Trout Disease at Wild Rose and Other Hatcheries, Report Wisconsin Commission Fisheries for 1911–1912." *Wisconsin Fisheries Commission*, 1912, pp. 12–22.

Ferguson, F.F., Richards, C.S., and Palmer, J.R. "Control of *Australorbis glabratus* by Acrolein in Puerto Rico." *Public Health Report, 76(6)*: 461–468, 1961.

Finegold, S.M., Davis, A., Ziment, I., and Jacobs, I. *Outline Guide to Chemotherapy*. Oradell, New Jersey, Medical Economics Book Division, 1970.

Fischthal, J. "*Epistylis:* A Peritrichous Protozoan on Hatchery Brook

Trout." *Prog Fish-Cult, 11(2):*122–124, 1949.

Fish, F.F. "The Chemical Disinfection of Trout Ponds." *Trans Am Fish Soc, 63:*158–162, 1933.

———. "Simplified Methods for the Prolonged Treatment of Fish Diseases." *Trans Am Fish Soc, 68:*178–187, 1939.

———. "Formalin for External Protozoan Parasites." *Prog Fish-Cult, 48:* 1–10, 1940.

Fish, F.F. and Burrows, R. "Experiments Upon the Control of Trichodiniasis of Salmonid Fishes by the Prolonged Recirculation of Formalin Solutions." *Trans Am Fish Soc, 69:*94–100, 1940.

Fletcher, A. "Anchor Worm (Aquarium Pest)." *All Pets, 32(2):*27–28, 1961.

Floch, A., Deschiens, R., and Le Corroller, Y. "Sue l'action Molluscicide Elective de l'oxyde Cuivreux du Ciuvre Metal et du Chlorure Cuivereux." *Bull Soc Pathol Exot, 57:*124–138, 1964. Also in *Helm Abstr, 34,* Abs. 1007, 1964.

Foster, R.F. and Olson, P.A. "An Incident of High Mortality Among Large Rainbow Trout After Treatment With PyridylMercuric Acetate." *Prog Fish-Cult, 13(3):*129–130, 1951.

Foster, F.J. and Woodbury, L. "The Use of Malachite Green as a Fish Fungicide and Antiseptic." *Prog Fish-Cult, 18:*7–9, 1936.

Foye, R.E. "The Effects of a Low Dosage Application of Antimycin A on Several Species of Fish in Crater Pond, Aroostook County, Maine." *Prog Fish-Cult, 30(4):*216–219, 1968.

Frear, D.E.H. *Pesticide Index.* State College, Pennsylvania, College Science Publishers, 1961.

Fremling, C.R. *Acute Toxicity of the Lampricide 3-Trifluoromethyl4-Nitrophenol (TFM) to Nymphs of Mayflies (Hexagonia sp.).* Investigations in Fish Control, BSFW, U.S. Dept. Interior, Washington, D.C., No. 58, 1975, pp. 1–8.

Friborough, J.H., Robinson, J.A., and Meyer, F.P. *Oxytetracycline Residues in Tissues of Blue and Channel Catfishes.* BSFW, U.S. Dept. Interior, Washington, D.C., Technical Papers No. 38, 1969a, pp. 1–7.

———. *Oxytetracycline Levels Produced in Catfish Serum by Three Methods of Treatment.* BSFW, U.S. Dept. Interior, Washington, D.C., Technical Papers No. 39, 1969b, pp. 1–6.

———. *Oxytetracycline Leaching from Medicated Fish Feeds.* BSFW, U.S. Dept. Interior, Washington, D.C., Technical Papers No. 40, 1969c, pp. 1–7.

Frick, L.P., Ritchie, L.S., Fox, I., and Jiminez, W. "Molluscicidal Qualities of Copper Protoxide (Cu_2O) as Revealed by Tests on Stages of *Australorbis glabratus.*" *Bull WHO, 30:*295–298, 1964.

Funnikova, S.V. and Krivova, M.I. "Action of Chlorophos on the Lower Crustaceans." *Uchenye Zapiske Kazanskoga Veterinaria Instituta, 96:*228–233, 1966.

Gamet, A., Brottes, H., and Mvogo, L. "Premiers Essais de Lutte Contre

les Vecteurs des Bilharzioses dans les Etangs D'une Station de Piscicul-
ture au Cameroun." *Bull Soc Pathol Exot, 57*:118–124, 1964.

Gardner, W. and Cooke, E.I. *Chemical Synonyms and Trade Names.*
Cleveland, Ohio, Chemical Rubber Co., 1968.

Garibaldi, L. "Chlorine +3." *Drum & Croaker, 12(1)*:15–19, 1971.

Gee, L. and Sarles, W. "The Disinfection of Trout Eggs Contaminated
With *Bacterium salmonicida.*" *Journal Bacteriology, 44*:111–126, 1942.

"General Anesthesia in Exotics." *Veterinary Medicine/Small Animal Clini-
cian,* Sept. 1974, pp. 1184–1185.

Gerard, J.P. and de Kinkelin, P. "Traitment de l'Acanthocephalose de la
Truite Arc-en-ciel." *La Piscicult* (Francaise), No. 26, 1971, pp. 22–27.

Ghadially, F.N. "Treatments for White Spot Disease, Part I." *The Aquarist, 28*:98–100, 1963.

Ghadially, F.N. "Treatments for White Spot Disease, Part II." *The
Aquarist, 29*:116–118, 1964.

Ghittino, P. "Systemic Control of Hexamitiasis in Trout Fingerlings." *Ri-
vista Italiana Piscicultura Ittiopatologia, 3(1)*:8–10, 1968.

Ghittino, P. *Piscicoltura e Ittiopatologia, 2-Ittiopatologia.* Edited by *Rivi-
sta Zootecnia Veterinaria.* Giovanni, Stampa Strada, Sesto 5, 1970.

Ghittino, P. and Arcarese, G. "*Argulosi e Lerneosi* dei Pesci Trattate in Ex-
tenso con Masoten Bayer." *Riv Ital Piscicult Ittiopatol, 5(4)*:93–96, 1970.

Gibbs, E.L. "An Effective Treatment for Red Leg Disease in *Rana pipiens.*"
Laboratory Animal Care, 13(6):781–783, 1963.

Gilderhus, P.A., Berger, B.L., and Lennon, R.E. *Field Trials of Antimycin
A as a Fish Toxicant.* Investigations in Fish Control, BSFW, FWS, U.S.
Dept. Interior, Washington, D.C., No. 27, 1969, pp. 1–21.

Gilderhus, P.A., Berger, B.L., Sills, J.B., and Harman, P.D. *The Efficacy of
Quinaldine Sulfate as an Anesthetic for Freshwater Fish.* Investigations
in Fish Control, BSFW, U.S. Dept. Interior, Washington, D.C., No. 49,
1973a, pp. 1–9.

Gilderhus, P.A., Berger, B.L., Sills, J.B., and Harman, P.D. *The Efficacy
of Quinaldine Sulfate: MS-222 Mixtures for the Anesthetization of Freshwater Fish.* Investigations in Fish Control, BSFW, U.S. Interior, Washington, D.C., No. 54, 1973b, pp. 1–9.

Gilderhus, P.A., Sills, J.B., and Allen, J.L. *Residues of 3-Trifluoromethyl-4-
Nitrophenol (TFM) in a Stream Ecosystem After Treatment for Control
of Sea Lampreys.* Investigations in Fish Control, BSFW, U.S. Dept. Interior, Washington, D.C., No. 66, 1975, pp. 1–7.

Giudice, J.J. "Control of *Lernaea carassii* Tidd, Parasitic Copepod Infesting
Goldfish in Hatchery Ponds, With Related Observations on Crayfish and
the 'Fish Louse,' *Argulus sp.*" Master's Thesis, University of Missouri
(Columbia), 1950.

Glagoleva, T.P. and Malikova, E.M. "The Effect of Malachite Green on the
Blood Composition of Young Baltic Salmon." *Ryb Khoz, 44(5)*:15–18,
1968.

Gnadeberg, W. "Beiträge zur Biologie und Entwicklung des *Ergasilus sieboldi* v. Nordmann (Copepoda: Parasitica)." *Zeitschrift Parasitenkunde, 14(1,2):*103–180, 1949.

Goldstein, R.J. "Aquarist Goldstein States Fear of Drugged Fish All Wet." *Marine Hobbyist News, 1(3):*1, 6, 1973.

Goncharov, G.D. "Effect of Chloramine-B on Ectoparasites." *Trudy Biologic Cheskogo Instituta.* Sibirshoe Otdelfnie. [*Trudy Biol Inland Waters*]. An SSSR, *10:*338–340, 1966 (English translation by *Fish Res Bd Can Lib Bull, 5(2):*2, 1966).

Goncharov, G.D. and Mikryakov, V.R. "The Effect of Low Concentrations of Phenol on Antibody Formation in Carp, *Cyprinus carpio L.*" In *Problems of Aquatic Toxicology.* Moscow, 'Nauka,' 1970 (English translation by BSFW, Division of Fish Research, 1971).

Gopalakrishnan, V. "Controlling Pest and Diseases of Cultured Fishes." *Indian Livestock, 1(1):*51–54, 1963.

——. "Recent Developments in the Prevention and Control of Parasites of Fishes Cultured in Indian Waters." *Proceedings Zoological Society Calcutta, 17:*95–100, 1964.

——. "Diseases and Parasites of Fishes in Warm Water Ponds in Asia and the Far East." *FAO World Symp Warmwater Pond Fish Cult,* FR:IX/ R-4:319–343, 1966.

Gottwald, M. "Die Anwendung von Malachitgrün und Kochsalz Bein Erbrüten und Hältern von Laichfischen in Polen." *Dtsch Fisch Ztg, 8(2):* 48–52, 1961.

Gowanloch, J.N. "Notes on the Occurrence and Control of the Trematode *Gyrodactylus,* Ectoparasitic on *Fundulus.*" *Transactions Nova Scotian Institute of Science, 16:*126–131, 1927.

Grabda, J. and Grabda, E. "An Attempt to Control Dactylogyrosis of Carp With Neguvon," *FAO Fish Report, 5(44)*IX/E7:377–379, 1966, 1968.

Grétillat, S. "Prophylaxie de la Dracunulose par Destruction des *Cyclops* au Moyen d'un Dérive Organique de Synthése, le Dimethyldithiocarbamate de Zinc ou Zirame." *Biologie Medicale, 54(5):*529–539, 1965. Also in *Helm Abstr, 36, (1):*518, 1965.

Guberlet, J.E., Hansen, H.A., and Kavanaugh, J.A. "Studies on the Control of *Gyrodactylus.*" *Fisheries Publications, University of Washington,* College of Fisheries, 2:17–29, 1927.

Gutsell, J. "Sulfa Drugs and the Treatment of Furunculosis in Trout." *Science, 104:*85–86, 1946.

Gutsell, J. "The Value of Certain Drugs, Especially Sulfa Drugs, in the Treatment of Furunculosis in Brook Trout, *Salvelinus fontinalis.*" *Trans Am Fish Soc, 75:*186–199, 1948.

Gutsell, J. and Snieszko, S.F. "Dosage of Sulfamerazine in the Treatment of Furunculosis in Brook Trout *(Salvelinus fontinalis).*" *Trans Am Fish Soc, 76:*82–96, 1949a.

Gutsell, J. and Snieszko, S.F. "Response of Brook, Rainbow, and Brown

Trout to Various Dosages of Sulfamerazine." *Trans Am Fish Soc, 77:* 93–101, 1949b.

Harris, E.J. "Quantitative Determination of Copper in a Natural Receiving Water With 2,2 biguinoline." *New York Fish & Game Journal, 7(2):* 149–155, 1960.

Havelka, J.V. and Petrovicky, I. "Curing Ich (*Ichthyophthirius multifiliis*) With Malachite Green." *Tropical Fish Hobbyist*, January, 1967, pp. 11–19.

Havelka, J.V. and Tesarick, J. "Investigation of New Endoparasiticides With Special Regard to *Cryptobia cyprini* (Plehn, 1903) [Syn.: *Trypanoplasma cyprini* (Plehn, 1903)]." *Prace VUR (Vodnany), 5:*68–87, 1965 (In Czech; English and German summaries included).

Herbert, D.W.M. and Mann, H.T. "The Tolerance of Some Freshwater Fish for Seawater." *Salmon Trout Magazine, 153:*99–101, 1958.

Herman, R.L. *Oxytetracycline in Fish Culture: A Review.* BSFW, FWS, U.S. Dept. Interior, Washington, D.C., Technical Papers No. 31, 1969a, pp. 1–9.

——. *Oxytetracycline Toxicity to Trout.* BSFW, FWS, U.S. Dept. Interior, Washington, D.C., Technical Papers No. 33, 1969b, pp. 1–4.

——. "The Principles of Therapy in Fish Diseases." In Mawdesley-Thomas (Ed.). *Diseases of Fish.* Symposium Zoological Society London, No. 30, 1972, pp. 141-151.

Herman, R.L., Collis, D., and Bullock, G.L.: *Oxytetracycline Residues in Different Tissues of Trout.* BSFW, FWS, U.S. Dept. Interior, Washington, D.C., Technical Papers No. 37, 1969, pp. 1–6.

Herman, R.L. and Degurse, P.E. "Sulfamerazine Residues in Trout Tissues." *Ichthyologica, 39:*73–79, 1967.

Herwig, N. "Starvation, A Cyanide Syndrome." *The Marine Aquarist, 7(5):* 5–11, 1976.

Hess, W.N. "Control of External Fluke Parasites on Fish." *Journal Parasitology, 16:*131–136, 1930.

Hesselberg, R.J. and Burress, R.M. *Labor-Saving Devices for Bio-assay Laboratories.* Investigations in Fish Control, BSFW, FWS, U.S. Dept. Interior, Washington, D.C., No. 21, 1967; pp. 1–8.

Hewitt, E.R. "Fin Rot Eliminated by Continued Tank Sterilization." *Prog Fish-Cult,* No. 33, 1937, pp. 19–20.

Hickling, C.F. *Fish Culture.* London, Faber & Faber, 1962.

Higgins, C. and Lovelace, J. "Effects of X-Irradiation on Jewel Cichlid Eggs and Fry." *Today's Aquarist, 1(1):*39–44, 1969.

Hilliard, D.K. "The Effects of Low Temperatures on Larval Cestodes and Other Helminths in Fish." *J Parasitol, 45:*291–294, 1959.

Hindle, E. "Notes on the Treatment of Fish Infected With *Argulus.*" *Proceeding Zoological Society London, 119:*79–81, 1949.

Hnath, J.G. "Di-*n*-Butyl Tin Oxide as a Vermifuge on *Eubothrium crassum* (Bloch, 1779) in Rainbow Trout." *Prog Fish-Cult, 32(1):*47–50, 1970.

Hnath, J.G. "A Summary of the Fish Diseases and Treatments Administered in a Cool Water Diet Testing Program." *Prog Fish-Cult, 37(2)*:106-107, 1975.

Hoffman, G.L. *Recommended Treatment for Fish Parasite Diseases.* FWS, U.S. Dept. Interior, Washington, D.C., Fishery Leaflet No. 486, 1959.

———. *Parasites of Freshwater Fish. I. Fungi (Saprolegnia and Relatives) of Fish and Fish Eggs.* FWS, U.S. Dept. Interior, Washington, DC., Fish Disease Leaflet No. 21, pp. 1–6 (Fishery Leaflet 564), 1969.

———. *Control and Treatment of Parasitic Diseases of Freshwater Fishes.* FWS, U.S. Dept. Interior, Washington, D.C., Fish Disease Leaflet No. 28, 1970, pp. 1–7.

———. *Annual Report.* Eastern Fish Disease Laboratory, Division Fishery Research, BSFW, U.S. Dept. Interior, Washington, D.C., 1972, pp. 1–20.

Hoffman, G.L. and Hoffman, G.L. Jr. "Studies of the Control of Whirling Disease (*Myxosoma cerebralis*). I. The Effects of Chemicals on Spores in Vitro, and of Calcium Oxide as a Disinfectant in Simulated Ponds." *Journal Wildlife Diseases, 8*:49–53, 1972.

Hoffman, G.L. and Meyer, F.P. *Parasites of Freshwater Fishes.* Neptune, New Jersey, T.F.H. Publications, 1974.

Hogan, J.W. *Toxicity of Hyamine 3500 to Fish.* Investigations in Fish Control, BSFW, FWS, U.S. Dept. Interior, Washington, D.C., No. 32, 1969, pp. 1–9.

Højgaard, M. "Experiences Made in Danmarks Akvarium Concerning the Treatment of *Oodinium ocellatum*." *Bulletin of Institute of Oceanography,* Monaco, Premier Congrès International d'Aquariologie, Numéro Special IA, Vol. A, 1962, pp. 77–79.

Holt, R.A., Conrad, J.F., and Fryer, J.L. "Furanace for Control of *Cytophaga psychrophila*, the Causative Agent of Coldwater Disease in Coho Salmon." *Prog Fish-Cult, 37(3)*:137–139, 1975.

Hora, S.L. and Pillay, T.V.R. *Handbook of Fish Culture in the Indo-Pacific Region. FAO Fishery Biologist Technical Papers,* No. 14, 1962, pp. 1–504.

Hoshina, T. "On Monogenetic Trematodes." *Gyobyokenkyu [Journal Fish Pathology], 1(1)*:47–57, 1966 (English translation by Bureau of Commercial Fisheries, U.S. Dept. Interior, Washington, D.C.).

Howell, J.H., King, E.L. Jr., Smith, Allen J., and Hanson, Lee H. *Synergism of 5,2'-Dichloro-4'-Nitro-Salicylanalide and 3-Trifluoromethyl-4-Nitrophenol in a Selective Lamprey Larvicide.* Ann Arbor, Michigan, Great Lakes Fishery Commission, Technical Report No. 8, 1964, pp. 1–21.

Howland, R.M. "Interaction of Antimycin A and Rotenone in Fish Bioassays." *Prog Fish-Cult,* January 1969a, pp. 33–34.

Howland, R.M. *Laboratory Studies on Possible Fish Collecting Aids With Some Toxicities for the Isomers of Cresol.* Investigations in Fish Control, BSFW, U.S. Dept. Interior, Washington, D.C., No. 34, 1969b, pp. 1–10.

Howland, R.M. and Schoettger, R.A. *Efficacy of Methylpentynol as an Anesthetic on Four Salmonids.* Investigations in Fish Control, BSFW, U.S. Dept. Interior, Washington, D.C., No. 29, 1969, pp. 1–11.

Hsu Me-Keng and Jen Yung-Feng. "A Preliminary Report of the Chemical Control of the Parasitic Copepod, *Sinergasilus yui.*" *Acta Hydrobiology Sin,* No. 2, 1955, pp. 59–68 (In Chinese; English summary included).

Hublou, W.F. "The Use of Malachite Green to Control *Trichodina.*" *Prog Fish-Cult, 20(3):*129–132, 1958.

Hunn, J.B. *Dynamics of MS-222 in the Blood and Brain of Freshwater Fishes During Anesthesia.* Investigations in Fish Control, BSFW, FWS, U.S. Dept. Interior, Washington, D.C., No. 42, 1970, pp. 1–8.

Irwin, W. "Terramycin as a Control for Fin Rot in Fishes." *Prog Fish-Cult, 21(2):*89–90, 1959.

Iaksov, L.S. and Shulman, S.S. "On the Resistance of Some Ectoparasites of Sticklebacks to Changes in Salinity." *Trudy Karelofinsk Filial Akademyia Nauk USSR.* An S.S.S.R., Vol. 4, 1956.

Ivasik, V.M. and Karpenko, I.M. "The Application of Lime for Combatting Ichthyophthiriasis." *Veterinariia,* No. 6, 1965 (English translation by BSFW, Division Fish Research, U.S. Dept. Interior, Washington, D.C.).

Ivasik, V.M., Stryzhak, O.I., and Turkevich, V.N. "On Diplostomosis in the Trout." *Ryb Kohz,* 11:27–28, 1968 (English translation by BSFW, U.S. Dept. Interior, Washington, D.C.).

Ivasik, V.M. and Sutyagin, V.S. "How to Make Sanitary Carp Fishery Enterprises." *Ryb Kohz,* 7:23, 1967 (English translation by U.S. Dept. Commerce).

Ivasik, V.M. and Svirepo, B.G. "New Therapeutics and Prophylactic Chemical Used Directly in the Ponds." *Ryb Khoz, 40(11):*19–20, 1964 (In Russian).

Jen Yung-Feng and Hsu Me-Keng. "Factors Influencing the Application of Copper Sulfate and Ferrous Sulphate as a Parasiticide in Ponds." *Acta Hydrobiol Sin,* 1958, pp. 1–8 (In Chinese; English summary included).

Jobin, W.R. and Unrau, G.O. "Chemical Control of *Australorbis glabratus.*" *Public Health Report, 82(1):*63–71, 1967.

Johnson, A.K. "Ichthyophthiriasis in a Recirculating Closed Water Hatchery." *Prog Fish-Cult, 23(2):*79–82, 1961.

Johnson, D.W. "Pesticides and Fishes: A Review of Selected Literature." *Trans Am Fish Soc, 97(4):*398–424, 1968.

Johnson, H.E. "Treatment of Trichodinid Infections of Chinook Salmon Fingerlings." *Prog Fish-Cult, 18(2):*94, 1956.

Johnson, H.E., Adams, C.D., and McElrath, R.J. "A New Method of Treating Salmon Eggs and Fry With Malachite Green." *Prog Fish-Cult, 17(2):* 76–78, 1955.

Johnson, H.E. and Bruce, R.F. "Mortality of Silver Salmon From Treatments With Sulfamerazine." *Prog Fish-Cult, 15:*31–32, 1953.

Kabata, Z. "Crustacea as Enemies of Fish." In Sneiszko, S.F. and Axelrod,

H.R. (Eds.). *Diseases of Fishes*, Vol. I. Neptune, New Jersey, T.F.H. Publications, 1970.

Kanaev, A. "Advances in Fish Disease Research." *Rybovodstvo i Rybolovstvo, 4(3):3–4*, 1967.

Kanayama, R.K. *The Use of Alkalinity and Conductivity Measurements to Estimate Concentrations of 3-Trifluoromethyl-4-Nitrophenol Required for Treating Lamprey Streams.* Ann Arbor, Michigan, Great Lakes Fishery Commission, 1963, pp. 1–10.

Kasahara, S. "Studies on the Biology of the Parasitic Copepod, *Lernaea cyprinacea* Linnaeus, and the Method for Controlling This Parasite in the Fish Culture Ponds." *Contributions Fisheries Laboratories Faculty Agriculture*, University of Tokyo, No. 3, 1962, pp. 103–106 (English summary included).

Kasahara, S. "On the Sodium Pyrophosphate Peroxyhydrate Treatment for Ectoparasitic Trematodes on the Yellow Tail." *Fish Pathology, 1(2):48–53*, 1967.

Kasahara, S. "Some External Treatments for External Parasites of Cultured Fish." *Agriculture and Horticulture, 43(8):1235–1238*, 1968 (In Japanese).

Kashchenko, N.F. "Measures Against Diseases of Fishes Caused by the Ligulid Worms." *Vestnik Obshchestvennye Akklimatiz* (from *Akklimatiz Botanika Zoologica Syezd*), 1893.

Katz, M. "Advises on Copepods." *U.S. Trout News*, July-Aug., 1961.

Kawatski, J.A., Ledvina, M.M., and Hansen, C.R. Jr. *Acute Toxicities of 3-Trifluoromethyl-4-Nitrophenol (TFM) and 2',5-Dichloro-4'-Nitrosalicylanilide (Bayer 73) to Larvae of the Midge, Chironomus tentans.* Investigations in Fish Control, FWS, U.S. Dept. Interior, Washington, D.C., No. 57, 1975, pp. 1–7.

Kelly, W.H. "Controlling *Argulus* on Aquarium Carp." *NY Fish & Game J, 9(2):118–126*, 1962.

Kemp, P.S.J.T. "Trout in Southern Rhodesia. IV. On the Toxicity of Copper Sulfate to Trout." *Rhodesian Agricultural Journal, 55:637–640*, 1958. Also in *Sport Fisheries Abstracts, 6(2):95*, 1961.

Kemper, H. "Versuche Über Die Wirkung von Pyrethrumblütenpulver." *Zeitschrift Gesundheitstechein un Stadte Hygiene, 25:149–164*, 1933.

Kennedy, H.D., Eller, L.L., and Walsh, D.F. *Chronic Effects of Methoxychlor on Bluegills and Aquatic Invertebrates.* BSFW, FWS, U.S. Dept. Interior, Washington, D.C., Technical Papers No. 53, 1970, 1–18.

Kennedy, H.D. and Walsh, D.F. *Effects of Malathion on Two Warmwater Fishes and Aquatic Invertebrates in Ponds.* BSFW, FWS, U.S. Dept. Interior, Washington, D.C., Technical Papers No. 55, 1970, pp. 1–13.

Khan, H. "Studies in Diseases of Fish: Infestation of Fish With Leeches and Fish Lice." *Proceedings Indian Academy Science, (B)19(5):171–175*, 1944.

Kimura, S. "Control of the Fish Louse, *Argulus japonicus* Thiele, with Dipterex." *Agriculture (Tokyo),* 8(3):141–150, 1967 (In Japanese).

Kingsbury, O.R. "A Possible Control for Furunculosis." *Prog Fish-Cult, 23 (3):*136–137, 1961.

Kingsbury, O.R. and Embody, G.C. *The Prevention and Control of Hatchery Diseases by Treating the Water Supply.* New York State Conservation Department, 1932.

Kingsford, E. *Treatment of Exotic Marine Fish Diseases.* Pet Reference Series, No. 1, St. Petersburg, Florida, Palmetto Publishing Co., 1975.

Kislev, I.V. and Ivleva, V.K. "Control Measures Against *Argulus* Under Conditions of Pond Fishes." *Ryb Khoz, 12:*52, 1950 (In Russian).

Kislev, I.V. and Ivleva, V.K. "Some Data on the Biology of the Carp Louse and Measures of its Control Under Conditions of Pond Fisheries." *Trudy Nauchno-Isseledovatelis Institute Prudovogo i Ozernogo Rechnogo Rybnogo Khozyaistva Ukranian SSK, 9:*61–77, 1953.

Klenov, A.P. "Testing of Anthelminthics Against Bothriocephaliasis of White Amur." *Veterinariia, 7:*71–72, 1970 (In Russian).

Klontz, G.W. and Anderson, D.P. *Oral Immunization of Salmonids: A Review,* American Fisheries Society, Special Pub. No. 5, 1970, pp. 16–20.

Knittel, M.D. "Topical Application of Malachite Green for Control of Common Fungus Infections in Adult Spring Chinook Salmon." *Prog Fish-Cult, 28(1):*51–53, 1966.

Kocytowski, B. and Antychowicz. "Anatomo– and Histopathological Lesions in Ichthyophthiriosis of Carp in Sick Fish and in Those Treated With Malachite Green." *Bulletin Veterinary Institute Pulaway* (Poland), *8 (3rd quarter):*136–145, 1964.

Kokhanskaya, Y.M. "The Use of Ultraviolet Radiation for the Control of Disease in Eggs and Fishes (The MBU-3 Compact Bactericidal Plant)." *Journal Ichthyology, 10(3):*386–393, 1970 (English Translation by American Fisheries Society).

Krabec, J., Lucky, Z., and Dyk V. "Treatment of Dermatomycoses in Aquarial Fish," *Sborn Vyssk Zemed,* Bron Ser. B, 2:197–201, 1966. Also in Calcott, E.J. and Smithcors, J.F. (Eds.): *Progress in Feline Practice,* Vol. 2. Wheaton, Illinois, American Veterinary Publications, 1971, Abstract 1799.

Krug, E.E. and McGuigan, H.A. *Pharmacology in Nursing,* 1st ed. St. Louis, C.V. Mosby, 1955.

Kubu, F. "Heilung der mit *Ichthyophthirius* Befallen Durch Malachitgrun." *Dtsch Fisch Ztg, 9:*290, 1962.

Kubota, S.S. and Hagita, K. "Studies on the Diseases of Marine Culture Fishes. II. Pharmacodynamic Effects of Nitrofurazone for Fish Diseases (I)." *Journal Faculty Fisheries,* University of Mie Prefect, 6:125–144, 1963.

Kulow, H. and Spangenberg, R. "Eigenschaften und Bedeutung der Nitrofurane fur die Prophylaxie und Therapie von Fischkrankheiten." *Dtsch Fisch Ztg, 16(12):*365–371, 1969.

Kumar, A.K. "Control of *Gyrodactylus sp.* on Goldfish." Master's Thesis

Abstract, Auburn University, Auburn, Alabama, 1958.

Lahav, M. and Sarig, S. *"Ergasilus sieboldi* Nordmann Infestation of Grey Mullet in Israel Fish Ponds." *Bamidgeh, 19(4)*:69–80, 1967.

Lahav, M., Sarig, S., and Shilo, M. "The Eradication of *Lernaea* in Storage Ponds of Carp Through Destruction of the Copepodidal Stage by Dipterex." *Bamidgeh, 16(3)*:87–94, 1964.

Lahav, M., Sarig, S., and Shilo, M. "Experiments in the Use of Bromex-50 as a Means of Eradicating the Ectoparasites of Carp." *Bamidgeh, 18 (3, 4)*:57–66, 1966.

Lahav, M., Shilo, M., and Sarig, S. "Development of Resistance to Lindane in *Argulus* Populations of Fish Ponds." *Bamidgeh, 14(4)*:67–76, 1962.

Laird, J. and Embody, G.C. "Controlling the Trout Gill Worm *(Discocotyle salmonis*, Schaffer)." *Trans Am Fish Soc, 61*:189–191, 1931.

Lal, M. "Acanthocephala of Trout and Anthelmintics: Behavior in Vitro." *Nature (London), 159*:4042, 1947.

Lane, T.H. and Jackson, H.M. *Voidance Times for 23 Species of Fish*. Investigations in Fish Control, BSFW, U.S. Dept. Interior, Washington, D.C., No. 33, 1969, pp. 1–9.

Lanzing, W.J.R. "Observations on Malachite Green in Relation to its Application to Fish Diseases." *Hydrobiology, 25*:426-440, 1965.

Larsen, H.N. "Comparison of Various Methods of Hemoglobin Determination on Catfish Blood." *Prog Fish-Cult, 26(1)*:n.p., 1964.

Lavrovskii, V. and Uspenskaya, A. "An Effective Method of Controlling Dactylogyriasis." *Rybovodstvo i Rybolovstvo, 6*:31–32, 1959. Also in *Biological Abstracts, 46(19)*, Abs. 83061.

Lawler, G.H. "Biology and Control of the Pike Whitefish Parasitic Worm, *Triaenophorus crassus*, in Canada." *Progress Report Biological Station and Technical Unit, London*, Fisheries Research Board Canada, *1*:31–37, 1959.

Lawrence, J.M. "Preliminary Results on the Use of Potassium permanganate to Counteract the Effects of Rotenone on Fish." *Prog Fish-Cult, 18(1)*:15–21, 1956.

Layman, E.M. and Sadkovskay, O.D. "The Black Spot Disease of Carp and Measures Against It." *Trudy Naucho-Issled Inst Prud Ozern Rech Ryb Khoz Ukr SSR*, Vol. 8, 1952.

Leger, L. "La Costiase et son Traitement Chez les Jeunes Alevins de Truite." *Comptes Rendus Hebdomadaires des Seances de l'Academie des Sciences* [D] *(Paris), 148(19)*:1284–1286, 1909.

Leifson, E. "The Effect of Formaldehyde on the Shape of Bacterial Flagella." *Journal General Microbiology, 25*:131–133, 1961.

Leith, D.A. and Moore, K.D. *Pelton Pilot Hatchery*. 1967 Progress Report, Portland, Oregon, Oregon Fish Commission Research Division, Nov. 1966 –Oct. 1967.

Leitritz, E. *Trout and Salmon Culture*. Department of Fish & Game, State of California, Fish Bulletin No. 107, 1960.

Lennon, R.E. and Berger, B.L. *A Resume on Field Applications of Antimycin A to Control Fish.* Investigations in Fish Control, BSFW, FWS, U.S. Dept. Interior, Washington, D.C., No. 40, 1970, pp. 1–19.

Lennon, R.E. and Walker, C.R. *Laboratories and Methods for Screening Fish Control Chemicals.* Investigations in Fish Control, BSFW, FWS, U.S. Dept. Interior, Washington, D.C., No. 1, 1964, pp. 1–15.

Leteux, F. and Meyer, F.P. "Mixtures of Malachite Green and Formalin for Controlling *Ichthyophthirius* and Other Protozoan Parasites of Fish." *Prog Fish-Cult, 34(1)*:21–26, 1972.

Lewis, S. "Prophylactic Treatment of Minnow Hatchery Ponds With Paraformaldehyde to Prevent Epizootics of *Gyrodactylus.*" *Prog Fish-Cult, 29(3)*:160–161, 1967.

Lewis, W.M. "Benzene Hexachloride vs. Lindane in the Control of the Anchor Worm." *Prog Fish-Cult, 23(2)*:69, 1961.

Lewis, W.M. and Lewis, S. "Control of Epizootics of *Gyrodactylus elegans* in Golden Shiner Populations." *Trans Am Fish Soc, 92(1)*:60–62, 1963.

Lewis, W.M. and Parker, J.D. "Paraformaldehyde for Control of *Gyrodactylus* and *Dactylogyrus.*" *Proc 19th Ann Conf SE Assoc Game & Fish Comm,* 1962, pp. 222–225.

Lewis, W.M. and Ulrich, M.G. "Chlorine as a Quick-Dip Treatment for the Control of Gyrodactylids on the Golden Shiner." *Prog Fish-Cult, 29 (4)*:229–231, 1967.

Lientz, J.C. and Springer, J.E. "Neutralization Tests of Infectious Pancreatic Necrosis Virus With Polyvalent Antiserum." *J Wildlife Dis, 9*:120–124, 1973.

Loader, J.D. "The Use of Chemicals for the Aquarist." *The Aquarist, 28*: 28–29, 1963.

Lobel, P.S. "Letter to the Editor." *Marine Hobbyist News, 2(2)*, 6, 1974.

Locke, D.O. *Quinaldine as an Anesthetic for Brook Trout, Lake Trout and Atlantic Salmon.* Investigations in Fish Control, BSFW, U.S. Dept. Interior, Washington, D.C., No. 24, 1969, pp. 1–5.

Lotan, R. "Adaptability of *Tilapia nilotica* to Various Saline Conditions." *Bamidgeh, 12(4)*:96–100, 1960.

Lüdemann, D. "Beiträge zur Toxizität von Herbiziden auf Die Lebensgemeinschaft Der Gewässer, Tiel. I., Fische." *Wasser-Abwasser, 106(8)*:220–223, 1965.

Lüdemann, D. and Kayser, H. "Die Toxische Wirkung des Insektiziden Wirkstoffes S1752 (Baytex, Lebaycid) Auf Tiere des Susswassers." *Zeitschrift Fuer Angewandte Zoologie, 49*:447–463, 1962.

Luhning, C.W. *Methods for Simultaneous Determination and Identification of MS-222 and Metabolites in Fish Tissues.* Investigations in Fish Control, BSFW, FWS, U.S. Dept. Interior, Washington, D.C., No. 51, 1974a, pp. 1–10.

Luhning, C.W. *Residues of MS-222, Benzocaine and Their Metabolites in Stripped Bass Following Anesthesia.* Investigations in Fish Control,

BSFW, FWS, U.S. Dept. Interior, Washington, D.C., No. 52, 1974b, pp. 1–11.

McElwain, I.B. and Post, G. "Efficacy of Cyzine for Trout Hexamitiasis." *Prog Fish-Cult, 30(2)*:84–91, 1968.

McKee, J.E. and Wolf, H.W. *Water Quality Criteria.* California State Water Quality Control Board, Pub. No. 3A, 1963.

Mackenthun, K.M. *The Chemical Control of Aquatic Nuisances.* Madison, Wisconsin, Commission on Water Pollution, State Board of Health, 1958.

Mckernan, D.L. "A Treatment for Tapeworms in Trout." *Prog Fish-Cult, 50:*33–35, 1940.

McNeil, P.L. Jr. "The Use of Benzene Hexachloride as a Copepodicide and Some Observations on Lernean Parasites in Trout Rearing Units." *Prog Fish-Cult, 23:*127–133, 1961.

Makai, A.W., Geissel, L.D., and Johnson, H.E. *Toxicity of the Lampricide 3-Trifluoromethyl-4-Nitrophenol (TFM) to 10 Species of Algae.* Investigations in Fish Control, FWS, U.S. Dept. Interior, Washington, D.C., No. 56, 1975, pp. 1–17.

Makai, A.W. and Johnson, H.E. *The Freshwater Mussel (Anodonta sp.) as an Indicator of Environmental Levels of 3-Trifluoromethyl-4-Nitrophenol (TFM).* Investigations in Fish Control, FWS, U.S. Dept. Interior, Washington, D.C., No. 70, 1976, pp. 1–5.

Malacca Research Institute, *Report Tropical Fish Culture Research Institute, Malacca, Malaysia, 1962.* Batu Berendam, 1963.

Mann, H. "Zur Frage der Geschmacksbeinflussung Durch Phenole." *Fischwirt, 1:*164–165, 1951.

Markevich, A.P. "Carp Louse and Measures Against it Under the Conditions of Pond Fisheries." *Za Rybnoe Industr Severa*, 1934.

Marking, L.L. *Evaluation of p,p'-DDT as a Reference Toxicant in Bioassays.* Investigations in Fish Control, BSFW, U.S. Dept. Interior, Washington, D.C., No. 10, 1966, pp. 1–10.

——. *Toxicity of MS-222 to Selected Fishes.* Investigations in Fish Control, BSFW, FWS, U.S. Dept. Interior, Washington, D.C., No. 12, 1967, pp. 1–10.

——. *Toxicity of Quinaldine to Selected Fishes.* Investigations in Fish Control, BSFW, FWS, U.S. Dept. Interior, Washington, D.C., No. 23, 1969a, pp. 1–10.

——. *Toxicity of Methylpentynol to Selected Fishes.* Investigations in Fish Control, BSFW, FWS, U.S. Dept. Interior, Washington, D.C., No. 30, 1969b, pp. 1–7.

——. *A Method for Rating Chemicals for Potency Against Fish and Other Organisms.* Investigations in Fish Control, BSFW, FWS, U.S. Dept. Interior, Washington, D.C., No. 36, 1970, pp. 1–8.

——. *Methods of Estimating the Half-life of Biological Activity of Toxic Chemicals in Water.* Investigations in Fish Control, BSFW, FWS, U.S. Dept. Interior, Washington, D.C., No. 46, 1972, pp. 1–9.

Marking, L.L., Bills, T.D., and Chandler, J.H. *Toxicity of the Lampricide 3-Trifluoromethyl-4-Nitrophenol (TFM) to Nontarget Fish in Flow-Through Tests.* Investigations in Fish Control, BSFW, FWS, U.S. Dept. Interior, Washington, D.C., No. 61, 1975, pp. 1–9.

Marking, L.L. and Dawson, V.K. *Toxicity of Quinaldine Sulfate to Fish.* Investigations in Fish Control, BSFW, FWS, U.S. Dept. Interior, Washington, D.C., No. 48, 1973, pp. 1–8.

Marking, L.L. and Dawson, V.K. *Method for Assessment of Toxicity or Efficacy of Mixtures of Chemicals.* Investigations in Fish Control, BSFW, FWS, U.S. Dept. Interior, Washington, D.C., No. 67, 1975, pp. 1–8.

Marking, L.L. and Hogan, J.W. *Toxicity of Bayer 73 to Fish.* Investigations in Fish Control, BSFW, FWS, U.S. Dept. Interior, Washington, D.C., No. 19, 1967, pp. 1–13.

Marking, L.L., King, E.L., Walker, C.R., and Howell, J.H. *Toxicity of 33NCS (3'-Chloro-3-Nitrosalicylanilide) to Freshwater Fish and Sea Lampreys.* Investigations in Fish Control, BSFW, FWS, U.S. Dept. Interior, Washington, D.C., No. 38, 1970, pp. 1–16.

Marking, L.L. and Olson, L.E. *Toxicity of the Lampricide 3-Trifluoromethyl-4-Nitrophenol (TFM) to Non-Target Fish in Static Tests.* Investigations in Fish Control, BSFW, FWS, U.S. Dept. Interior, Washington, D.C., No. 60, 1975, pp. 1–27.

Marking, L.L. and Willford, W.A. *Comparative Toxicity of 29 Nitrosalicylanilides and Related Compounds to Eight Species of Fish.* Investigations in Fish Control, BSFW, FWS, U.S. Dept. Interior, Washington, D.C., No. 37, 1970, pp. 1–11.

Martin, R.L. "Comparison of Effects of Concentration of Malachite Green and Acriflavine on Fungi Associated With Diseased Fish." *Prog Fish-Cult, 30(3)*:153–158, 1968.

Mattheis, T. "*d*-Chloronitrin Als Heilmittel bei Bakterieller Flossenfäule" [*d*-chlorontrin as a remedy in bacterial fin rot]. *Aggar unt Terrarien,* July 8, 1961, p. 212 (English translation by BSFW, U.S. Dept. Interior, Washington, D.C.).

Mawdesley-Thomas, L.E. "Toxic Chemicals: The Risk to Fish." *New Scientist, 49*:74–75, 1971.

Mawdesley-Thomas, L.E. and Leahy, J.S. "Organochlorine Pesticide Residues in Pike." *Prog Fish-Cult, 29*:64, 1967.

Meehan, O.L. "*Dactylogyrus* Control in Ponds." *Prog Fish-Cult,* Memorial ed. 1–131, *32*:10–12, 1937.

Meinken, H. *Die Aquarien-und Terrarien Zeitschrift,* 7:50–51, 1954.

Meister, A.L. and Ritzi, C.F. "Effects of Chloretone and MS-222 on Eastern Brook Trout." *Prog Fish-Cult, 20(3)*:104–110, 1958.

Mellen, I. "The Treatment of Fish Diseases." *Zoopathologica,* 2:1–31, 1928.

Menn, C.T. *Rotenone: Its Use in Fisheries Management.* Austin, Texas, Texas Parks and Wildlife Department, 1976, pp. 1–7.

Merriner, J.V. "Constant Bath Malachite Green Solution for Incubating Sunfish Eggs." *Prog Fish-Cult, 31(4)*:223–225, 1969.

Meyer, F.P. "Field Treatments of *Aeromonas liquefaciens* Infections in Golden Shiners." *Prog Fish-Cult, 26:33–35,* 1964.

———. "A New Control for the Anchor Parasite, *Lernaea cyprinacea." Prog Fish-Cult, 28:33–39*, 1966a.

———. *Parasites of Freshwater Fish. II. Protozoa. 3. Ichthyophthirius multifiliis.* BSFW, U.S. Dept. Interior, Washington, D.C., Fish Disease Leaflet No. 2, 1966b.

———. "A Review of the Parasites and Diseases of Fish In Warmwater Ponds in North America." *FAO World Symp Warmwater Pond Fish Cult,* FR: IX/R3:290–318, 1966c.

———. "Chemical Control of Fish Diseases in Warmwater Ponds." *Proceedings Fish Farming Conference,* Feb. 1–2, 1967, College Station, Texas A & M University, Texas Agricultural Extension Service, 1967, pp. 35–39.

———. *Treatment Tips, RP-66* [Formerly FWS Circular 209]. BSFW, FWS, U.S. Dept. Interior, Washington, D.C., No. 66, 1968, pp. 1–16.

———. "A Potential Control for Leeches." *Prog Fish-Cult, 31(3)*:160–163, 1969a.

———. *Lernaea Control Studies, Progress in Sport Fishery Research in 1969.* BSFW, U.S. Dept. Interior, Washington, D.C., 1969b, pp. 160–161.

———. "Dylox as a Control for Ectoparasites of Fish." *Proc 22nd Ann Conf SE Assoc Game & Fish Comm,* 1970, pp. 392–396.

———. "Anthelminthic Treatment of Channel Catfish for Tapeworm Infections." *Prog Fish-Cult, 35(4)*:205–206, 1973.

Meyer, F.P. and Collar, J. "Description and Treatment of a *Pseudomonas* Infection in White Catfish." *J Appl Microbiol, 12(3)*:201–203, 1964.

Meyer, F.P., Schnick, R.A., Cumming, K.B., and Berger, B.L. "Registration Status of Fishery Chemicals: February, 1976." *Prog Fish-Cult, 38(1)*:3–7, 1976.

Mitchum, D.L. and Moore, T.D. "Efficacy of Di-*n*-Butyl Tin Oxide on an Intestinal Fluke, *Crepidistomum farionis,* in Golden Trout." *Prog Fish-Cult, 31(3)*:143–148, 1966.

Moore, J.P. *A Method for Combatting Blood-sucking Leeches in Bodies of Water Controlled by Dams.* BSFW, FWS, U.S. Dept. Interior, Washington, D.C., Pub. No. T-267A, 1923.

Mount, D.I. and Stephan, C.E. "A Method for Establishing Acceptable Toxicant Limits for Fish: Malathion and the Butoxyethanol ester of 2, 4-D." *Trans Am Fish Soc, 96(2)*:185–193, 1967.

Moyle, J.B. *The Use of Copper Sulfate for Algal Control and its Biological Implications, Limnological Aspects of Water Supply and Water Disposal.* American Association Advancement Sciences, 1949, pp. 79–87.

Musselius, V.A. *Parasites and Diseases of Herbivorous Fishes and Their Control Measures.* Moscow, Kolos, 1967 (In Russian).

Musselius, V.A. "Test of New Preparations in Control of Ichthyophthiriasis in Fish Farms." *Voprosy Prudovro Rybovodstva, 16*:288–301, 1969 (In Russian; English Summary included).

Musselius, V.A. and Flippova, N.T. "New Preparations for Combatting Ichthyophthiriasis in Pond Fish." *Ryb Khozyaistvo, 44(1)*:19–20, 1968.

Musselius, V.A. and Laptev, V.I. "Experimental Application of Chlorophos for Mollusc Control at Pond Farms." Moscow, *Pishchevaya Promyshlennost, Trudy Vesesoyuznogo Nauchno-Issledovatelis Kogo Instituta Prudovogo Rybnogo Khozyaistva Voprosy Prudovogo Rybovodstva, 15*:294–298, 1967 (English translation by BSFW, U.S. Dept. Interior, Washington, D.C.).

Musselius, V.A. and Strelkov, I.A. *Diseases and Control Measures for Fishes of the Far East Complex in Farms of the U.S.S.R.* Third Symposium Commission Office International Epizootics for Study Fish Diseases, Contribution No. 7, 1968. Also in *Bull Off Int Epizoot, 69(9–10)*:1603–1611, 1968.

Muzykovskii, A.M. "Un Anthelminthique Pour la Bothriocephalose des Carpes: le *n*-12′-Chlor-4′-nitrophenyl 5-Chlorsalicylamide." *Bull Off Int Epizoot, 69(9–10)*, 1539–1540, 1968.

Muzykovskii, A.M. "The Testing of Phenasal in Bothriocephalosis in Carp." *Prudovogo Rybnogo Khozyaistva, Trudy Vsesoyuznogo Nauchno-Issledovatelis Kogo Instituta, 18*:146–148, 1971. (English translation by BSFW, U.S. Dept. Interior, Washington, D.C., Fish Report TR-73-02).

Nakai, N. and Kokai, E. "On the Biological Study of a Parasitic Copepod, *Lernaea elegans* Leigh-Sharpe, Infesting Japanese Freshwater Fishes." *Journal Imperial Fish Experimental Station, 1(2)*:123–128, 1931.

National Drug Code Directory, Public Health Service, U.S. Department of Health, Education and Welfare, Washington, D.C., 1972 (Prepared by the Office of Scientific Coordination, Bureau of Drugs, Food and Drug Administration).

Naumova, A.M. "Parasites of Carp in Pond Fisheries and the Diseases They Cause." *Zooparazitologiya*, Itogi Nauki, 1966. Also in *VINTA* (Moscow), 1968, pp. 66–82.

Naumova, A.M. and Kanaev, A.I. "Experience in the Treatment of Carp Infected With Coccidiosis." *Vopr Ikhtiol, 2(4)*:749–751, 1962.

Nazarova, N.S., Musikovski, A.M., Sorokin, A.N., Marchenckio, R.N., and Sen, V.I. "The Use of Fenasal Against Bothriocephaliasis in Carp." *Veterinariia, 6*:57–59, 1969 (In Russian).

Nelson, E.C. "Carbarsone Treatments for *Octomitus*." *Prog Fish-Cult, 55*: 1–5, 1941.

Nichols, M.S., Henkel, T., and McNail, D. "Copper in Lake Muds From Lakes of the Madison Area." *Transactions Wisconsin Academy of Science, 38*:333–350, 1946.

Nigrelli, R.F. and Ruggieri, G.D. "Enzootics in the New York Aquarium Caused by *Cryptocaryon irritans* (Brown, 1951) [= *Ichthyophthirius marinus* (Sikama, 1961)], a Histophagous Ciliate in the Skin, Eyes and Gills of Marine Fishes." *Zoologica (New York),* 51(3):97–102, 1966.

Noyes, J.C. "Yellowhead Jawfish." *Marine Aquarist,* 5(2):43–51, 1974.

O'Donnell, D.J. "The Disinfection and Maintenance of Trout Hatcheries for the Control of Disease With Special Reference to Furunculosis." *Trans Am Fish Soc,* 74:26–34, 1947.

Osborn, P. "Effective Chemical Control of Some Parasites of Goldfish and Other Pond Fish." 1966 Annual Meeting of the Wildlife Diseases Association, Osage Catfisheries, Osage Beach, Missouri. Mimeographed.

Pasovski, A.I. "Use of Ammonia Against Dactylogyrosis of Carp. *Trudy Nauchno — Issled Institute Prudovogo i Ozernogo Rechnogo Rybnogo Khozyaistva SSSR,* Vol. 9, 1953.

Patterson, E.E. "Effects of Acriflavine on Birth Rate." *The Aquarium Journal,* 21:36, 1950.

Paulini, E. "Reports on Molluscicide Tests Carried out in Belo Horizonte, Brazil." *1964 WHO, Bilharziasis Research Division,* MOL/INF/20.65, p. III/1–23, 1965.

Paulini, E. and Camey, T. "Un Novo Tipo de Moluscicida com Acao Sistemica." *Rev Bras Malariol Doencas Trop,* 17(4):349–353, 1965 (English summary on p. 352).

Peterson, E.J., Steucke, E.W. Jr., and Lynch, W.H. "Disease Treatment at Gavin Point Aquarium." *The Dorsal Fin,* 6(1):18–19, 1966.

Petrie, C.J. and Ehlinger, N.F. "A Convenient Method of Medicating Dry Diets." *Prog Fish-Cult,* 37(4):236, 1975.

Petrushevski, G.K. and Bauer, O.N. "Measures Against Diseases of Trout in Pond Fisheries." *Bull Inst Freshw Fish (Leningr.),* Vol. 27, 1948.

Pfeifer, K. "Erfolgreiche Behandlung der Ichthyophthiriasis Mit Atebrin." *Aqua Terr Z,* Vol. 5, 1952.

Piavis, G.V. and Howell, J.H. *Effects of 3-Trifluoromethyl-4-Nitrophenol (TFM) on Developmental Stages of the Sea Lamprey.* Investigations in Fish Control, BSFW, FWS, U.S. Dept. Interior, Washington, D.C., No. 64, 1975, pp. 1–8.

Piper, R.G. "Toxic Effects of Erythromycin thiocyanate on Rainbow Trout." *Prog Fish-Cult,* 23(3):134–135, 1961.

Plate, G. "Masoten Für die Bekämpfung von Ektoparasiten Bei Fischen." *Archiv Fuer Fischereiwissenschaft,* 21(3):258–267, 1970.

Plehn, M. *Praktikum der Fischkrankheiten.* Stuttgart, Germany, E. Schweizerbartsche Verlagshandlung, 1924.

Popov, A.T. and Jankov, G.Y. *"Information Sur les Maladies des Poissons et l'organization de la Lutte Contre ces Maladies en Bulgarie.* Third Symposium, Commission Office International Epizootics for Study Fish Diseases. Also in *Bull Off Int Epizoot,* 69(9–10):1571–1576, 1968.

Post, G. "A Preliminary Report on the Use of Nitrofuran Compounds for Furunculosis of Trout, with Special Emphasis on Furoxone." *Prog Fish-Cult,* 21(1):30–33, 1959.

Post, G. and Beck, M.M. "Toxicity Tissue Residue, and Efficacy of Enhep-

tin Given Orally to Rainbow Trout for Hexamitiasis." *Prog Fish-Cult,*
28(2):83–88, 1966.

Post, G. and Keiss, R.E. "Further Laboratory Studies on the Use of Furazolidone for the Control of Furunculosis of Trout." *Prog Fish-Cult, 62*
(1):16–21, 1962.

Postema, J.L. "Ichthyophthiriose." *Tijdschrift voor Diergeneeskunde, 81*
(1):519–524, 1956 (English summary included).

Prevost, G. "A Criticism of the Use of Potassium Permanganate in Fish
Culture." *Trans Am Fish Soc, 64*:304–306, 1934.

Prokhorchik, M.I. and Lukyanovich, D.N. "Measures Against *Ichthyophthirius.*" *Fish Ind (Moscow)*, Vol. 11, 1953.

Prost, M. and Studnicka, M. "Badania nad Zastosowaniem Estrów Organi-
ićznych Kwasu Fosforowego w Zwalczaniu, Zewnetrznych Ryb Hodow-
lanych. III. Zwalczanic Inwazji Pierwotniakow z Rodzaju *Chilodonella,
Ichthyophthirius* i *Trichodina.*" *Medycyna Weterynaryjna, 23(4)*:201–
203, 1967.

Prost, M. and Studnicka, M. "Investigations on the Use of Pyro-phosphate
for Control of Ectoparasites of Cultured Fishes. IV. Therapeutic Value
of the Polish Preparation 'Foschlor.'" *Medycyna Weterynaryjna, 24(2)*:
97–101, 1968.

Prost, H. and Studnicka, M. "Badania nad Wartoscia Terapentyczng Niek-
torych Preparatow Przy ichtioftriozie Karpi." *Medycyna Weterynaryjna,
28(2)*:69–73, 1971 (In Polish; English summary).

Prowse, G.A. *Annual Report of the Tropical Fish-Cultural Research Institute.* Malacca Research Institute, Batu Berendam, Malacca, Malaysia,
1965.

Putz, R.E. and Bowen, J.T. *Parasites of Freshwater Fishes. IV. Miscellaneous. The Anchor Worm (Lernaea cyprinacea) and Related Species.*
BSFW, FWS, U.S. Dept. Interior, Washington, D.C., Fishery Leaflet No.
575, 1964, pp. 1–4 (available as Fish Disease Leaflet No. 12, 1968).

Quebec Game & Fisheries Department. "Control of Leeches." *Sixth Annual Report Biological Bureau.* Montreal, Quebec Game & Fisheries
Department, 1948, pp. 85–87.

Rankin, M. "Treating Fish Affected by Gill Flukes." *Water Life (London)*, Dec., 1952, pp. 297–298.

Rankin, M. "New Cure For Fin Rot." *Water Life (London)*, 1953.

Reddecliff, J.M. "Formalin as a Fungicide in the Jar Method of Egg Incu-
bation: Notes for Fish Culturists." Benner Spring Fish Research Station, Pennsylvania Fish Commission. Unpublished, 1958, 1961.

Reichelt, H.W. Jr. "Use of Copper Sulfate at Millen Aquarium." *Drum
& Croaker, 12(1)*:26, 1971.

Reichenbach-Klinke, H.H. *Krankheiten un Schädigungen der Fische.* Stuttgart, Germany, Fischer Verlag, 1966.

Reichenbach-Klinke, H.H. and Elkan, E. *The Principal Diseases of Lower
Vertebrates.* New York, Academic Press, 1965 (out of print). Also pub-

lished by T.F.H. Publications (Neptune, New Jersey), Vol. 1, 1972.

Reichenbach-Klinke, H.H. and Landolt, M. *Fish Pathology.* Neptune, New Jersey, T.F.H. Publications, 1973.

Robertson, R. "Malachite Green Used to Prevent Fungus on Lake Trout Eggs." *Prog Fish-Cult, 16(1):*38, 1954.

Robinson, J.A., Meyer, F.P., and Friborough, J.H. *Oxytetracycline Efficacy Against Bacterial Infections in Blue and Channel Catfishes.* BSFW, U.S. Dept. Interior, Washington, D.C., Technical Papers No. 35, 1969, pp. 1–7.

Roegner-Aust, S. "Über die Wirkung der Neuen Kontaktinsektizide auf Fische." *Verhandlungen der Deutschen Gesellschaft fur Angewandte Entomologische,* 1949/1951.

Rogers, E., Hazen, B., Friddle, S., and Snieszko, S.F. "The Toxicity of Pyridylmercuric Acetate Technical (PMA) to Rainbow Trout *(Salmo gairdneri).*" *Prog Fish-Cult, 13:*71–73, 1951.

Rogers, W.A. "The Biology and Control of the Anchor Worm, *Learnaea cyprinacea* L." *FAO World Symp Warmwater Pond Fish Cult,* FR:IX/ E10:393–398, 1966.

Romey, D.B. "Treatment of Salmon and Steelhead With Sulfonamides." *Proceedings NW Fish Culturists Conference,* 1964, pp. 7–13.

Rosewater, J. "An Effective Anesthetic for Giant Clams and Other Mollusks." *Turtox News, 41(12):*300–302, 1963.

Rossoff, I.S. *Handbook of Veterinary Drugs.* New York, Springer Publishing Co., 1974.

Roth, W. "Das Formalin als Vertilgungsmittel Fur Aussenschmarotjer." *Deutsche Fischerei-Correspondenz, 14:*7–9, 1910.

Rucker, R.R. "New Compounds for the Control of Bacterial Gill Disease." *Prog Fish-Cult, 10(1):*19–22, 1948.

——. "Some Problems of Private Trout Hatchery Operators." *Trans Am Fish Soc, 87:*374–379, 1957.

——. "The Use of Merthiolate on Green Eggs of the Chinook Salmon." *Prog Fish-Cult,* July, 1961, pp. 138–141.

Rucker, R.R., Bernier, A.F., Whipple, W.J., and Burrows, R. "Sulfadiazine for Kidney Disease." *Prog Fish-Cult, 13(3):*135–137, 1951.

Rucker, R.R., Earp, B., and Burrows, R. "Lignasan for Bacterial Gill Disease." *Prog Fish-Cult, 18(2):*75–77, 1956.

Rucker, R.R., Johnson, H., and Ordal, E. "An Investigation of The Bactericidal Action and Fish Toxicity of Two Homologous Series of Quaternary Compounds." *J Bacteriol, 57:*225–234, 1949.

Rucker, R.R., Taylor, W.O., and Toney, D.P. "Formalin in the Hatchery." *Prog Fish-Cult, 25(4):*203–207, 1963.

Rucker, R.R. and Whipple, W.J. "Effects of Bactericides on Steelhead Trout Fry." *Prog Fish-Cult, 13(1):*43–44, 1951.

Rychlicki, Z. "Eradication of *Ichthyophthirius multifiliis* in Carp." *FAO World Symp Warmwater Pond Fish Cult,* FR: IX/E–3:361–364, 1966.

Sachachte, J.H. Jr. "A Short Term Treatment of Malachite Green and Formalin for the Control of *Ichthyophthirius multifiliis* on Channel Catfish in Holding Tanks." *Prog Fish-Cult, 36(2):*103–104, 1974.

Safonov, A.T. "Measures Against Piscicolisis of Carp." *Fish Ind (Moscow),* Vol. 12, 1950.

Safonov, A.T. "A New Method of Controlling Carp Louse." *Ryb Khoz,* No. 11, 1952, p. 60.

Saha, K.C., and Chakraborty, S.K. "Gammexane in the Treatment of a New Parasitic Infection in Fish." *Science & Culture, 25(2):*159, 1959.

Saha, K.C. and Sen, D.P. "Gammexane in the Treatment of *Argulus* and Fish Leech Infection in Trout." *Annals Biochemistry & Experimental Medicine, 15:*71–72, 1958.

Sakowicz, S. and Gottwald, S. "Zapobieganie i Zwalczanie Plesni u Tarlakow Troci i Lososi przy Pomocy Kapieli w Roztworze Zieleni Malachitowej." *Roczniki Nauk Rolniczych, 73B:*281–293, 1958.

Sampson, G.R., Young, D.C., Gregory, R.P., and Rathmacher, R.P. "Clinical Evaluation of Cephaloridine Injectible Antibiotic in Dogs and Cats." *Vet Med Small Anim Clin,* Nov., 1973, pp. 1302–1306.

Sanders, H.O. and Walsh, D.F. *Toxicity and Residue Dynamics of the Lampricide 3-Trifluoromethyl-4-Nitrophenol (TFM) in Aquatic Invertebrates.* Investigations in Fish Control, BSFW, U.S. Dept. Interior, Washington, D.C., No. 59, 1975, pp. 1–9.

Sandler, A. "Diseases of Tropical Fish." In Catcott, E.J. and Smithcors, J.F. (Eds.). *Progress in Feline Practice,* Vol. 1. Wheaton, Illinois, American Veterinary Publications, 1966.

Sarig, S. "Carp Diseases: Their Prevention and Treatment." *Proceedings General Fish Council of Mediterranean, 6:*207–212, 1961.

——. "A Review of Diseases and Parasites of Fishes in Warmwater Ponds in the Near East and Africa." *FAO Fishery Report, 5(44):*278–289, 1966.

——. "Possibilities of Prophylaxis and Control of Ectoparasites Under Conditions of Intensive Warmwater Pond Fish Culture in Israel." *Bull Off Int Epizoot, 69(9–10):*1577–1590, 1968.

——. "Pesticide Concentrations for Pond Spraying Effective Against Various Ectoparasites Attached to Carp." Mimeographed. Jerusalem, The Hebrew University, Hadassah Medical School, Department of Microbiological Chemistry and the Field Laboratory at Nir David, 1969.

——. "Prevention and Treatment of Diseases of Warmwater Fishes Under Subtropical Condition, With Emphasis on Intensive Fish Farming." In Snieszko, S.F. and Axelrod, H.R. (Eds.). Book 3. *Diseases of Fishes.* Neptune, New Jersey, T.F.H. Publications, 1971.

Sarig, S. and Lahav, M. "The Treatment With Lindane of Carp and Fish Ponds Infected With the Fish Louse *Argulus.*" *Proc Gen Fish Coun Medit, 5:*151–156, 1959.

Sarig, S. and Lahav, M. "New Substances for Control of *Pyrmnesium, B. Lignasan.*" *Bamidgeh, 13(1):*3–8, 1961.

Sarig, S., Lahav, M., and Shilo, M. "Control of *Dactylogyrus vastator* on Carp Fingerlings With Dipterex." *Bamidgeh, 17(2):*47–52, 1965.

Sarig, S., Lahav, M., and Vardina, G. "New Substances for Control of *Pyrmnesium.* A. Liquid Ammonia." *Bamidgeh, 12(4):*84–92, 1960.

Schäperclaus, W. "Die Drehkrankheit und ihre Bekämpfung. Mitt der Fischereivereine." *Westausgabe, 2:*26–33, 1932.

Schäperclaus, W. "Fischfuttervergiftung Durch DDT und Benzol Hexachlorid." *"W",* Vol. 43, 1949.

——. "Auswirkungen der Insektenbekämpfung Mit DDT und Benzol Hexachlorid auf Fischgewässer." *Abhandlung Aus Der Fischerei und Deren Hilfswissenschaften,* Part III, 1950.

——. "Fischerkrankungen und Fischsterben Durch Massentwicklung von Phytoplankton bei Anwesneheit von Ammonium Verbindungen." *Abhand A D Fisch Hilfs,* Part V, 1952.

——. *Fischkrankheiten,* 3rd ed. Berlin, Akademie Verlag, 1954.

——. "Ergebnisse der Versuche Zur Bekämpfung der Infektiösen Bauchwassersucht in Karpenfenteichen Mit Choloronitrin im Jahre 1956." *Dtsch Fisch Ztg,* Vol. 4, 1957.

——. "Bewährung des Chloronitrins in der Teichwirtschaftlichen Praxis und Neue Versuche Über die Anwendbarkeit Weiterer Breitspektrum-Antibiotica bei der Bekämpfung der Infektiösen Bauchwassersucht des Karpfens." *Z Fisch,* 7 (New Series):599–628, 1958.

Scheneberger, E. "Fishery Research in Wisconsin." *Prog Fish-Cult,* No. 56, 1941, pp. 14–17.

Schneider, J.A. "Dispersion of a Fintrol Concentrate-Dye Mixture Applied to the Surface of a Dimictic Lake at Fall Overturn." *Prog Fish-Cult, 36 (4):*192–194, 1974.

Schnick, R.A. *A Review of Literature on TFM (3-Trifluoromethyl-4-Nitrophenol) as a Lamprey Larvicide.* Investigations in Fish Control, BSFW, FWS, U.S. Dept. Interior, Washington, D.C., No. 44, 1972, pp. 1–31.

Schoettger, R.A. *Annotated Bibliography on MS-222.* Investigations in Fish Control, BSFW, FWS, U.S. Dept. Interior, Washington, D.C., No. 16, 1967, pp. 1–15.

Schoettger, R.A. *Toxicology of Thiodan in Several Fish and Aquatic Invertebrates.* Investigations in Fish Control, BSFW, FWS, U.S. Dept. Interior, Washington, D.C., No. 35, 1970, pp. 1–31.

Schoettger, R.A. and Julin, A.M. *Efficacy of MS-222 as an Anesthetic on Four Salmonids.* Investigations in Fish Control, BSFW, FWS, U.S. Dept. Interior, Washington, D.C., No. 13, 1967, pp. 1–15.

Schoettger, R.A. and Julin, A.M. *Efficacy of Quinaldine as an Anesthetic for Seven Species of Fish.* Investigations in Fish Control, BSFW, FWS, U.S. Dept. Interior, Washington, D.C., No. 22, 1969, pp. 1–10.

Schoettger, R.A. and Svendsen, G.E. *Effects of Antimycin A on Tissue Respiration of Rainbow Trout and Channel Catfish.* Investigations in Fish Control, BSFW, FWS, U.S. Dept. Interior, Washington, D.C., No. 39,

1970, pp. 1–10.

Schoettger, R.A., Walker, C.R., Marking, L.L., and Julin, A.M. *MS-222 as an Anesthetic for Channel Catfish: Its Toxicity, Efficacy and Muscle Residues.* Investigations in Fish Control, BSFW, FWS, U.S. Dept. Interior, Washington, D.C., No. 17, 1967, pp. 1–14.

Schubert, G. *Cure and Recognize Aquarium Fish Diseases.* Neptune, New Jersey, T.F.H. Publications, 1974.

Schulz, D. "Studien Über Nebenwirküngen des Herbizids NATA (Na-Trichloracetat) Auf Karpfen." *Zentralblatt fur Veterinaermedizin;* Reihe A, *17:*230–251, 1970.

Scott, W.W. and Warren, C.O. Jr. "Studies on the Host Range and Chemical Control of Fungi Associated With Diseased Tropical Fish." *Virginia Agricultural Experimental Station Technical Bulletin, 171:*1–24, 1964.

Shcherbina, A.K. *Prophylaxis and Hygiene in Fisheries.* Moscow, Pishchevaya Promyshlennost, 1939.

Shcherbina, A.K. and Ilin, V.M. "Veterinary and Husbandry Measures Against Chilodonasis." *Fish Ind (Moscow),* Vol. 9, 1950.

Shchupakov, I.G. "The Way They Combat *Ichthyophthirius* in Pond Fisheries." *Fish Ind (Moscow),* Vol. 5, 1951.

Shchupakov, I.G. "New Data on the Biology and Ecology of *Ichthyophthirius* Fouquet and Their Significance in Measures Against This Parasite of Fishes." *Trudy Problemn i Temat Soveshch Zoologica Instituta Akademiya Nauk USSR,* An S.S.S.R., Vol. 4, 1954.

Shilo, M. "Study on the Isolation and Control of Blue-green Algae From Fish Ponds." *Bamidgeh, 17(4):*83–93, 1965.

Shilo, M., Sarig, C., and Rosenberger, R. "Ton Scale Treatment of *Lernea* Infected Carp." *Bamidgeh, 12(2):*37–42, 1960.

Shilo, M., Sarig, S., Shilo, M., and Zeev, H. "Control of *Pyrmnesium parvum* in Fish Ponds With the Aid of Copper Sulfate." *Bamidgeh, 6(3):* 99–102, 1954.

Shilo, M. and Shilo, M. "Conditions Which Determine the Efficiency of Ammonium Sulfate in the Control of *Pyrmnesium parvum* in Fish Breeding Ponds." *Appl Microbiol, 1(6):*330–333, 1953.

Shilo, M. and Shilo, M. "Control of the Phytoflagellate *Pyrmnesium parvum.*" *Proceedings International Association Theory & Applied Technology, 12:*233–240, 1955.

Shimizu, M. and Takase, Y. "A Potent Chemotherapeutic Agent Against Fish Diseases: 6-Hydroxy-methyl-2-[2-(5-Nitro-2-Furyl) Vinyl] pyridine, (P-7138)." *Bulletin Japanese Society Scientific Fisheries, 33(6):*544–554, 1967.

Shumilova, A.M. *Experimental Studies on the Prophylaxis Against Opisthorchis.* Omsk Medical Institute, 1954.

Sills, J.B. and Allen, J.L. *Accumulation and Loss of Residues of 3-Trifluoromethyl-4-Nitrophenol (TFM) in Fish Muscle Tissue: Laboratory Studies.* Investigations in Fish Control, BSFW, FWS, U.S. Dept. Interior, Washington, D.C., No. 65, 1975, pp. 1–10.

Sills, J.B., Allen, J.L., Harman, P.D., and Luhning, C.W. *Residues of Quinaldine in Ten Species of Fish Following Anesthesia With Quinaldine Sulfate.* Investigations in Fish Control, BSFW, FWS, U.S. Dept. Interior. Washington, D.C., No. 50, 1973a, pp. 1–9.

Sills, J.B., Allen, J.L., Harman, P.D., and Luhning, C.W. *Residues of Quinaldine and MS-222 in Fish Following Anesthesia With Mixtures of Quinaldine Sulfate: MS-222.* Investigations in Fish Control, BSFW, FWS, U.S. Dept. Interior, Washington, D.C., No. 55, 1973b, pp. 1–12.

Skidmore, J.F. "Toxicity of Zinc Compounds to Aquatic Animals With Special Reference to Fish." *Quarterly Review Biology, 39:*227–248, 1964.

Slater, D.C. "New Treatment for White Spot." *Water Life,* June, 1952, p. 122.

Smith, H.W. "Chloromycetin in the Treatment of Red Leg." *Science, 112:* 274–275, 1950.

Smith, R.T. and Quistorff, E. "The Control of *Octomitus:* Calomel in the Diet of Hatchery Salmon." *Prog Fish-Cult, 51:*24–26, 1940.

Smith, W.W. "Action of Alkaline Acriflavine Solution on *Bacterium salmonicida* and Trout Eggs." *Proceedings Society For Experimental Biology & Medicine, 51:*324–326, 1942.

Snieszko, S.F. "Pyridylmercuric Acetate Technical: Its Use in Control of Gill Disease and Some External Parasitic Infections." *Prog Fish-Cult, 11(3):*153–155, 1949.

———. "Therapy of Bacterial Fish Diseases." *Trans Am Fish Soc, 83:*313–330, 1953.

———. "Use of Antibiotics in the Diet of Salmonid Fishes." *Prog Fish-Cult, 19:*81–84, 1957.

———. "Antibiotics in Fish Diseases and Fish Nutrition." *Antibiotics and Chemotherapy, 9(9):*541–545, 1959.

———. "A Comprehensive List of the Most Important Diseases of Fishes and the Drugs and Chemicals Used for Their Control." *Tropical Fish Hobbyist,* Dec. 1975, pp. 14–34.

Snieszko, S.F. and Bullock, G.L. "Determination of the Susceptibility of *Aeromonas salmonicida* to Sulphonamides and Antibiotics, With a Summary Report on the Treatment and Prevention of Furunculosis." *Prog Fish-Cult, 19(2):*99–107, 1957.

Snieszko, S.F. and Friddle, S.B. "Disinfection of Rainbow Trout Eggs With Sulfomerthiolate." *Prog Fish-Cult, 10(3):*143–149, 1948.

———. "Prophylaxis of Furunculosis in Brook Trout (*Salvelinus fontinalis*) by Oral Immunization and Sulfamerazine." *Prog Fish-Cult, 11(3):*161–168, 1949.

———. "Tissue Levels of Various Sulfonamides in Trout." *Trans Am Fish Soc, 80:*240–250, 1951.

———. "Further Studies on Factors Determining Tissue Levels of Sulfamerazine in Trout." *Trans Am Fish Soc, 81:*101–110, 1952.

Snieszko, S.F. and Griffin, P.J. "Successful Treatment of Ulcer Disease in

Brook Trout With Terramycin." *Science, 113*:717–718, 1951.

Snieszko, S.F. and Griffin, P.J. "Kidney Disease in Brook Trout and Its Treatment." *Prog Fish-Cult, 17(1)*:3–13, 1955.

Snieszko, S.F., Griffin, P.J., and Friddle, S.B. "Antibiotic Treatment of Ulcer Disease and Furunculosis in Trout." *Transactions North American Wildlife Conference, 17*:197–213, 1952.

Snieszko, S.F., Gutsell, J.S., and Friddle, S.B. "Various Sulfonamide Treatments of Furunculosis in Brook Trout, *Salvelinus fontinalis.*" *Trans Am Fish Soc, 78*:181–188, 1950.

Snieszko, S.F. and Wood, E. "The Effect of Some Sulfonamides on the Growth of Brook Trout, Brown Trout, and Rainbow Trout." *Trans Am Fish Soc, 84*:86–92, 1955.

Sokolov, P.M. and Maslyukova, N.G. "The Use of Malachite Green in Gyrodactylosis of Carp." *Vsesoyunznogo Nauchno-Issledovatelis Kogo Instituta Prudovoga Rybnogo Khozyaistva, 18*:179–180, 1971 (English translation by SFWR-TR-73-01, Division of Fish Research, U.S. Dept. Interior, Washington, D.C.).

Speyer, W. "Die Wirkung von Dinitrokresolen Auf Fische." *Nachr Bl Dtsch Pflanzenschutzd, 19*:43–44, 1939.

Sproston, N. "The Effect of the Insecticide '666' on Some Fish Pests and Other Animals in the Fish Ponds." *Acta Hydrobiologica Sinica*, No. 1, 1956, pp. 89–97.

Stammer, H.J. "Beiträge Zur Morphologie, Biologie und Bekämpfung der Karpenlaus." *Z Parasitenkd, 19*:135–208, 1959.

Steffens, W. "Verhütung des Saprolegnia-Befalls von Forellenneiern Durch Formalin." *Dtsch Fisch Ztg, 9*:287–289, 1962.

Steffens, W., Lieder, U., Nehring, D., and Hattop, H.W. "Möglichkeiten und Gefahren der Anwendung von Malachitgrün in der Fischerei." *Z Fisch, 10* (New Series):745–771, 1961.

Sukhenko, G.E. "*Argulus pellucidus* — Wagler, 1935 (Crustacea, Branchiura): A Species New to the Fauna of the U.S.S.R., Found in the Ponds of the Ukraine." *Zool Zh, 42*:621–622, 1963 (In Russian).

Sukhoverkhov, F.M. "The Effect of Cobalt, Vitamins, Tissue Preparations and Antibiotics on Carp Production." *FAO World Symp Warmwater Pond Fish Cult.* Also in *FAO Fishery Report, 44(3)*:400–407, 1967.

Surber, E.W. "Chemical Control Agents and Their Effects on Fish." *Prog Fish-Cult, 10(3)*:125–131, 1948.

Surber, E.W. and Pickering, Q.H. "Acute Toxicity of Endothal, Diquat, Hyamine, Dalapon and Silvex to Fish." *Prog Fish-Cult, 24*:164–171, 1962.

Svendsen, G.E. *Annotated Bibliography on Methylpentynol.* Investigations in Fish Control, BSFW, U.S. Dept. Interior, Washington, D.C., No. 31, 1969, pp. 1–7.

Tack, E. "Bekämpfung der Drenkrankheit Mit Kalkstickstoff." *Fischwirt, 5(1)*:123–129, 1951.

Takase, Y., Kouno, K., and Shimizu, M. "Effect of Nifurpirinol Against

Diseases Caused by Bacteria and Protozoa in Hobbyfishes." *Fish Pathology (Japan)*, *5(2)*:81–84, 1971.

Taylor, R.E.L., Coli, S.J., and Junnel, D.R. "Attempts to Control Whirling Disease by Continuous Drug Feeding." *J Wildlife Dis*, *9*:302–305, 1973.

Tebo, L.B. and McCoy, E.G. "Effect of Seawater Concentration on the Reproduction and Survival of Largemouth Bass and Bluegills." *Prog Fish-Cult*, *26(3)*:99–106, 1964.

Tesarick, J. and Havelka, J. "Pruzkum Antiparazitarnich a Protiplisnovych Opatreni." *Prace VUR (Vodnany)*, *6*:97–122, 1966.

Tesarick, J. and Havelka, J. "Prevention and Cure of Fish Diseases." *Ustav Vedeckotechnickych Informaci NZLH*, 1967 (In Czech).

Tesarick, J. and Mares, J. "The Applicability of an Antiparasitic Bath in Malachite Green of the Sheatfish Fry *(Siluris glanis L.)*." Bulletin VURH *(Vodnany)*, *2(3)*:13–15, 1966 (In Czech– English summary on p. p. 15).

Thienpoint, D. and Niemegeers, C.J.E. "R7464: A New Potent Anesthetic in Fish." *Int Zoo Year Book*, *5*:202–205, 1965.

Thompson, F.M. and Socolof, R.B. "Metabolism Inhibitors in the Shipment of Fish." *Int Zoo Year Book*, *3*:120–121, 1961.

Toth, R. "Fish Anesthetics." In Calhoun, A. (Ed.). *Inland Fisheries Management*, Department of Fish & Game, State of California, 1966, pp. 148–149.

Tripathi, Y.R. "Studies on Parasites of Indian Fishes. III. Protozoa. 2. (Mastigophora and Cilophora)." *Records Indian Museum*, *52:(2–4)*:221–230, 1954.

Van Duijn, C. Jr. *Diseases of Fish*, 3rd ed. London, Butterworth & Co.; Springfield, Thomas, 1973.

Van Horn, M. and Katz, M. "Pyridylmercuric Acetate as a Prophylactic in Fisheries Management." *Science*, *104*:557, 1946.

Van Roekel, H. "Acetic Acid as a Control Agent for *Cyclochaeta* and *Gyrodactylus* in Hatchery Trout." *California Fish & Game*, *15(3)*:230–233, 1929.

Venulet, J. and Schultz, G.O. "A New Molluscicide 1-(*p*-nitrophenyl)-2-amidineurea hydrochloride (T72)." *Nature*, *204*(4961):900–901, 1964.

Verigin, B.V. "Measures Against *Ichthyophthirius*." *Fish Ind (Moscow)*, Vol. 6, 1954.

Vik, R. "Studies on the Helminth Fauna of Norway. VI. An Experiment in the Control of *Diphyllobothrium* Infections in Trout." *Mod Fra Zoological Museum (Oslo)*, Contribution No. 75, 1965, pp. 76–78 (In English).

Villiere, de J.P. and Mackenzie, J.C. "Structure and Activity in Molluscicides; The Phenacyl Halides, A Group of Potentially Useful Molluscicides." *Bull WHO*, *29(3)*:424–427, 1963.

Walker, C.R., Lennon, R.E., and Berger, B.L. *Preliminary Observations on the Toxicity of Antimycin A to Fish and Other Aquatic Animals.* Investigations in Fish Control, BSFW, FWS, U.S. Dept. Interior, Washington, D.C., No. 2, 1964, pp. 1–18.

Walker, C.R. and Schoettger, R.A. *Method for Determining MS-222 Residues in Fish.* Investigations in Fish Control, BSFW, FWS, U.S. Dept. Interior, Washington, D.C., No. 14, 1967a, pp. 1–10.

Walker, C.R. and Schoettger, R.A. *Residues of MS-222 in Four Salmonids Following Anesthesia.* Investigations in Fish Control, BSFW, FWS, U.S. Dept. Interior, Washington, D.C., No. 15, 1967b, pp. 1–11.

Walker, C.R., Starkey, R.J., and Marking, L.L. *Relation of Chemical Structure to Fish Toxicity in Nitrosalicylanilides and Related Compounds.* Investigations in Fish Control, BSFW, FWS, U.S. Dept. Interior, Washington, D.C., No. 9, 1966, pp. 1–9.

Warren, J. "Toxicity Tests of Erythromycin Thiocyanate in Rainbow Trout." *Prog Fish-Cult, 25(2):*88–92, 1963.

Watanabe, M. "Salmon Culture in Japan." *Prog Fish-Cult, 48:*14–18, 1940.

Weber, D. and Ridgway, G.J. "Marking Pacific Salmon With Tetracycline Antibiotics." *J Fish Res Bd Can, 24:*849–865, 1967.

Weber, E. "Einwirkung von Pentachlorphenolnatrium auf Fische und Fischnährtiere." *Biol Zentralbl, 84:*81–93, 1965.

Wellborn, T.L. Jr. "*Trichodina* (Ciliata: Urceolariidae) of Freshwater Fishes of the Southeastern United States." *Journal Protozoology, 14:*399–412, 1967.

——. "The Toxicity of Nine Therapeutic and Herbicidal Compounds to Striped Bass." *Prog Fish-Cult, 31(1):*27–32, 1969.

——. "Toxicity of Some Compounds to Striped Bass Fingerlings." *Prog Fish-Cult, 33(1):*32–36, 1971.

Willford, W.A. *Toxicity of 22 Therapeutic Compounds to Six Fishes.* Investigations in Fish Control, BSFW, FWS, U.S. Dept. Interior, Washington, D.C., No. 18, 1967a, pp. 1–10.

——. *Toxicity of Dimethyl Sulfoxide (DMSO) to Fish.* Investigations in Fish Control, BSFW, FWS, U.S. Dept. Interior, Washington, D.C., No. 20, 1967b, pp. 1–18.

——. *Effect of MS-222 on Electrolyte and Water Content in the Brain of Rainbow Trout.* Investigations in Fish Control, BSFW, FWS, U.S. Dept. Interior, Washington, D.C., No. 43, 1970, pp. 1–7.

Wilson, C.O. and Jones, T.E. *American Drug Index.* Philadelphia, J.B. Lippincott, 1962.

Wolf, K. "Physiological Salines for Freshwater Teleosts." *Prog Fish-Cult, 25(3):*135–140, 1963.

Wolf, K. and Dunbar, C.E. "Test of 34 Therapeutic Agents for Control of Kidney Disease in Trout." *Trans Am Fish Soc, 88(2):*117–124, 1959.

Wolf, K. and Snieszko, S.F. "The Use of Antibiotics and Other Antimicrobials in Therapy of Diseases of Fishes." *Antimicrobial Agents & Chemotherapy, 1963:*597–603, 1964.

Wolf, L.E. "The Use of Potassium Permanganate in the Control of Fish

Parasites." *Prog Fish-Cult,* No. 11, 1935a, pp. 20–21.
——. "The Use of Potassium Permanganate in the Control of Fish Parasites." *Trans Am Fish Soc, 65:*88–100, 1935b.
——. "Sulfamerazine in the Treatment of Trout for Furunculosis and Ulcer Disease." *Prog Fish-Cult, 9(3):*115–124, 1947.
——. "Development of Disease-Resistant Strains of Fish." *Trans Am Fish Soc, 83:*342–349, 1954.
Wonderlin, C.C. "Editorial: Shock in Marine Fish." *Marine Hobbyist News, 2(2):*2, 1974.
Wood, E.M., Yasutake, W.T., and Johnson, S.F. "Acute Sulfamethazine Toxicity in Young Salmon." *Prog Fish-Cult, 19(2):*64–67, 1955.
Wood, E.M., Yasutake, W.T., and Snieszko, S.F. "Sulfonamide Toxicity in Brook Trout." *Trans Am Fish Soc, 84:*155–160, 1957.
Wood, J.W. *Diseases of Pacific Salmon: Their Prevention and Treatment.* Olympia, Washington, Department of Fish, Hatchery Division, 1968.
Woyanarovich, E. "Eine Neue Methods Zur Bekämpfung der Ektoparasiten von Karpfen." *Acta Veterinaria Academiae Scientiarum Hungaricae,* Vol. 4, No. 1, 1954.
Yasutake, W.T., Buhler, D.R., and Shanks, W.E. "Chemotherapy of Hexamitiasis in Fish." *J Parasitol, 47(1):*81–86, 1961.
Yin, Weng Yin, Ling, M.E., Hsu, G.A., Chen, I.S., Kuang, P.R., and Chu, S.L. "Studies on the Lernaeosis (*Lernaea,* Copepoda parasitica) of Freshwater Fishes of China." *Acta Hydrobiol Sin,* 1963:48–117, 1963 (In Chinese; English summary included).
Yousuf–Ali, M. "Investigations of Fish Diseases and Parasites in East Pakistan." *Third Symp Comm Inst Epizoot Etud Malad Poissons (Stockholm),* Contribution No. 27, Sept. 23–27, 1968, pp. 1–5.
Yui-fan et al. "Fishing Industry of the Inland Waters of China." (Cited by Musselius, V.A., 1967).
Zakhvatkin, V.A. and Ivasik, V.M. "An Attempt at Eradication of Costiasis and Dactylogyrosis in a Fish Pond." *Fish Ind (Moscow),* Vol. 2, 1954.
Zeiler, W. "Anthium Oxide: A New Disinfectant Compound for Aquaria." *Ichthyologica, 37:*107–110, 1966.
Zeiller, W. "Quinaldine: A Ray of Hope for an Old Enigma." *Drum & Croaker, 13(2):*65–67, 1972.
Zschiesche, A. "Eizellen in der Haut von Macropoden." *Zoologischer Anzeiger, 36:*294–298, 1910 (English summary included).